FROM PRACTICE TO GROUNDED THEORY: QUALITATIVE RESEARCH IN NURSING

is the *only* book available that focuses on *how* to conduct qualitative research using grounded theory in nursing. It discusses the entire research process in grounded theory—from conceptualization and proposal, through data collection and analysis, to the actual writing of the report. These are some of the practical topics addressed:

- Collecting data: observation and interviewing
- Analyzing data
- Coding, diagramming, and memo-writing
- Organizing categories into theory
- Ethical issues for the nurse using grounded theory
- Critiquing grounded theory studies

Plus: five examples of actual grounded theory studies that illustrate the method and show the different levels of analysis that are possible. A final chapter discusses the application of one grounded theory study to clinical practice and shows how grounded theory research can be used to improve nursing care.

FROM PRACTICE TO GROUNDED THEORY

is a practical as well as theoretical guide that demystifies grounded theory and puts it to work for nurses in clinical practice and education. The text is designed for:

- graduate nursing students
- nurse researchers
- educators
- nurses practicing in clinical settings who wish to conduct and apply qualitative research studies using grounded theory

FROM PRACTICE TO GROUNDED THEORY

will also be a valuable resource for students and researchers in public health, health education, social work, sociology, and other health-related fields.

Titles of Related Interest

Research in Nursing, Holly Wilson
Code 09739/575 pp/Hardbound/1985

Applying Research in Nursing, Holly Wilson and Sally Hutchinson
Code 09738/350 pp/Paperbound/1985

**From Proposal to Publication: An Informal Guide to Writing About
Nursing Research,** Elizabeth Tornquist
Code 08012/160 pp/Paperbound/March 1986

**From Novice to Expert: Excellence and Power in Clinical Nursing
Practice,** Patricia Benner
Code 00299/307 pp/Paperbound/1984

FROM PRACTICE TO GROUNDED THEORY

qualitative
research
in nursing

W. Carole Chenitz, RN, EdD
Janice M. Swanson, RN, PhD

ADDISON-WESLEY PUBLISHING COMPANY
Health Sciences Division, Menlo Park, California
Reading, Massachusetts ● Don Mills, Ontario ● Wokingham, UK
Amsterdam ● Sydney ● Singapore ● Tokyo ● Madrid
Bogota ● Santiago ● San Juan

Sponsoring Editor: Thomas Eoyang
Production and Design: Michael Bass & Associates
Copy Editor: Lori Donohue

Library of Congress Cataloging in Publication Data
Main entry under title:

Chenitz, W. Carole, 1946-
    From practice to grounded theory.

    Bibliography: p. 241
    Includes index.
    1. Nursing—Research—Methodology.   2. Sociology—
Research—Methodology.   I. Swanson, Janice M.
II. Title.   III. Title: Grounded theory.   IV. Title:
Qualitative research in nursing. [DNLM: 1. Nursing.
2. Research—nurses' instruction.   WY 20.5 C518f]
RT81.5.C49   1986   610.73'072   85-26855

ISBN 0-201-12960-4

5 6 7 8 9 10 AL 9594939291

The authors and publishers have exerted every effort to ensure
that drug selection and dosage set forth in this text are in accord
with current recommendations and practice at the time of publication. However, in view of ongoing research, changes in govern-
ment regulations and the constant flow of information relating to
drug therapy and drug reactions, the reader is urged to check the
package insert for each drug for any change in indications of
dosage and for added warnings and precautions. This is particularly important where the recommended agent is a new and/or
infrequently employed drug.

Addison-Wesley Publishing Company
Health Sciences Division
2725 Sand Hill Road
Menlo Park, California 94025

Contributors

Patricia Archbold, RN, DNS, FAAN
Professor
Oregon Health Sciences University
School of Nursing
Portland, Oregon

Barbara Artinian, RN, PhD
Associate Professor
Azusa Pacific University
College of Nursing
Azusa, California

W. Carole Chenitz, RN, EdD
Associate Chief Nursing Service for Research
Veterans Administration Medical Center
San Francisco, California

Julie Corbin, RN, DNS
Research Associate
Department of Social and Behavioral Sciences
University of California at San Francisco
School of Nursing
San Francisco, California

Marcella Z. Davis, RN, DNS, FAAN
Associate Chief Nursing Service for Research
Veterans Administration Medical Center
La Jolla, California

Shizuko Y. Fagerhaugh, RN, DNS
Research Nurse, Visiting Lecturer
University of California at San Francisco
School of Nursing
San Francisco, California

Sally A. Hutchinson, RN, PhD
Associate Processor
Jacksonville Health Education Programs and
University of Florida
College of Nursing
Jacksonville, Florida

Robert J. Kus, RN, PhD
Assistant Professor
The University of Iowa
College of Nursing
Iowa City, Iowa

Katharyn Antle May, RN, DNS, FAAN
Associate Professor
Department of Family Health Care Nursing
University of California at San Francisco
School of Nursing
San Francisco, California

Phyllis N. Stern, RN, DNS, FAAN
Professor and Director
School of Nursing
Dalhousie University
Halifax, Nova Scotia, Canada

Janice M. Swanson, RN, PhD
Brigadier General Lillian Dunlap Professor of Nursing
Incarnate Word College
Division of Nursing
San Antonio, Texas

Holly S. Wilson, RN, PhD, FAAN
Professor
Department of Mental Health and Community Nursing
University of California at San Francisco
School of Nursing
San Francisco, California

Contents

Preface

PURPOSE

This book is designed to assist nurses in understanding qualitative research using grounded theory methodology.

The term *qualitative research* represents many theoretical orientations that have led to a range of approaches to research in the social sciences. Qualitative research includes phenomenology, existentialism, symbolic interactionism, and ethnomethodology. In this book, we view qualitative research in a symbolic interactionist framework. Symbolic interactionism is both a philosophy of human life and social experience and a distinctive approach to the study of human life. A methodology research using symbolic interaction was developed by Glaser and Strauss in *The Discovery of Grounded Theory* (Glaser, Strauss, 1968).

Grounded theory is theory developed from data systematically collected through social research (Glaser, 1978). The methodology for grounded theory provides research tools that lead to theory development. Grounded theory can assist us to identify and order nursing phenomena and generate theory relevant to our practice and research.

Theory development in nursing has been a concern of nurse scholars and scientists. There is an acknowledged need in the discipline to develop, test, and use theory in order to improve practice. We present the methodology of grounded theory as a means to this end. One of the objectives of this book is to encourage theory-generating research by demystifying the process of theory generation.

This book provides information and specific guidelines for nurses on how to conduct and apply qualitative research to nursing research using grounded theory methodology.

We present our understanding of the grounded theory process to nurses in its present state of development by social scientists. In particular, we have stressed the issues and adaptation of grounded theory to nursing by nurses.

We have laid out the principles that we, as nurse-researchers, have learned from social scientists or have discovered ourselves while conducting research. Throughout this book, these principles are presented and recommendations are made.

As we worked on the material presented here, we became aware that this book and others on the subject of qualitative research in nursing represent a benchmark in the development of scientific inquiry in nursing. As such, this book marks the progress within the discipline toward a fuller and deeper understanding of nursing and the phenomena of concern to nurses. We present this book with our hope that it stimulates thinking and discourse on methodology and encourages research activity for the purpose of generating theory.

Grounded theory is but one way to approach phenomena for scientific investigation. It is complementary to other research approaches rather than a replacement for them. The phenomena of concern for nurses are complex, and multiple research strategies are necessary to fully understand them. Grounded theory has a place in nursing research and in this spirit we present this book.

AUDIENCE

This book is designed for graduate students in nursing, nurse researchers, educators, faculty who teach research courses, and nurses practicing in clinical settings who wish to conduct qualitative research. It will be of interest also to students and researchers in public health, health education, social work, sociology, and other health-related fields.

CONTENT

This book is divided into two parts. Part I presents the methodology of grounded theory research. The first three chapters provide an overview of grounded theory, a discussion of the research process in grounded theory, and a rationale for generating theory from nursing practice. Chapters 4 through 13 discuss the process of grounded theory research beginning with the research proposal and continuing through the various techniques of data collection and data analysis, and ending with discussions of the writing process and ethical issues.

Part II shifts from the research process to illustrations of grounded theory studies. All but one of these chapters have been published elsewhere. They were selected as examples of the types of research problems that can be addressed using grounded theory. These chapters also illustrate different levels of analytic complexity and they provide the reader with models of written reports of grounded theory that demonstrate the kind of insight this methodology can contribute to nursing.

The bibliography includes relevant articles, books, and dissertations for further reading in grounded theory and qualitative research.

ACKNOWLEDGEMENTS

There are many people responsible for the completion of this volume. First there are the contributors who supported this work from the beginning and without whom this volume would not exist. We thank Thomas Eoyang of Addison-Wesley Publishing Company for his patience, encouragement, and belief in this project.

The idea for this book originated while we were in the post-doctoral fellowship program at the University of California, San Francisco, School of Nursing. We acknowledge our debt to Susan Gortner, of the Office of Research for creating an environment for research, to students and colleagues in the School of Nursing, and especially to Anselm Strauss and Shizuko Fagerhaugh, our mentors in grounded theory.

Major ideas in this book were first presented in a conference at the Veterans Administration Medical Center in San Francisco. This conference was sponsored by the Veterans Administration Medical District 27 Nursing Research Committee. Barbara Sater deserves special thanks for her work in making that conference possible.

Heartfelt thanks to Nancy Strouse whose belief in nursing research and in this work sustained us throughout this project. We thank Fay Bower and Marcella Davis for their support. Jim Swanson and John Harvey get special mention for their work on the manuscripts.

To our families we owe a special debt. The encouragement and understanding of Richard Swanson and Lucille Allison made this book possible. Our love and thanks to our daughters Karen and Betsy Swanson and Becky Chenitz for their belief in us.

We would like to thank the following reviewers for their constructive comments: Ivo Abraham, Case Western Reserve University; Donna Diers, Yale University; Jacqueline Fawcett, University of Pennsylvania; Carol Lindeman, Oregon Health Sciences University.

References

Glaser BG, Strauss AL: *The Discovery of Grounded Theory: Strategies for Qualitative Research.* New York, Aldine Publishing Co, 1967.
Glaser BG: *Theoretical Sensitivity.* Mill Valley, California, The Sociology Press, 1978.

DEDICATION

To all nurses who raise questions and search for answers in order to improve nursing and nursing care.

Part I

The

Grounded Theory

Method

Part I of this book presents the research process in grounded theory. Chapters 1, 2, and 3 provide a theoretical backdrop for grounded theory research. Chapter 1 presents an overview of grounded theory and describes its foundations in the symbolic interactionist perspective. Key issues addressed include theoretical sampling and validity and reliability.

Chapter 2 discusses two modes the research process can take in a grounded theory study: the discovery mode and the emergent fit mode.

Chapter 3 presents a method for generating theory through identification of the many processes that nurses use daily in their work. This method, called surfacing nursing process, is offered as one of the many ways to arrive at theory that contributes to the understanding of nursing practice.

Chapters 4 through 12 cover the entire process of grounded theory research. The research proposal, presented in chapter 4, is the focus of a discussion of the early stages of a project, beginning with an idea and progressing through the problem statement, the statement of purpose, the specific aims, the literature review, and the theoretical framework.

Chapters 5, 6, and 7 present methods for data collection: participant observation and formal and informal interviewing. In each of these chapters, each method is presented with particular attention to issues for nurse researchers.

Data analysis is presented in chapters 8 through 11. These chapters are organized to guide the reader through the analytic process. An overview of analysis is presented in chapter 8. Chapter 9 deals with coding and memo writing. With this background, the analyst moves to develop categories and a process that organizes the categories into theory. Chapter 10 focuses on analysis for categories and description, while chapter 11 discusses analysis for basic social processes. Chapter 11 also makes a lucid distinction between core categories and basic social processes (BSP), which will be highly useful to researchers whose goal is to identify the *processes* that comprise nursing practice.

Chapter 12 provides suggestions for writing the grounded theory study as well as guidelines for evaluating completed studies. Finally, chapter 13 discusses some of the ethical issues raised by grounded theory research. Some of these issues are identified in other chapters in the book. The issues will focus on five areas of concern: problem identification, investigator/sponsor relationship, investigator/subject relationship, data collection, and publication of results.

We hope that the reader will find Part I to be a useful and explicit guide to a research methodology capable of elucidating nursing problems. Some of the problems that grounded theory researchers have already addressed are presented as examples in Part II.

1
Qualitative research using grounded theory

W. Carole Chenitz
Janice M. Swanson

Grounded theory is a highly systematic research approach for the collection and analysis of qualitative data for the purpose of generating explanatory theory that furthers the understanding of social and psychological phenomena. The objective of grounded theory is the development of theory that explains basic patterns common in social life. Grounded theory represents an advance in the technology for handling qualitative data gathered in the natural, everyday world. It describes a method to study fundamental patterns known as basic social-psychological processes which account for variation in interaction around a phenomenon or problem. Grounded theory has its roots in the social sciences, specifically, in the symbolic interaction tradition of social psychology and sociology. The aim of grounded theory is to generate theory about social and psychological phenomena.

THE NATURE OF THEORY

All theories by nature are symbolic constructions of reality (Kaplan, 1964). Theory creates an abstract conception about phenomena in the empirical world through the use of symbols. As Kaplan notes,

Theoretical concepts are contrasted with observational ones, and theoretical laws with empirical generalizations. Though all conception involves the use of symbols and is thereby distinguished from perception, in some cases the symbols relate directly to the perceptual materials while in other cases the relation is mediated by still further symbolic processes (1964, p 296).

Theories consist of concepts and propositions about the relationships between concepts. Concepts are theoretical terms used to denote abstract material or phenomena and are related to the facts at the empirical level and to the abstract constructs about those facts at the theoretical level. Propositions in theory are used to denote relationships. At the empirical level, premises relate to the empirical facts. At the conceptual level, propositions specify relationships between concepts. Theory is related to both the abstract and empirical level. The degree of abstraction of a theory will indicate the extent of symbolic processes used to mediate between the empirical world and the concepts and propositions in a theory (Kaplan, 1964).

Theories function to interpret or explain and predict phenomena. Theory serves to fulfill the need to organize facts and knowledge, interpret and understand events or phenomena in the empirical world, predict events, and guide action in relation to phenomena. Theories are developed to fulfill a need within a scientific discipline. A given theory may be developed to fill one or more of the needs of a discipline. The material of the theory in each discipline is related to the phenomena of concern to the group.

SYMBOLIC INTERACTION

Symbolic interaction is a theory about human behavior. In addition, it is an approach to the study of human conduct and human group life. Symbolic interaction focuses on the meaning of events to people in natural or everyday settings and is therefore akin to the school of philosophy known as *phenomenology*. Both phenomenology and symbolic interaction are concerned with the study of the inner or "experiental" aspects of human behavior, that is, how people define events or reality and how they act in relation to their beliefs. For symbolic interactionists, meaning guides behavior and a stage of deliberation or definition of the situation precedes action (Morris, 1977). The reality or meaning of the situation is created by people and leads to action and the consequences of action.

George Herbert Mead (1934), a social psychologist, advanced the symbolic interactionist school of thought by postulating a social process whereby a biological organism develops a mind and a self and becomes, through social interaction and society, a rational being. It is in social interaction that the individual achieves a sense of self. Through role taking, the individual is capable of being an object to self and achieves a sense of self. As the individual "takes the role of other" the ability to look back at self, a distinctly human capacity, is learned. This human capacity of seeing self from the perspective of other enables the individual to hold a concept of self (Mead, 1934). This concept of self is learned during childhood and through social interaction.

Mead's contribution to symbolic interaction is his description of the process whereby a sense of self develops. The child develops the concept of self in play and games. During play, the child takes on many roles. As the child takes on a role, all others that hold this role in the child's world are subsumed in the play role. The child is learning to play a part that includes multiple others who hold the role.

Herbert Blumer (1969) further elaborated on the symbolic interaction tradition. According to Blumer, symbolic interaction rests on three basic premises.

First, that "human beings act toward things on the basis of the meanings that the things have for them" (Blumer, 1969, p 2). These things may be objects, other human beings, institutions, guiding ideals, activities of others and situations, or a combination of these.

Second, the "meaning of such things is derived from, or arises out of the social interaction that one has with one's fellows" (Blumer, 1969, p 2).

And third, "these meanings are handled in, and modified through, an interpretive process used by the person in dealing with the things he encounters" (Blumer, 1969, p 2).

These premises rest on the belief that, as Blumer notes,

The human being is not a mere responding organism, only responding to the play of factors from his world or from himself; he is an acting organism who has to cope with and handle such factors and who in so doing has to forge and direct his line of action (1969, p 55).

Like Mead, Blumer focused on the concept of self which is central to symbolic interaction. The concept of self leads to meaning and "self-directed" behavior. According to symbolic interactionists, the concept of self is unique to humans. A human has a concept of self and also acts toward self as toward others and communicates with self. The human ability to hold a concept of self and for self-interaction is the basis for the formulation of meaning and experience in the world.

Nothing in the world, that is, objects, people, or events, has intrinsic meaning or inherent value in and of itself. Meaning is created by experience. Through interaction with the object and with self, the object is defined. Once defined, meaning can be attached to it. The meaning the object has to the individual gives it a value. Therefore, Blumer (1969) sees action or behavior toward the object as planned, based on the meaning and value it has to the individual.

Symbolic interactionists view human behavior as the result of process. According to Blumer, all human behavior is the result of "a vast interpretive process in which people, singly and collectively, guide themselves by defining the objects, events and situations they encounter" (Blumer, 1969, p 132).

For social life, group action is essential. Individuals must align their behavior with others and with groups. Therefore, meaning must be shared. As Blumer notes,

. . . an institution carries on its complicated activity through an articulated complex of such stabilized meanings. . . . The process of interpretation may be viewed as a

vast digestive process through which the confrontations of experience are trans-
formed into activity . . . it is, I think, the chief means through which human group
life goes on and takes shape (Blumer, 1969, p 133).

Communication and a common language for communication provides the mechanisms for meaning to be shared.

Humans learn through self and social interaction the definitions and meanings of objects, events, and people. Through socialization and a common language, the learning of shared meaning is accomplished. In this way, individual behavior is appropriate to the group and the individual's behavior has meaning in the group.

A process of consensus about definitions explains group behavior. Group consensus is reached when there is universal agreement by members on definitions of objects, events, and situations. Group consensus on definitions creates shared meaning in the group. Individuals can then plan their behavior with those of others.

Society, organizations, families, and other forms of group life are based on consensus and shared meanings about relevant phenomena and people. These shared meanings create collective behavior. The individual as part of the collective aligns his or her self-definition with those of others and acts according to shared meaning.

All phenomena and people are subject to redefinition and new meanings through interaction. Since meaning is created through the self, new definitions of phenomena create new self-definitions. Experience changes self and hence, changes behavior (Blumer, 1969; Denzin, 1970).

The symbolic interactionist studies behavior on two levels: the behavioral or the interactional level and the symbolic level. Studies in this framework must include observations of behavior in a specific situation. The full range and variation in the behavior is sought. The focus of observation is on the interaction since it is in both verbal and nonverbal behavior that the symbolic meaning of the event is transmitted. The analysis of interaction includes participants' self-definitions and shared meaning. Observation focuses on the interaction in a situation and analysis focuses on the symbolic meaning that is transmitted via action. Analysis focuses on interaction, patterns of interaction, and their consequences. In order to obtain participants' definition and shared meaning, microscopic analysis of the interaction is conducted. In addition, a macroscopic analysis for contextual circumstances in the setting and conditions that preclude the interaction is done to establish larger symbolic events that create definitions and shared meaning in the situation. Still larger contexts are included in the macroscopic analysis to include shared meanings of groups, populations, and society. Analysis is complete when both the symbolic and the behavioral events in a situation are understood (Denzin, 1970).

The symbolic interactionist perspective has several implications for research activity. First, human behavior, to be understood, must be examined in interaction. The setting, the implications in the setting, and the larger social forces such as ideologies and events that affect behavior, are analyzed. The full range and variation of behavior in a setting or in relation to a phenomenon is examined to produce self and group definitions and shared meanings. In order to do this, the researcher describes social behavior as it takes place in natural settings. The actual setting is examined for social rules, ideologies, and events that illustrate shared meaning held by people in the interaction and, thus, affect their behavior in the interaction (Blumer, 1969; Denzin, 1970).

Second, the researcher needs to understand behavior as the participants understand it, learn about their world, learn their interpretation of self in the interaction and share their definitions. In order to accomplish this, the researcher must "take the role of other" and understand the world from the participants' perspective. The researcher, therefore, must be both a participant in the world and an observer of the participants in that world. Finally, in order for the knowledge to be understood and accepted by the researcher's discipline, the researcher, as observer, must translate the meaning derived from the researcher as participant into the language of the research discipline (Blumer, 1969; Denzin, 1970).

Using a symbolic interactionist perspective, grounded theory provides a way to study human behavior and interaction. This approach is particularly useful to conceptualize behavior in complex situations, to understand unresolved or emerging social problems, and to understand the impact of new ideologies. This approach is useful to health practitioners where the interaction with the health care system is only one factor in how a health care problem is managed by a client. The health care scene is one of rapid change. In health care systems, new ideologies that impact on treatment lead to new or changed treatment modalities. These complex interactions can be studied with grounded theory. Conceptualization of the impact of change on the health care system, the community, and the client can be understood using the grounded theory approach. Finally, grounded theory creates a new perspective or viewpoint on familiar problems. The focus of a grounded theory study on interaction allows us to understand behavior in new and different ways.

AN OVERVIEW OF GROUNDED THEORY

Grounded theory is a research method developed from the implications of the symbolic interactionist view of human behavior. As a systematic way to derive theories that illuminate human behavior and the social world, grounded theory has many uses. Like most forms of qualitative research, grounded theory makes its greatest contribution in areas in which little research has been done. In these areas, theory testing cannot be done since the variables relevant to the concepts have not yet been identified (Stern, 1980). Therefore, one of the major uses of grounded theory has been in preliminary, exploratory, and descriptive studies (Glaser, Strauss, 1966). In these situations, grounded theory and other forms of qualitative research are widely acceptable since they are considered precursors for further investigation.

In this view, grounded theory studies are complementary to other approaches. However, when grounded theory is viewed as only a precursor for other research, its full capability is limited. The specific focus of grounded theory on theory generation adds an important dimension to data analysis. In fact, Glaser and Strauss (1966) point out that there may be little research done after a grounded theory study in an area. They attribute this to the usefulness and density of grounded theory.

The grounded theory study is done to produce abstract concepts and propositions about the relationships between them. Grounded theory studies have been reported at both the descriptive and theoretical or process levels. The researcher may stop at any level of analysis and report findings. For example, the researcher may report one descriptive category (Melia, 1982), a process (Wilson, 1982) or multiple processes (Fagerhaugh, Strauss, 1977) (See chapters 10 and 11). There are several levels of analytic complexity that the researcher will pursue during the study to reach a theory that is ''grounded.'' A brief overview will be given here.

Grounded theory uses the constant comparative method of analysis throughout, that is, comparisons are made continuously. For example, the first two interviews or field notes are compared for similarities and differences in the lives of those interviewed or observed. Data is then initially coded with substantive codes that reflect the substance of what people said or the observed events, actions, or other dimensions of the phenomena. Often, the words of the subjects themselves are used. Codes are then compared; similar codes are clustered and given an initial label and a category is formed.

Further data collection and analysis will produce other categories; some will be later recoded and some categories will be combined with others. The data is then analyzed for patterns of relationships between two or more categories. These patterns of relationships form initial hypotheses to be tested in the field. Substantive codes are then compared to a ''family'' of theoretical codes; those best depicting the nature of the code are matched according to conceptual categories (theoretical codes) such as conditions, strategies, and consequences (Glaser, 1978). The theoretical code gives order to the relationships between categories thus leading to a theory.

Relationships between categories continue to be developed until a pattern among relationships is conceptualized. Analysis now focuses on the interrelationships and a general theory about these relationships is produced. Thus, at each phase of the analysis for a grounded theory, the researcher generates hypotheses about categories, their relationships and interrelationships, and tests these hypotheses with data. Therefore, the joint collection and analysis of data is an essential strategy of grounded theory research.

Data collection continues until categories become saturated, that is, no new data and no additions are added to the category and one overriding or core category can explain the relationship between all of the others. The core category best explains how a problem is processed.

Writing the theory is also part of the research process in grounded theory. Writing is done throughout the study and is stored in memos. Memos are the written capsules of the analysis and serve to store the ideas generated about the data. Through memo sorting and resorting, the researcher begins to organize the ideas for writing. Memo writing and sorting point out areas for further clarification, refinement, and verification, and lead to further data collection.

Theoretical Sampling

All sampling procedures rest on the notion of representativeness. However, this usually refers to the population and the sampling frame being sought. In standard sampling procedures, representativeness is assured by clarifying the critical variable(s) to be sought in the sample and assuring that there is a way to ascertain that the sample selected reflects these variables in the same way as does the population (Kerlinger, 1973). The desire for representativeness has led to extensive, carefully developed strategies for sampling procedures.

In grounded theory study, the sample is not selected from the population based on certain variables prior to the study. Rather, the initial sample is determined to examine the phenomena where it is found to exist. Then, data collection is guided by a sampling strategy called *theoretical sampling*.

Theoretical sampling is based on the need to collect more data to examine categories and their relationships and to assure that representativeness in the category exists. Simultaneous data collection and analysis are critical elements in grounded theory research. The full range and variation in a category is sought to guide the emerging theory. Each category needs to be tested against incoming data as a full range in a category is sought. Sampling proceeds to produce this range. Sampling to test, elaborate, and refine a category is done for verification or to test the validity of a category. Further sampling is done to develop the categories and their relationships and interrelationships.

Theoretical sampling or sampling to test the conceptualization from analysis can lead the researcher into varied sites which are often substantively different from the initial site. For example, in a study of how elderly people respond to relocation, the researcher may begin data collection in a site where relocation is known to occur. The researcher may collect data in nursing homes, retirement communities, or anywhere where elders have recently relocated. During analysis, a category is generated that relates to crisis and how crisis is managed by elders. In order to assess the full range and variation in this category under different structural conditions, the researcher may collect data on elders who have not relocated but who are experiencing a crisis situation. This may lead to data collection in day centers or in private homes with elders who have had a major loss or several losses. The point here is that the logic of sampling and the site for data collection are guided by analysis. The researcher needs to examine the conceptualization for validity and accuracy. This is done by generating hypotheses and testing them. The site for hypotheses testing varies with the analysis and is determined by the concepts that are being tested.

VALIDITY AND RELIABILITY

Validity and reliability are critical issues in evaluating research findings. In most forms of research, validity and reliability are established through the use of certain procedures for data collection and analysis. In qualitative research, these issues are not addressed in the same way as in quantitative forms of research since the nature of the research process is different. However, qualitative researchers are sensitive to these issues and have developed what could be called "rough analogs" to quantitative measures of reliability and validity, usually referred to as establishing adequacy of evidence and credibility. (See R. M. Emerson, 1983, for a review.)

Major problems in addressing these areas in grounded theory are noted by Charmaz (1983): (1) the lack of a language that describes the analysis of qualitative data using grounded theory and the reliance of often confusing quantitative terms to describe the analytic steps, such as *coding* and *theoretical sampling;* and (2) the rough passage from an oral tradition or a tutorial method of teaching grounded theory to a written tradition which was initiated by Glaser and Strauss (1967) nearly 20 years ago. Inevitably, some written steps are missing. It is the purpose of this book to make explicit some of those steps to nurse researchers who use this method.

Observations and interviews in natural settings allow the researcher to get close to ongoing life of persons interacting under normal, everyday social constraints. This is in contrast to a laboratory setting or other abnormal constraint (Emerson, 1983). As meaningful behavior is derived from social interaction and environmental contexts, the researcher is able to capture both the behavior and the context that gives the behavior background and meaning (see Davis, chapter 5). However, the adequacy of data and analysis must still be addressed and communicated.

Validity

Kerlinger points out that "The subject of validity is complex, controversial and peculiarly important in behavioral research. Here perhaps more than anywhere else, the nature of reality is questioned" (1973, p 456). Cook and Campbell (1979) note that validity refers to the best available approximation to the truth of propositions. They stress the importance of the word approximation when referring to validity, since no one can ever be certain about truth.

There are many types of validity and many names have been used to define the different types of validity (Kerlinger, 1979). Campbell and Stanley (1966) have defined two major forms of validity that encompass the many types. They refer to "internal" and "external" validity. Internal validity refers to the approximate truth in a proposition about the relationship between two variables when cause is inferred (Cook, Campbell, 1979). Internal validity includes the issue of covariance. In internal validity, the construct or theoretical label used to describe the variables and proposition is evaluated. External validity refers to the generalizability of a proposition about a causal relationship across populations (Cook, Campbell, 1979).

Validity during data collection   Denzin (1970) used the distinction between internal and external validity and applied it to qualitative research. According to Denzin, internal validity is threatened during data collection by a number of factors. These factors include the following:

1. History or events that occurred before data collection or those that inter-
    vene during data collection. Historical factors that impinge on the phenom-
    ena under study affect internal validity if they are not accounted for and if
    their impact is not assessed. These factors are addressed by assessing the
    meaning and importance of events which occurred and are occurring, and
    through the use of multiple sources of data, such as document analysis,
    interviews, and participant observation.

2. Subject maturation as a result of the relationship with the investigator and
    the research. Qualitative researchers are particularly sensitive to the effect
    their relationship with informants has on the data and the type of data
    being collected. Detailed field notes about researcher-informant relation-
    ships are used to examine the effects of maturation and changes over the
    course of the study.

3. Subject bias or the difference between the kinds of people studied and
    those not studied. Standard face sheet data that includes biographical infor-
    mation can be collected to assess the extent of subject bias. However, this is
    not the main concern of qualitative researchers using grounded theory;
    they are pursuing theoretical concepts rather than social units (such as race
    and age) which vary over time. Interviews, field notes, and comparative
    analysis are used to examine the extent of bias and to determine ways (that
    is, sites and subjects) to correct this threat to validity.

4. Subject mortality or those subjects who leave the study for whatever rea-
    son (e.g., death, job change, or different living situation). These subjects
    are routinely recorded in field notes with extensive detail. These notes are
    analyzed for the effects these subjects have on validity and the effects
    their coming and going have on others and on the setting. Often, the
    issue of subject mortality can point out further avenues for study. For
    example, in a study of nursing in the intensive care unit, subject mortality
    can suggest hypotheses about stress, nurse retention, and other factors
    the researcher should examine.

5. Reactive effects of the researcher is the factor with which qualitative
    researchers are most concerned. Participant observation, a central
    method of data collection, is by definition interactive. Reactive effects of
    the researcher's presence (ie., the ways the researcher's presence in the
    scene affects the participants) and action needs to be carefully examined.
    Some researchers attempt to minimize or control the effects they produce
    on the situation being studied. Others suggest that they are part of the
    reality and it is taken for granted that they alter what is observed. In the
    first view, reactivity is seen as interference, and in the second it is seen as
    data (Emerson, 1983). In both views, reactivity as a result of the research-
    er's presence is addressed through careful, detailed description and analy-
    sis of the situation. Researchers are aware of and sensitive to how they are
    treated and seen by those in the scene. Gussow (1964) said that the inter-

action of the researcher in the setting is expected and should be viewed as process, the effects of which are analyzed by the researcher.

6. Changes in the observer or the extent the observer is affected by the participants and the scene. One term used to describe this threat to validity in field data is "going native" or assuming the attitudes and behavior of those under study. It is expected that the observer will change as a result of the study and the interaction with participants. One method used to control for the effects of changes is to record changes over time. Researchers keep personal notes on their actions, interactions, and subjective states in the field. Conscious introspection and analysis of field notes permit researchers to be aware of these changes and use their own changes and subjective states to further heighten the sensitivity of the analysis. The following excerpt from a field note illustrates the type of note and data that is recorded to monitor, assess, and analyze changes in the observer. This field note was written more than a year after the relationship with the informant had been established.

FIELD NOTES

Effects on Researcher

June 3, 1981

The first person I met in this nursing home was Grace. I remember, I was waiting to meet the administrator to explain the study. I had to wait and so I sat in the front hallway and began chatting with Grace who sat in a wheelchair there. So began the relationship with this woman who was to teach me so much, not only about life in nursing homes but about life in general. Grace had been a resident for many years in this nursing home. Her pragmatic view of life, her confiding in me about happenings in the home when I wasn't there, and her belief in life all led me to like her and then become friends with her. When she started her downward physical course that was to lead to her death eight agonizing months later, I knew (because I experienced it) how staff feel when they watch their special, beloved patients die. It is more than a professional relationship that develops between people here. You share your life with them and they share theirs with you. . . . The effects that this woman and our relationship had on my life, the things she taught me, told me, shared with me, have affected me profoundly. Not only do I see people and relationships in nursing homes differently but I now understand life more. This feels like a lasting effect. My perceptions on relationships have changed. . . . I miss Grace.

In this case, the relationship between informant and researcher increased the researcher's sensitivity about relationships between staff and residents in nursing homes.

External validity rests on the generalizability of the observations to other populations (Denzin, 1970). Denzin notes that in order to handle this threat to validity, the researcher needs to "demonstrate that the case(s) he studies are representative of the class of units to which generalizations are made" (1970, p 200). In grounded theory, generalizability is handled by detailed description during the data collection and assigning membership to a class or unit to the case under study. In grounded theory, external validity rests on internal variety. The greater the range and the variation sought through theoretical sampling, the more certain that the data is generalizable to other members of the same class or units as the phenomena under study. The greater the internal variety, the greater the likelihood the researcher has sought out and addressed the "negative case," that is, the case that does not fit an existing category or proposition (Glaser, 1978).

Validity of data analysis   The credibility of the theory is also important. Grounded theory is based on data collected through research and is intimately linked to data. A grounded theory must "fit" the phenomena under study, have "grab," and "work" when put to use (Glaser, Strauss, 1967). "Fit" in a grounded theory means that the categories that are generated must be indicated by the data and applied readily to the data. "Grab" means that the theory speaks to or is relevant to the social or practice world and to persons in that world. "Work" refers to the relevance or usefulness of the theory to explain, interpret, and predict phenomena under study (Glaser, Strauss, 1967). Modifiability is another criteria of a grounded theory. This refers to the need to qualify a theory over time and to adapt to rapidly changing social conditions. Glaser points out that with time,

> *always something emerges that requires generating qualification of what came before . . . Though basic social processes remain in general. Their variation and relevance is ever changing in our world (1978, p 4).*

As theory, grounded theory is abstract and able to interpret, explain and predict phenomena.

Reliability

Reliability in quantitative research refers to the accuracy of a measuring instrument over repeated measures (Kerlinger, 1973). Reliability and replicability are associated. Another way of addressing reliability is through replicating the study. The lack of replicability in grounded theory has been a major critique of this method. Grounded theorists are often asked, "If I were to repeat this study would I find or generate the same results, that is, theory?" There is no simple answer to this question. Perhaps the best answer to the question of exact replication is "no." Since grounded theory is derived from the researcher's best analysis which includes the researcher's skill, creativity, time, resources, and analytic ability, no two analyses will be exactly alike, since no two researchers are exactly alike. A more appropriate question to ask about grounded theory is, "If I apply this theory to a similar situation will it work, that is, allow me to interpret, understand, and predict phenomena?" The answer to this question would be "yes." The test for reliability in theory is through the use of the theory and its applicability to similar settings and to other types of problems over time.

It must be noted that Denzin's effort to specifically address the issues of validity and reliability in qualitative field research is an attempt to create a rough analog between these research approaches. Qualitative researchers generally avoid the terms *validity* and *reliability*. As stated, these issues, that is, the truth and accuracy of the data and analysis, are usually handled by terms such as *evidence* and *credibility* of the data and analysis.

NURSING AND GROUNDED THEORY

The development of a scientific basis for nursing practice has been the goal of nursing for the past 25 years. Research in nursing is the major means through which a science of nursing is to be developed. Nursing is a practice profession and the science of nursing must be relevant to the practice of nursing. Research in nursing is expected to generate new knowledge that can ultimately be used to guide nursing action and interventions. Relevancy of nursing science is a critical issue for the profession. Yet, as Wilson points out, "Voices in the vanguard of leadership in nursing call for bridging the gap between research and practice, a gap sometimes viewed as an abyss" (1985, p 32).

Grounded theory offers a systematic method to collect, organize and analyze data from the empirical world of nursing practice. Grounded theory is an approach to theory development based on the study of human conduct and the contexts and forces that impinge on human conduct. Benoliel notes that such theory can provide "one means of conceptualizing the interacting influences of personal characteristics, social processes, and cultural circumstances as they bear on the adaptation of individuals and groups to crisis and change" (1983, p 184).

Grounded theory holds promise for a fuller and deeper understanding of nursing knowledge and a method to generate theory in a practice profession. It is not surprising that interest in grounded theory is increasing among nurses and other health care professionals. This interest should spark further theory development and understanding of the world of nurses and their clients.

References

Benoliel JQ: Grounded theory and qualitative data: The socializing influences of life threatening disease on identity development, in Wooldridge PJ, Schmitt MH, Skipper JK et al (eds): *Behavioral Science and Nursing Theory:* St. Louis, C. V. Mosby Co, 1983.
Blumer, H: *Symbolic Interaction: Perspective and Method.* Englewood Cliffs, New Jersey, Prentice-Hall Publishing Co, 1969.

Campbell DT, Stanley JC: *Experimental and Quasi-Experimental Designs for Research.* Chicago, Rand McNally, 1966.

Charmaz K: The grounded theory method: An explication and interpretation, in Emerson RM (ed): *Contemporary Field Research: A Collection of Readings.* Boston, Little Brown and Co, 1983.

Cook TD, Campbell DT: *Quasi-Experimentation: Design and Analysis Issues for Field Settings.* Boston, Houghton Mifflin Co, 1979.

Denzin NK: *The Research Act.* Chicago, Aldine Publishing Co, 1970.

Emerson RM: *Contemporary Field Research: A Collection of Readings.* Boston, Little Brown and Co, 1983.

Fagerhaugh SY, Strauss A: *The Politics of Pain Management: Staff Patient Interaction.* Menlo Park, California, Addison-Wesley Publishing Co, 1977.

Glaser B: *Theoretical Sensitivity.* Mill Valley, California, The Sociology Press, 1978.

Glaser B, Strauss A: *The Discovery of Grounded Theory.* Chicago, Aldine Publishing Co, 1967.

Glaser B, Strauss AL: The purpose and credibility of qualitative research. *Nurs Res* 1966; 15:56–61.

Gussow Z: The observer-observed relationship as information about structure in small group research: A comparative study of urban elementary school classrooms. *Psychiatry* 1964; 27:230–247.

Kaplan A: *The Conduct of Inquiry: Methodology for Behavioral Science.* Scranton, Pennsylvania, Chandler Publishing Co, 1964.

Kerlinger FN: *Foundations of Behavioral Research.* New York, Holt, Rinehart and Winston, Inc, 1973.

Kerlinger FN: *Behavioral Research: A Conceptual Approach.* New York, Holt, Rinehart and Winston, Inc, 1979.

Mead GH: *Mind, Self and Society.* Chicago, University of Chicago Press, 1934.

Melia KM: "Tell it as it is"—qualitative methodology and nursing research: Understanding the student nurse's world. *J Adv Nurs* 1982; 7:327–335.

Morris MB: *An Excursion Into Creative Sociology.* New York, Columbia University Press, 1977.

Stern PN: Grounded theory methodology: Its uses and processes. *Image* 1980; 12:20–23.

Wilson HS: (1985). *Research in Nursing.* Menlo Park, California, Addison-Wesley Publishing Co, 1985.

Wilson HS: Limiting intrusion: social control of outsiders in a healing community, an illustration of qualitative comparative analysis. *Nurs Res* 1982; 26:103–111.

2

The research process in grounded theory

Barbara Artinian

Research is a process, not an act. It begins with an initial curiosity about what is happening or how or why something happens in a particular way. Over time, questions can take on many forms as more is known about the phenomenon under study. In this chapter, we will examine two modes of grounded theory: the discovery mode and the emergent fit mode.

The basic question that needs to be addressed in order to decide the form the research will take is, "What do you want to know about the problem?" For example, within the general problem area of adaptation to a chronic illness there are many different questions that can be asked. As an illustration, the specific situation of adaptation to renal dialysis will be used.

THE DISCOVERY MODE

The discovery mode asks the question, "What patterns can I identify in the problem and how are these patterns related?" This is the type of research often referred to as *grounded theory* (Glaser, Strauss, 1967) or the *discovery model* (Glaser, 1978). If prior descriptive research has not been done for a particular problem area, this is the type of research to use. The purpose of the research is to identify the core variable or the process that describes the characteristics of a particular social world. This approach, which has as its aim the study of human group life and human conduct, is done within the paradigm termed *symbolic interactionism*. Blumer states that the two parts of the methodology used by symbolic interactionists—the direct naturalistic examination of the empirical social world—are exploration and inspection. He writes that exploration is:

> the means of developing and sharpening his inquiry so that his problem, his directions of inquiry, data, analytical relations, and interpretations arise out of, and remain grounded in, the empirical life under study. Exploration is by definition a flexible procedure in which the scholar shifts from one to another line of inquiry, adopts new points of observation as his study progresses, moves in new directions previously unthought of, and changes his recognition of what are relevant data as he acquires more information and better understanding. . . . The purpose of exploratory investigation is to move toward a clearer understanding of how one's problem is to be posed, to learn what are the appropriate data, to develop ideas of what are significant lines of relation, and to evolve one's conceptual tools in the light of what one is learning about the area of life (1969, p 40).

Inspection is the other part of direct naturalistic examination of data. By inspection, Blumer (1969) means an analysis of the empirical content of the analytic elements and an examination of the nature of the relation between such elements.

Both exploration and inspection are used to generate a tentative theory using the discovery mode. This mode allows the researcher to answer the general question of what is going on and how. When the core variable or basic social process which "accounts for most of the variation in the behavior about the problem" is identified, the focus of the research changes from studying the social unit in general to studying the process (Glaser, 1978, p 107). The question is now focused on one specific aspect of behavior.

One way to approach the general problem area of adaptation to renal dialysis is to ask a broad general question about the experience of adaptation to a selected group of dialysis patients. The question should explore varying dimensions of the problem. I asked the question, "How does end-stage renal disease affect the patient's ability to accomplish the normal developmental tasks of young adulthood?" An interview guide was developed that focused on six specific areas: (1) family interaction patterns, (2) social networks and peer relationships, (3) vocational and educational accomplishments, (4) involvement in community and political activities, (5) attitude toward self, and (6) compliance with the dialysis regimen. Specific attention was given to identifying how the young adults integrated the demands of illness into the demands of daily living. Attention was also paid to understanding the patients' definition of self as normal or not normal. Over a 3-year period, 45 young adults between the ages of 18 and 35 were interviewed on several occasions in dialysis units or in their homes. Observations of nurse-patient interactions in the units were made. In addition, physicians, social workers, nurses, and family members were interviewed and observations were made at public meetings held for renal patients and their families. Qualitative data analysis methods were used to develop categories of data which described the process of adaptation to dialysis.

The first question answered was, "What are the various forms adaptation can take?" A conceptual map was developed to describe the process of identity formation for each type of adaptation. A conceptual map is a diagram of the relationships among the variables under study. It shows how the independent variable is linked to the dependent variable. Its major purpose is to organize all the information the researcher has about a phenomenon into a clear statement of the relationships among the variables under investigation. Therefore, it is a useful technique to organize and clarify the concepts in the research problem under study (Artinian, 1982). The conceptual map is similar to the diagram noted by Corbin in chapter 9.

The conceptual map that was constructed related the independent variable of renal failure to a number of dependent or outcome variables which represent the various modes of adaptation the patient may use (Fig. 2-1). Roles identified as specific modes of adaptation include the "Undecided" role, the "Waiter" role, the "Worker" role, the "True Dialysis Patient" role, and the "Emancipated" role (Artinian, 1983). Some of these roles are more adaptive than others; therefore, the next question addressed was, "In terms of the quality of life, what are the consequences for the patient if he takes on one of these roles?" This question is still under investigation.

Another question was asked: "How do interactions with nurses affect the process of taking on a particular role?" The concept of a partnership relationship between the patient and nurse was identified as one that would help the patient accomplish what he identified as important for himself. During the simultaneous collection and analysis of data that takes place in grounded theory, literature related to the conceptual category is often helpful in focusing the research. In this study, the core category, "maintaining control," was identified as contributing to an adaptive response to dialysis which would make it possible for the young adult to accomplish his developmental tasks.

The method of constant comparative analysis used to generate grounded theory makes it possible to progressively focus the research as the data becomes clearer. What can result is the generation of a theory which describes the core category that characterizes the behaviors of the group. Since the theory generated is derived from the observation of only a small group of subjects, it can only be considered as tentative. Through theoretical sampling techniques, the theory can be clarified and refined by asking questions which can provide more in-depth knowledge about the identified core category.

EMERGENT FIT MODE

When a theory has already been developed about the phenomenon under study, the question can be asked within the emergent fit mode. Using this mode, the researcher has identified a theory that was developed by someone else and asks a

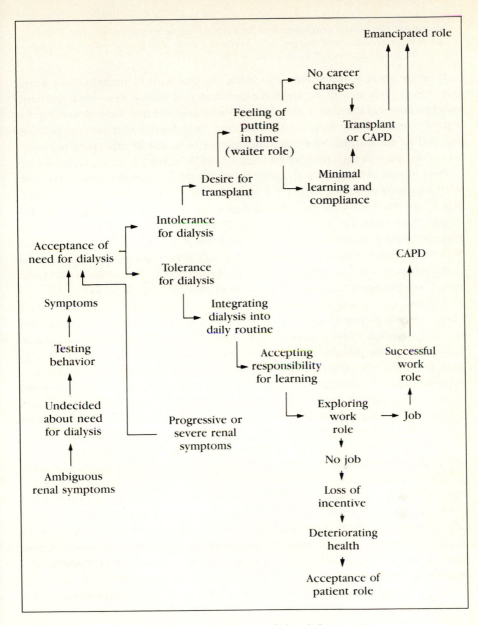

FIGURE 2–1.   Conceptual map: the career of the dialysis patient.

question that will help him extend the theory or refine it into a formal grounded theory. Using this mode, the researcher

does not start "empty" or "non-preconceived" as in the first model. He engages in pre-emergent analytic thinking, and sampling before approaching the field. But once in the field, he starts correcting his early thoughts and follows the grounding in his subsequent theoretical sampling. And he ends up as he would in the first model, searching for comparison groups, as it becomes clearer and clearer where to go for fit as the theory develops (Glaser, 1978, p 108).

However, there is some danger in using the emergent fit mode. Glaser warns that even if there is a fit between the predeveloped theory describing the basic social process and the observations, it cannot be assumed that the core variable for that phenomenon has been discovered since "the basic social process is being imposed for the purpose of generating a theory of it, not of explaining the variation of behavior in the unit studied" (Glaser, 1978, p 108).

Even though the emergent fit mode is not the mode of choice, Glaser says that it has a place in grounded theory if it is done carefully. Blumer supports the emergent fit approach as well if theories, models, or concepts are systematically studied to test their empirical validity. If the comparative analysis techniques of the grounded theory method allow the empirical world to "talk back" to our pictures of it or assertions about it (Blumer 1969, p 22), then earlier impressions can be corrected so that the actual experience of the subjects can be understood. However, Blumer believes "this is not the order of the day" (1969, p 34).

The use of existing theoretical constructs can be valuable in developing a research problem only if they are viewed as tentative and in need of verification from the empirical world of social interaction. And Blumer writes that the theoretical constructs are valuable if the "given research inquiry is guided by a conscientious and continuous effort to test and revise one's images" (1969, p 37).

In the study of adaptation to renal dialysis, maintaining control was identified as the core category central to the process of adaptation to the dialysis regimen. The next research questions that can be asked are, "What are the conditions under which maintaining control is possible?" and "Are there specific characteristics of the subjects or of their interactions with others that enhance the likelihood of maintaining control?" In my study of dialysis patients, my next step is to ask the question, "Are there stages that occur in maintaining control?" A reanalysis of the interviews and field notes with this focus allows the data to be recategorized to answer the new questions. The research questions at this stage direct a more specific investigation of the dimensions of the core category or basic social process.

Ideas for an in-depth investigation can come from a variety of sources. A new group of subjects experiencing a similar life situation can be studied. Nursing literature or the literature of other disciplines may suggest characteristics to be investigated. For example, Seligman has developed the idea of "learned helplessness." He says that the very independent person finds it difficult to submit to the losses he faces because he still has the expectation that he can exert control over his situation (Seligman, 1975, p 60). If Seligman is correct, how is this refusal to submit to losses carried out by dialysis patients? Are there variations in independence that can be measured? To what extent is independence affected by the institutional climate of the dialysis unit?

Another theoretical construct that may be of use in conceptualizing the process of maintaining control is that of "revaluing of self" developed by Woodward

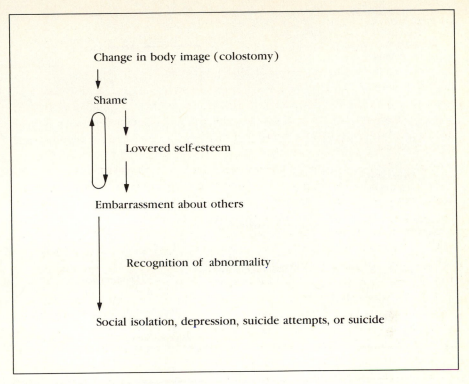

FIGURE 2-2.   Relationship of variables in colostomy literature.

(1982). In her study focusing on how colostomates handle the embarrassment of the colostomy, Woodward initially identified shame and lowered self-esteem as being associated with the experience of embarrassment since others were aware of the colostomy (Fig. 2–2). After an intensive study of the colostomates' experience, Woodward discovered these variables to be important. She identified the process through which colostomates were able to revalue themselves; this process led to acceptance of responsibility for the colostomy and acceptance of themselves as "normals with a physical problem" (Fig. 2–3).

If Woodward wished to extend, refine, or clarify her theory of the revaluing of self, she could select another group of patients also experiencing a body image problem such as the dialysis patients. She could ask the question, "To what extent do dialysis patients go through the experience of devaluing and revaluing self?" For my study, I am interested in the question, "How is revaluing of self related to maintaining control over life?"

In other words, is maintaining control really the basic social process of regaining control? Further examination of the process of regaining control will either establish it as being able to "differentiate and account for variations in the problematic pattern of behavior" (Glaser, 1978, p 97) or not. If it does not, Glaser says the stages to be identified will collapse and there is no basic social process.

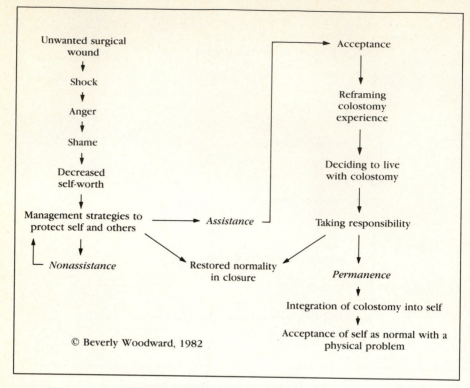

FIGURE 2-3.   The phenomenon of revaluing of self.

CONCLUSION

Each of the modes of approaching research which is described can be carried out using the research methods in this book. It is stressed that the discovery mode is the approach associated most often with grounded theory. There are real dangers of assuming the frame of a preconceived theory in the emergent fit mode. For researchers beginning to use qualitative methods, emergent fit is not recommended.

References

Artinian B: Conceptual mapping: The development of the strategy. *West J Nurs Res* 1982; 4: 379–393.
Artinian B: Role identities of the dialysis patient. *Nephrol Nurse* 1983, 5: 10–14.
Blumer H: *Symbolic Interactionism: Perspective and Method.* Englewood Cliffs, New Jersey: Prentice Hall, Inc, 1969.
Glaser B, Strauss A: *The Discovery of Grounded Theory: Strategies for Qualitative Research.* Chicago, Aldine Publishing Co, 1967.

Glaser B: *Theoretical Sensitivity: Advances in the Methodology of Grounded Theory.* Mill Valley, California, The Sociology Press, 1978.

Seligman M: *Helplessness.* San Francisco, W. H. Freeman and Co, 1975.

Woodward B: *A Descriptive Study on the Phenomenon of Revaluing of Self in Colostomates,* thesis. California State University, Los Angeles, 1982.

3

Surfacing nursing process: A method for generating nursing theory from practice

W. Carole Chenitz
Janice M. Swanson

NURSING PROCESS

The nursing process has long been defined as "determining the client's problems, making plans to solve them, initiating the plan or assigning others to implement it, and evaluating the extent to which to plan was effective in resolving the problems identified" (Nursing Theories Conference Group, 1980). As Henderson (1982) points out, "it's fair to assume that the nursing process is now defined in the established steps of problem solving" (1982, p 103). She also notes that there is nothing unique to nursing about the nursing process, but rather, that we have adapted an analytic process that should and could be used by all health professionals. Unfortunately, acceptance of the nursing process as *the* process in nursing has stifled further examination and articulation of the process dimension of nursing. The nursing process consists of those problem-solving actions and interactions between nurse and client that are directed toward a specific end. These goal-directed behaviors are the ways in which nurses carry out the basic nursing process.

Reprinted with permission from *Journal of Advanced Nursing,* volume 9, number 7. Copyright © 1984, Blackwell Scientific Publications, Ltd.

The following is an example of a typical nurse-client interaction. While the practice site is a methadone maintenance clinic, this interaction can and does occur daily in nursing practice in many settings.

> *It is now 7:00 AM. Brenda Williams, RN, has been dispensing methadone since 6:30 AM. Joe S. steps to the counter. Without a word, Brenda interrupts her routine. She reaches for the breathalyzer and holds it up. Joe leans over and breathes into it. "You're not doing too well; when are you going to see your counselor?" she asks. He replies, "I've got an appointment today." "Okay," Brenda says as she passes him his daily dose of methadone.*

In this interaction, Brenda Williams was implementing the basic nursing process. She was also using the sub-processes of selectively attending (Sullivan, 1953), monitoring, evaluating, protecting, and dispatching (Wilson, 1981), in that order. All of these processes are inherent in this interaction. As in this example, all nursing practice is composed of multiple sub-processes such as these. These processes—that is, goal-directed actions—consist of multiple interactions and are an application of the basic nursing process.

However, the numerous applications of the basic nursing process used by nurses in daily practice cannot capture the level of sophistication and complexity that explains and predicts what nurses do and why, until systematic articulation of the nursing process is done.

This is a difficult but essential task. It is difficult because interactions are hard to capture or re-create and almost impossible to measure (Glaser, Strauss, 1967). It is essential since the basic nursing process has already been defined and analyzed, yet the sub-processes that compose this process are lacking. Nursing research has focused on nursing functions, roles, and specific nurse- or client-determined problems. This leaves gaps in nursing theory which depends heavily on research for development and refinement. Hitherto, the elusive nature of process has inhibited research. However, the need for theory, as well as outcome studies to determine the effects of nursing care, are becoming increasingly important for the discipline and the clients served.

This chapter purports to present a method whereby nursing theory is generated through careful study and analysis of the processes embedded in nursing practice. This method, termed *surfacing nursing process,* is the act of systematically identifying, describing, and analyzing the complex process dimension of nursing which is inherent and grounded in daily practice.

THE PROCESS DIMENSION

A major consequence of the under-development of process in nursing is the non-actualization of nursing as a profession. Without the process dimension more fully articulated, nursing is a discipline that lacks political, institutional, and professional power and hence, lacks control over practice (Fawcett, 1980) which is a basic element of a profession. For example, modern hospitals (where the majority of nurses practice), were created for the practice of medicine (Ashley, 1976). While nursing is essential to the practice of medicine, as well as to the maintenance and promotion of health, the number of nurses in hospitals is often determined by the needs of the medical regimen. Nurses are often frustrated that staffing patterns do not provide for implementation of the nursing care plan. For example, a nurse may give medication to a distressed patient, an angry patient, a fearful patient, and a patient with the need for knowledge, all in rapid succession. The medical regimen prescribes administration of a medication; the process of administration, however, is nursing. Due to staffing patterns and lack of attention to and knowledge of the process and sub-processes involved, this process may be cut short. The nurse may give the medication and carry out the medical regimen but may be forced to ignore the nursing needs of these patients.

As professionals, Schlotfeldt (1974) claims nurses are "to regard with certainty the mission they are expected to accomplish . . . grasp the significance of their corporate mission and the enduring responsibility it entails and be willing to be held accountable for fulfilling its obligations" (1974, p 20). How can nurses fulfill this dictum of professional practice without full, detailed descriptions and explanations of nursing process? Surfacing nursing process is the describing and analyzing via research, those processes submerged in practice. In order to do this, we need to shift our current epistemology of science from one dominated by theory-testing and problem-solving to one that captures the data inherent in nurse-client interactions. These interactions form the basis of nursing practice and theory development.

NURSING'S CURRENT EPISTEMOLOGY
OF SCIENCE

Another major consequence caused by lack of process knowledge is the generation of theory unique to nursing. Nursing research reflects and amplifies this consequence since nursing research is guided by existing theory. Thus, most published research reflects a deductive, theory-testing epistemology.

Theory consists of concepts and propositions that relate concepts (Blumer, 1969). Concepts and propositions are tested in the empirical world via research. Theory tells us not only what to look at, but why we look at it (Denzin, 1970). As new knowledge about concepts and propositions are generated, it is incorporated into existing theory. The organization of knowledge into theory provides explanations that allow for prediction and control over events in the empirical world (Kaplan, 1964). Thus, theory guides research and research feeds back into theory.

Much nursing research is guided by theory generated for the purpose of other disciplines. For example, Maslow's (1954) theory of human needs is a popular framework used in studies on nursing practice (Slocum et al., 1972). Other studies on the same subject operationalize a combination of Maslow's and Herzberg's theory to guide research (Longest, 1974; White, Maguire, 1973; Benton, White, 1972). The use of multiple theories to frame a study suggests that all variables under study in a nursing project may not be explained by theories from other disciplines.

Nursing research is also guided by nursing theory. However, many nursing theories rely heavily on concepts borrowed from others and adapted to nursing. For example, the theories of King, Roy, Rodgers, and Orem adapt systems theory to nursing (McFarlane, 1980). Paterson and Zeewald (1976) use Buber's concept of I-thou to conceptualize nursing interactions. We cannot expect to generate theory specific to nursing by testing theories and concepts developed for the purposes of other disciplines. In other words, research guided by Maslow's theory adapted to nursing will help to refine, elaborate, and correct Maslow's theory. The same notion can be applied to borrowed and applied concepts as well.

Finally, as Stevens (1979) points out, many nursing theories are based on fantasized ideals about what nursing should be rather than what nursing is. Research based on theories about nursing ideals may be blinded to the real phenomena under study.

Thus, this epistemology of science—which is the predominant orientation of nurse researchers, scholars, and educators—is based on assumptions problematic for nursing research for the purpose of theory development. These assumptions are: (1) theories can be generated from other disciplines and applied to nursing; (2) existing concepts adequately explain all variables under study; (3) and current nursing theory can be operationalized via models to guide both research and practice.

Shared Scientific Meaning

Concepts are the most critical elements in any theory since, as Blumer (1969) points out, "they are the means, and the only means of such connection (between theory and the empirical world), for it is the concept that points to such empirical instances about which a theoretical proposal is made" (Blumer, 1969, p 143). We know from nursing theories that concepts basic to nursing are man, environment, health, and nursing, in constant interaction (Flaskerud, Halloren, 1980). These concepts, however, are broad and general. A shared scientific meaning of these concepts is essential. Without consensual definition within a scientific community, concepts are subject to ambiguity. Ambiguity in a concept leads to weak theory since vaguely or broadly defined concepts will have different meanings for different people (Denzin, 1970; Blumer, 1969).

An example of a broadly defined concept is the development of the concept, "man." While man may encompass gender differences and apply to a woman as well as a man, it may apply not only to the individual but to all of mankind or humanity. There are many dimensions of the concept man as used in nursing literature. A broad range of physical, social, and psychological characteristics are inherent in this concept. Many of these characteristics we need and have borrowed from other disciplines, such as "personality" from psychology. Man may be seen as a mosaic which nursing has assembled from other disciplines. Development of the concept man must tell us what man is like, the nature, diversity, and range of variation embodied by this concept that reflects the holistic perspective of nursing (Swanson, 1980). Thus, concept development must be both specific and generalizable. Concepts are a bridge between the phenomenon under study in the empirical world and theory (Blumer, 1969). Therefore, concepts upon which nursing theory is shaped must be relevant to daily practice and have scientific meanings within the discipline of nursing. Nursing concepts must reflect the dynamic nature of man as experienced by nursing.

In the approach espoused here, man as a concept for a psychiatric nurse in a methadone maintenance clinic means a specific client with characteristics that epitomize a sub-population (alcohol and multiple drug abusers) within this population. This population has particular lifestyles, behavior patterns, norms, and expectations and experiences that have brought them to the clinic. While these are shared they may be different for each client (Nelson, 1973). Perhaps some of these characteristics of drug abusers could be generalizable to other "deviant" groups.

At more abstract levels, this concept of man for nurses specializing in substance abuse may share characteristics with other populations and groups of man who are at conflict with the values and norms of the larger society of man. Concepts based on process would provide both new understandings and awareness as well as provide a way to translate perceptions into meaningful language.

Scientific Discovery

Scientific discovery is based on the judicious use of induction, deduction, and intuition.

The development of quantum physics was a scientific discovery that had profound effects on our world. In order to generate this "new physics," basic paradoxes concerning the nature of subatomic matter had to be resolved. How could subatomic units of matter be both a particle and a wave (Capra, 1975)? As Capra notes about this discovery,

> *Every time the physicists asked nature a question about an atomic experiment, nature answered with a paradox. It took them a long time to accept the fact that these paradoxes belong to the intrinsic structure of atomic physics. . . . Once this was perceived, the physicists began to ask the right questions (1975, p 55).*

Physicists first had to intuitively accept the paradox intrinsic in the subatomic world in order to resolve it. Then through inductive logic the right questions were posed. Once the answers to these questions were forthcoming, deduction and induction enabled them to discover the "new physics."

In order for nurse researchers and scholars to make scientific discoveries, we must immerse ourselves in the practice world. Since induction, deduction, and intuition are inherent in practice, the "right" questions for nurse researchers will use all of these modes. In a discussion of theory development in nursing, Newman writes,

> *. . . there is a need to develop methods which will depict the holistic, dynamic nature of man as a living system in a constantly changing world . . . [and] which are reflective of the complexity of the real world situation of practitioner and client (1979, pp 69–70).*

SHIFTING TO SURFACING NURSING PROCESS

Nursing's approach to theory development—that of adaptation of knowledge and concepts—is common among disciplines new to the scientific/analytic world (Craig, 1980). In nursing, however, this approach is problematic because theories based on broad, borrowed concepts are not prescriptive since they fail to predict nursing action. For example, Underwood's model (Patricia Underwood, RN, D.N.S., personal communication, Nov. 1981) that adapts and refines Orem's (1980) self-care theory clearly provides guidelines based on ideals for psychiatric nursing practice in in-patient settings. Since the model is based on global concepts, however, interventions are not prescribed for the specific situations nurses frequently encounter. This can leave a nurse interacting with an increasingly frightened psychotic patient with only broad concepts to guide her interventions. While a nurse may understand theoretically what she should do, based on the Underwood/Orem model, she must rely on deduction, induction, and intuition to translate the model into the specific situation while filling in clinical gaps. This is done rapidly and under stress. Clear description of the central process that explains the action in the situation is needed. This description would include major processes that have been generated by similar situations, the interventions used, and outcomes of the use of these processes. This information would provide the specificity necessary for nursing interventions and the generalizability essential for theory development.

Shifting to surfacing nursing process means that attention in theory development is given to generation of theory through analysis of data systematically collected from observations of nursing as it occurs.

Surfacing Nursing Process Into Theory: The Method

Let us look at Brenda Williams, RN, an expert in substance abuse nursing that we examined earlier. We noted that Williams used multiple processes of selectively attending, monitoring, evaluating, protecting, and dispatching, in that order. Table 3–1 illustrates the analysis of this interaction from which these processes were identified.

The question raised here is, where can this approach to research lead us? Williams used multiple processes to carry out an intervention. Through analysis of this intervention, we have categorized it as "watchful monitoring." The definition of this intervention is the on-going selective assessment of specific problem areas and potential problem areas based on knowledge of the client population, disease processes, nursing assessment, and awareness of the individual client's history and current functional status in multiple areas. One could further conjecture that Williams's use of these processes and this intervention would shift and perhaps change with every client. If we were to observe her practice carefully, other processes would emerge. They, too, could be analyzed.

For example, later that morning, this same nurse engaged in the following interaction with Frank H., another client in the methadone clinic.

TABLE 3–1.   Line-by-line analysis of interaction

Interaction	Analysis	Processes
It is now 7:00 AM.	Setting: clinic Context: early morning dose for working clients.	
Brenda Williams, RN, has been dispensing methadone since 6:30 AM.	Clinic opens at this time schedule arranged for clients to hold jobs. Client determined hours.	Dispensing (clinic)
Joe S. steps to the counter.	He has been waiting his turn. Methadone distributed at a counter, clients wait in other area.	Distributing (clinic)
Without a word, Brenda interrupts her routine.	Why did she break routine? *Selectively attending* to something about this client.	Selectively attending (patient)
She reaches for the breathalyzer and holds it up. Joe leans over and breathes into it. "You're not doing too well;	Problem related to alcohol use/abuse *monitoring* his alcohol. Not a word spoken. Checked results *evaluating* this particular problem. She is concerned about this problem for him. Cannot dispense.	Monitoring (patient) Evaluating (patients)
when are you going to see your counselor?" she asks. He replies, "I've got an appointment today." "Okay," Brenda says as she passes him his daily dose of methadone.	*Protecting* him from persisting or going unchecked with this problem.	Protecting (patient)
	Sends him, *dispatches* him to appropriate person, then dispenses daily dose	Dispatching (patient) Dispensing (clinic)

As Frank opens his locked box and hands Brenda his empty bottles, she notes, "You're missing a bottle. What's going on that you don't have it?" "Last week I forgot my box; Alex picks me up at 5:30 in the morning, I just can't get it together that early," he explains. Brenda completes the interaction, "Well, bring it tomorrow or you know I can't help you." She hands him his drink dose and he leaves.

With this client, she again selectively attends, this time to the missing bottle. She was also probing, setting limits, and predicting consequences. In this interaction, her knowledge of this client and the population led her to suspect that a missing bottle may be a bottle sold on the street. She was also probing to assure that he wasn't "high" at this time and able to converse in a coherent manner. The processes she used culminated in a central process known as "calling a scam" (Christina Krumenaker, RN, Betty Green, RN, Cheryl Johnstone, RN, personal communication, April, 1982). Although neither she nor Frank mentions this, he is alerted that she suspects that he may be selling his bottles. She uses these multiple processes to complete the central process in a non-threatening and non-judgmental manner. Her expertise with this population makes her aware of the sensitivity of the ex-addict to judgment by the "straight" world. She is also aware that rule testing and rule breaking characterizes this population. She alerted him to his non-compliance by implementing calling a scam.

Further data collection would require us to closely examine other nurses practicing in methadone clinics. Comparisons between the processes they use and those Williams uses would be made.

For example, Pat Brody, another registered nurse in the clinic, has the following interaction with Daniel P.:

"Where's your box, Dan?" she asks as he steps up to the counter. "I don't have one yet," he answers. "You know that I have to take our box back today; you are supposed to have your box and lock today," she explains. "I never got it," he responded. Pat Brody concludes, "You've had plenty of time to get your box, we've told you all week to get it, now I can't give you your methadone until I see a box, with a lock." Dan hands the "loaner" box back to Pat and leaves.

While detailed analysis reveals that Pat was selectively attending, reviewing, imposing consequences, and forcing compliance, this interaction could also be analyzed to reveal the basic process Pat used with Dan called "jamming." In this process, the nurse is using an intervention that is more forceful than calling a scam. In this case, jamming is used to enforce clinic regulations, as well as to impose the consequences for non-compliance with regulations and the treatment program (C. Krumenaker, B. Green, C. Johnstone, personal communication, May, 1982).

We would then look for specific situations that call up these processes. We would examine the content, context, and interaction as they exist. In each of these cases, multiple processes were used. However, selectively attending, or specifically focusing in, emerged as a basic process used by nurses in a methadone clinic. Selectively attending could then lead to specific interventions, like calling a scam or jamming. We would then test these emerging concepts about process and intervention. For example, one of us in our daily practice suspected that two in-patients on a psychiatric unit had just smoked marijuana. Without hard evidence, there were no direct consequences, yet the potential scam or non-compliance had to be attended to. During the ensuing interaction, one of the clients became upset and defensive. The response was "I am not jamming you. I am letting you know." The client immediately relaxed, stating, "Oh, I thought you were gonna jam me." This interaction can be repeated or observed in multiple psychiatric settings with substance abusers. Their awareness of this intervention is obvious in this interaction. Since both the intervention and the name developed from multiple nurse-client interactions over time in multiple settings, it has meaning for both nurse and client.

Eventually, basic and central processes such as these would emerge. These processes may characterize nursing in a methadone clinic or nursing with substance abusers in a variety of mental health settings. We would understand how and why certain situations with certain clients will call up a specific set of processes. If our purposes were to develop a nursing theory of substance abuse, we would then go to other methadone clinics and repeat the observation, recording, analysis, and testing presented here. We would again compare processes after carefully isolating them. We would look for those processes that recur and explore until we understand why they recurred. We would then analyze for processes that led to an intervention, and describe the intervention and the processes that compose it. We would continue until no new data, no new processes could be uncovered. We would stop here if our focus was on nursing methadone clients. However, let us continue on in this approach.

Knowledge of the basic processes that characterize substance abuse nursing might then lead us to an alcohol treatment in-patient program or an alcohol out-patient program or both. We would again examine processes. We would observe, raise questions, compare, study, and carefully analyze the practice of alcohol nursing with that of nursing in a methadone clinic. Again, basic processes in both areas might be identified. That would lead us to elaboration and refinement of the emerging processes. For example, while conducting a group on the alcohol in-patient unit, Carlene, the registered nurse, noted that one of the residents may have taken a drink since she smelled alcohol on his breath. Immediately after the group, she and her nursing colleagues confronted him or "called the potential scam." Since this was a serious violation of the program, testing for the scam had to be done. After the resident completed the breathalyzer test, her suspicions were confirmed. She then explained what they would do and the specific consequences that could result. The following morning, the entire community would meet and discuss whether he should be expelled from the program. In this example, Carlene moved from calling a scam, called "confronting" on this unit, to possible expulsion from the treatment program, the most forceful intervention that can be used (C. Eniex, RN, W. Granfors, RN, personal communication, June 9, 1982).

We may then go to in-patient psychiatric units, day treatment centers, community mental health centers, and so on. Comparative analysis would lead us to an understanding of the basic processes used by psychiatric nurses. We can generalize from these processes and the conditions under which we observed them, a process-oriented theory of psychiatric nursing.

Multiple small theories from various clinical subspecialties could then be compared via their basic processes (Fig. 3–1). Links within and between subspecialty areas would be created by noting common processes. For example, protecting may emerge as a central process for geriatric nursing, psychiatric nursing, and pediatric nursing; selectively attending may be central to all of nursing practice. These clinical process theories would provide the basis for formulating a mid-range practice theory. Further abstraction could conceivably lead to a unified formal theory of nursing practice.

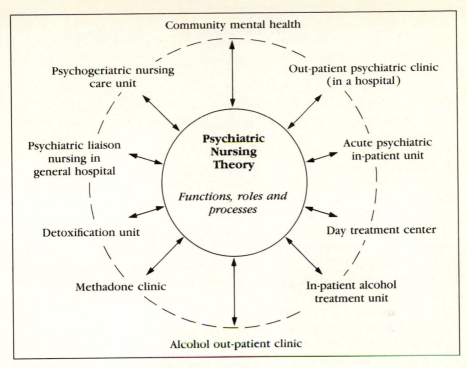

Community mental health

Psychogeriatric nursing
care unit

Out-patient psychiatric clinic
(in a hospital)

Psychiatric liaison
nursing in
general hospital

**Psychiatric
Nursing
Theory**

*Functions, roles and
processes*

Acute psychiatric
in-patient unit

Detoxification unit

Day treatment center

Methadone clinic

In-patient alcohol
treatment unit

Alcohol out-patient clinic

FIGURE 3–1.   Process linkage to formulate clinical theories in specialties. The processes within each structure that emerge as central: these are in constant interaction with generating theory, as processes may change to fit client needs or theory becomes refined. (------) The fitting and comparing of processes between subspecialties in psychiatric nursing. This is an open line since links may be made between one subspecialty and another.

Clinical, mid-range, and formal theory would be in constant interaction, subject to elaboration, correction, and verification as practice changes to fit the empirical world (Fig. 3–2).

Theories generated in this way would by their nature be prescriptive, that is, not only explaining but allowing for prediction, control, and nursing action. Since they are generated from the empirical world of nursing to explain the processes that are used under different conditions, surfaced theory would lead us to new understandings of the depths of nursing knowledge in action.

THE TASK OF THE RESEARCHER AND
SCHOLAR

Generating theory by surfacing nursing process requires not only an epistemological shift, but would emphasize the use and/or creation of methodology that would

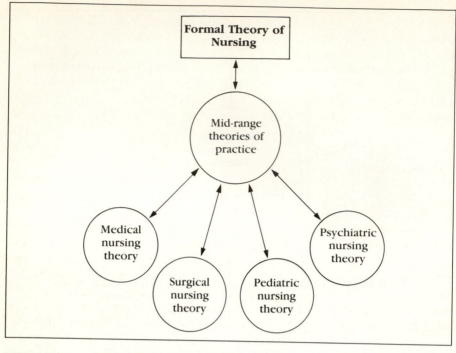

FIGURE 3–2.   Process linkage to formulate clinical theories from specialties into mid-range and formal theory. Only four specialty areas are represented for diagram clarity. The terms medical, surgical, pediatric, and psychiatric nursing theory are used since theory is generated from practice in specific sites. Conceptually, each area in nursing practice would be included and the subspecialties or structures that compose the subspecialty would be represented.

suit the task. Finely tuned descriptive, analytic, writing and interpersonal skills would be required of the researcher. For example, the researcher may decide that observation during methadone administration is insufficient to describe the scope of practice of nurses specializing in this area. Other techniques or methods for data collection would then be used, such as co-leading groups, participating in staff meetings, informal and formal interviews with staff and clients, and perhaps, at times, full participation in the practice setting.

Surfacing nursing process is a method that relies on both induction and deduction at different levels of theory development. An inductive approach is essential to comprehend the world of nursing practice and pursue the questions that arise naturally as one attempts to order the natural world through analysis (Melia, 1982). In this chapter, we presented only those processes and interventions that centered around "compliance" in a methadone clinic. The question the researcher may ask now is, what are those processes that compose interventions for the successful client in this program, one for whom compliance and management of daily functioning is no longer an important issue?

One would then focus on nurse interactions with successful clients. Theoretically, one could order the three case illustrations presented here in the form of a triangle. Most interventions, we could hypothesize, would resemble the first case and would use the processes that compose "watchful monitoring" in varying forms. This would be the base of the triangle. However, if this intervention uncovers a problem area, then calling a scam may be used. If this fails, jamming may be applied and after repeated jammings and other interventions failed to produce the desired outcomes, then expelling or detoxing from the program may be implemented. Conceptually and in practice, the tip of the triangle would represent expelling, the most forceful and least used intervention.

At the practice level or clinical level of analysis, induction would order the data analytically. Both induction and deduction would be used to formulate the research questions as they emerge. Induction and deduction may be used conjointly at the mid-range level of analysis to order the data into a comprehensive whole or a theory of practice. At the formal level, again deduction and induction would be used to refine, elaborate, quantify, and test the theories generated at the mid-range and clinical levels of analysis. The researchers' expertise in specific research approaches would vary depending upon the level of theory focused. However, in this method, without clinical theory from specific situations, theory development does not proceed. This method provides a built-in system of checks to assure the relatedness of research and practice.

Since it is from participation, observation, and immersion in nursing practice in a specialty area that surfaced theory emerges, surfacing nursing theory may appear similar to other inductive research approaches and qualitative methods for data collection and analysis; namely those used by phenomenologists (Oiler, 1982), ethnomethodologists (Evanseshko, Kay, 1982), and grounded theorists (Glaser, Strauss, 1967). In developing this method, we have availed ourselves of our research background in grounded theory. But more importantly, we have availed ourselves of our background in nursing and knowledge of the depth of nursing theory in action. While distinctly different from other inductive approaches, surfacing nursing process shares a common philosophical bond and methodologies (such as participant observation and interview data analyzed for basic social processes) with grounded theorists (Glaser, 1978).

The focus of the method proposed here is on nursing process and sub-processes which compose nursing interventions. This focus and specificity on nursing intervention make surfacing nursing process unique to nursing, as grounded theory is unique to sociology. Surfacing nursing process is an attempt to provide a systematic method for theory development. This approach can also be used to organize those interventions that are already surfaced and available in the clinical literature into process theories. An interactive link between the research and clinical literature could develop. Researchers would use clinical source material for analytic purposes. Clinicians would use the research literature to assist conceptualization, and thus a better understanding of their practice. Unfortunately, this interaction between the research and clinical sources does not currently exist (Downs, 1982).

In this method, the central purpose of the researcher is to fully and adequately describe a specific situation, analyze each situation for processes, develop basic and central processes, and identify how these processes are used in carrying out nursing interventions.

As Rubin noted:

> We *must* bring to the surface *the latent meanings that may lie outside the immediate awareness of the person who speaks them. And it's our task, too, to develop some system of ordering those words into a conceptual frame that permits a broader and deeper understanding than already exists (emphasis ours) (1981, p 102).*

This broader and deeper understanding can lead to scientific discovery in nursing.

CONCLUSION

We have attempted to present a method whereby nursing theory is generated through careful study and analysis of the processes submerged and imbedded in nursing. This method, called *surfacing nursing process,* requires a shift in our current epistemology of science. We have asserted that scientific discovery in nursing hinges on the use of deduction, induction, and intuition. These processes characterize nursing but are not used in research since our current epistemology of science relies heavily on deduction.

In order to point out the need for this shift in epistemology, we examined flaws in our current theories and weaknesses in concepts central to nursing theories. However, the purpose of this critical examination is not to detract from current theories—certainly benchmarks in the development of nursing—but to point out future directions that can be taken and the benefits to be gained by exploring alternatives to our current approach.

Having engaged in discourse with nurse colleagues over these subjects many times, we are aware that not all nursing scholars find tenable this presentation nor the method proposed. This is the fundamental basis of this paper. There is no simple way, no true path that will lead us to discovery. Dogma has no place in science. Attachment to theory or methodology by researchers and scholars impedes scientific progress.

Science is the search for truth. Theory organizes these truths into patterns that connect them into a meaningful whole. Theory is generated on different levels of abstraction for different purposes. In nursing, a discipline committed to human interaction as well as scientific knowledge, there are and must be many ways to arrive at theory.

We have presented one method, surfacing nursing process, as a way to provide the specificity required of a practice profession and the generalizability from the specific. This is necessary for theory development. When we understand how and why Brenda Williams, RN, uses certain processes in her practice, scientific discovery in nursing will not be far off.

References

Ashley JA: *Hospitals, Paternalism and the Role of the Nurse.* New York, Teachers College Press, 1976.

Benton DA, White HC: Satisfaction of job factors for registered nurses. *J Nurs Admin* 1972; 2:55–63.

Bower FL: *The Process of Planning Nursing Care.* St. Louis, CV Mosby, 1982.

Blumer H: *Symbolic Interactionism: Perspective and Method.* Englewood Cliffs, New Jersey, Prentice Hall, 1969.

Capra E: *The Tao of Physics.* New York, Bantam Books, 1975.

Craig S: Theory development and its relevance for nursing. *J Adv Nurs* 1980; 5:349–355.

Denzin NK: *The Research Act.* Chicago, Aldine Publishing Company, 1970.

Downs F: What's going on here? *Nurs Res* 1982; 31:323 (editorial).

Evanseshko V, Kay MA: The ethnoscience research technique. *West J Nurs Res* 1982; 4:49–64.

Fawcett J: A declaration of nursing independence: The relation of theory and research to nursing practice. *J Nurs Admin* 1980; 10:36–39.

Flaskerud JH, Halloran EJ: Areas of agreement in nursing theory development. *Adv Nurs Sci* 1980; 3:1–7.

Glaser B: *Theoretical Sensitivity.* Mill Valley, California, Sociology Press, 1978.

Glaser BG, Strauss A: *The Discovery of Grounded Theory.* Chicago, Aldine, 1967.

Henderson V: The nursing process: Is the title right? *J Adv Nurs* 1982; 7:103–109.

Kaplan A: *The Conduct of Inquiry: A Methodology for Behavioral Science.* Scranton, Pennsylvania, Chandler, 1964.

Longest B: Job satisfaction for registered nurses in the hospital setting. *J Nurs Admin* 1974; 4:46–52.

Maslow AH: *Motivation and Personality.* New York, Harper & Row, 1954.

McFarlane EA: (1980) Nursing theory: The comparison of four theoretical proposals. *J Adv Nurs* 1980; 5:3–19.

Melia KM: "Tell it as it is"—qualitative methodology and nursing research: Understanding the student nurse's world. *J Adv Nurs* 1982; 7:327–335.

Nelson KS: The nurse in a methadone maintenance program. *Am J Nurs* 1973; 73:870–874.

Newman M: *Theory Development in Nursing.* Philadelphia, FA Davis, 1979.

Nursing Theories Conference: Nursing Theories: The Base for Professional Nursing Practice, Englewood Cliffs, New Jersey, Prentice Hall, 1980.

Oiler C: The phenomenological approach in nursing research. *Nurs Res* 1982; 31:178–181.

Orem D: *Nursing: Concepts of Practice,* ed 2. New York, McGraw Hill, 1980.

Paterson J, Zeewald L: *Humanistic Nursing.* New York, John Wiley, 1976.

Rubin L: Sociological research: The subjective dimension: The 1980 SSSI distinguished lecture. *Symbolic Interaction* 1981; 4:97–112.

Schlotfeldt R: On the professional basis of nursing. *Nurs Forum* 1974; 13:16–31.

Slocum JW, Sussman GI, Sheridan JE: An analysis of need satisfaction and job performance among professional and paraprofessional hospital personnel. *Nurs Res* 1972; 21:338–341.

Stevens BJ: *Nursing Theory: Analysis. Application Evaluation.* Boston, Little Brown, 1979.

Sullivan HS: *The Interpersonal Theory of Psychiatry.* New York, W. W. Norton, 1953.

Swanson, J: Qualitative research using grounded theory. Presented at the Second Annual Patient Education Research Seminar, University of California. San Francisco, Dec 6, 1980.

White CH, Maguire MC: Job satisfaction and dissatisfaction among hospital nursing supervisors. *Nurs Res* 1973; 22:25–30.

Wilson HS: Usual hospital treatment in the community mental health system: A dispatching process. Presented at the American Public Health Association meeting, Los Angeles, Nov 3, 1981.

4

Getting started: The research proposal for a grounded theory study

W. Carole Chenitz

Getting started on a research project means going from an idea to a written proposal. Although much has been written on this subject in nursing research texts, there is little information available to assist nurses in developing a qualitative research project. In this chapter, the reader is guided through the early stages that lead from an idea toward a research proposal using grounded theory methodology. For purposes of organization, this chapter is arranged according to the steps in the process of developing a qualitative project using grounded theory, not necessarily in the order in which the research proposal will be written. We will address the following: recognizing the problem, stating research questions, purpose of the research, specific aims, statement of the problem, reviewing the literature, and the theoretical framework. Later chapters in this book will address the following sections in detail: methods of data collection, data analysis, and writing and critiquing the research report.

THE RESEARCH PROPOSAL

The research proposal is the researcher's plan to study a problem. Every research proposal contains certain key elements. The merit of a proposal is judged by how the researcher handles these elements, how well they interrelate, and how the overall plan relates to the problem addressed. These key elements are organized in a systematic way which allows reviewers to follow the researcher's understanding of the problem and thinking process.

The key elements of every proposal include the following: purpose of the research, statement of the problem, specific aims, review of the literature, theoretical framework, methods of study, and data analysis. Each of these key elements contains sub-elements or a subset of questions that are answered in a specific section of the proposal. It is important to note that the key elements for all proposals remain the same, while the sub-elements will differ considerably in a proposal for a grounded theory study. The relative importance of each element and the depth and detail required in the proposal depends on the reason the researcher has engaged in the work. For example, in a doctoral dissertation, the theoretical framework will be particularly valued. On the other hand, in a research proposal to the National Institutes of Health, the theoretical framework may have less importance relative to the problem's significance and the relationship of the problem to the methods of study. Over time, researchers learn to write a variety of proposals, to alter the elements, and to handle some elements more extensively than others depending upon the purpose of the proposal.

THE PROBLEM STATEMENT, PURPOSE AND SPECIFIC AIMS

All research begins with a question. The question is then translated into the problem statement or an exploration of the phenomena under study. The purpose of the study is the goal of the research in relation to the phenomena.

Once the clinical problem is recognized and research questions are stated, the purpose of the study, significance of the study and the specific aims to achieve the study purpose can be developed. This process is recognized as difficult and time consuming by researchers. In fact, some investigators suggest that almost 50% of the total research time should be given to the statement of the problem (Browne, Pallister, 1981).

The following example illustrates how a clinical problem raised questions which led to the study "Nursing Interventions in a Methadone Clinic." Clarifying the problem began through a series of notes similar to the one that follows:

> *I have observed the nurses in the methadone clinic now several times. With each client who approaches the dispensing window, there is a brief interaction between the nurse and client and then the methadone is given. With some clients, nurses initiate the interaction and question clients about a specific health, social, financial, or legal problem. With others, nurses will initiate the interaction with a question about the patient's compliance to program rules. Still other times, clients initiate the interaction. I have estimated that nurse/client interaction during methadone dispensing lasts about one minute and 52 seconds. Yet, during that time, there are a number of nursing actions taken. In other words, these nurses are making interventions.*

What are these interventions? Under what conditions and with what clients are specific interventions used? What are the specific outcomes for different interventions? Are there interventions to assure compliance for clients continuing an addict life style? What interventions are used with clients who are doing well on the program?

The questions about nursing interventions continued on; a long list of questions was developed. As in this example, it is helpful for the researcher to write down the events that stimulated the eventual research question. These events may come from clinical or research experiences, from the literature or a combination of both. From this, a list of questions can be generated.

These questions were examined to find the real question or the research question. In our example, the central research question was, "What are these interventions?" More specifically, the question was refined and again restated, "What are nursing interventions during methadone dispensing in a methadone maintenance clinic?"

The central research question was rewritten to form the purpose or goal for the study. In the example used, the purpose was "to identify, describe, and provide a theoretical analysis of nursing interventions in a methadone maintenance program." The purpose was written in a declarative statement. It was broad enough to satisfy all of the questions in the original list. This purpose included nursing interventions in the total program as well as during methadone dispensing.

This type of broad purpose is typical of a grounded theory study. If the purpose had been limited to nursing interventions during the dispensing of methadone only, the research would have no depth, background, or context. The grounded theory study is contextual, that is, the researcher documents that the actions and interactions occur in a specific setting under certain conditions. The researcher aims at capturing all of the variation in the phenomena under study and examining conditions under which the phenomena occurs, as well as conditions under which it varies.

Once the purpose of the study is clarified, a set of specific aims for the project are generated. Again, using the methadone nursing project as an example, the specific aims in this study were as follows: (1) to identify and describe nursing interventions directed at ensuring compliance by clients identified as noncompliant in methadone treatment; (2) to identify and describe those interventions that maximize self-care and self-direction in clients demonstrating progress in treatment; and (3) to describe the specific context and conditions under which specific interventions are used.

Again, the use of a set of specific aims with a broad purpose is typical of a grounded theory study. The specific aims include the research questions posed in the study. The research questions in a grounded theory study usually include the "6 C's" of cause, context, contingencies, consequences, covariances, and conditions (Glaser, 1978). Glaser points out that these codes are the "bread and butter" of theoretical analysis for social phenomena (Glaser, 1978).

Cause refers to the reason, source, or explanation for the occurrences of a phenomenon. *Consequences* is the result, outcome, or effects of the phenomena.

The cause-consequence model is familiar to nurse-investigators as the model of causal inference that includes independent and dependent variables.

When attempting to address the problem of causal inference in research, data must be included relevant to temporal order of events and covariance, while at least partially addressing rival causal factors (Denzin, 1970). *Covariance* is used to explain the nature and extent of the relationship between the variables. Variance is a fundamental concept in the social sciences used to describe variations in phenomena. Covariance explains the extent that variables systematically vary together (Kerlinger, 1979). *Contingencies* imply the direction of variance.

Context captures the social world of the individuals engaging in the phenomena under study. The context accounts for the setting as well as the events impinging on a particular setting. These events may be real occurrences or actual events, or they may be more global and symbolic such as the meaning of an event to the individuals involved. Included in questions and, hence, data on the context, the investigator examines the social world in which the phenomena occurs.

In order to capture the range and variation of a phenomenon, all of the *conditions* under which the phenomenon occurs are examined. Through study of the context and conditions, the phenomenon is placed in the perspective of the researcher who integrates the event both in the social world in which it occurs and within other social worlds that relate to or impinge upon it. Further, the social world is examined through the perspective of the interactants; it is their definitions, meanings, and values given to a phenomenon that are identified, described, and analyzed. Searching for conditions under which a phenomenon occurs or does not occur allows the researcher to account for variation and range in the phenomena.

Consequences are the events that happen as a result of the phenomena. The investigator searches for a range of consequences and organizes them into types or categories. They are then analyzed in relation to the conditions under which a type of consequence occurs.

Causes give reasons for the occurrences of a phenomenon. Context provides depth and background to the grounded theory. Conditions allow for range and variation. Consequences detail outcomes of a phenomenon. Covariance and contingencies account for variance. The investigator structures the research questions to meet the needs of later theory development. The research questions when structured in this way assure that essential data for a grounded theory will be collected.

After the purpose and specific aims are described, the statement of the problem to be studied is then developed. There are many ways to define the problem for study. One approach used in grounded theory studies is to conceptualize the problem in the broadest sense and continue to narrow the focus until the problem under study is stated. The statement of the problem may be done in one or several paragraphs. The purpose of the study is then presented in a declarative statement (Sweeney, Olivieri, 1981).

To continue with the example from the study of nursing in a methadone clinic, the following problem statement was used in the initial proposal.

"Nursing Interventions in a Methadone Maintenance Clinic"

Since its introduction in the early 1960s, methadone maintenance has become the most frequently used treatment for opiate addiction, since it is superior in drawing clients and preventing attrition program dropout (Rounsaville, 1983). The types of services offered with methadone maintenance range with each clinic. Most commonly, individual and group psychotherapy and counseling services are offered (Platt, Labate, 1976). In methadone maintenance programs, registered nurses are usually responsible for the management, distribution, and administration of methadone to clients. Nurses function as a central clearing source for information on clients' progress and overall health status. However, since Nelson's work in 1973 and Dy, et al., in 1975, there have been no published reports on the nurse's role, functions, and interventions during methadone administration. Little is known about what actually occurs between nurses and clients during this treatment time. The purpose of this study is to generate a detailed description and theoretical analysis of nursing interventions in methadone programs.

This is one approach to defining the purpose and stating the problem under study. These elements—problem statement, purpose, and specific aims—are interrelated. The researcher may use a variety of approaches to arrive at the definition of these elements in a specific proposal. Many of these elements are handled simultaneously by the researcher.

REVIEW OF THE LITERATURE

Once the problem is identified, the researcher needs to give the study background, explain the significance of the study, and develop how it will add to existing knowledge or theory. This is best done by using existing knowledge and information to document the development and importance of the problem. The literature is a valuable and essential source of this information.

In a grounded theory study, misconceptions abound concerning the literature review. This confusion is based on a lack of differentiation between research aimed at verification versus discovery. Most nursing research is directed at theory testing or verification of a preexisting theory. This is research based on existing theory that is then tested in the social world through research. The concepts in the theory are operationalized into variables. Hypotheses are developed to test the theoretical relationship between concepts. Assumptions critical to research aimed at theory testing are as follows: (1) the theory explains the phenomena under study; (2) the concepts in the theory are critical to the phenomena under study; (3) the relationships between concepts to be tested are preestablished by the theory; and (4) operationalization of the concepts into variables accounts for all of the variables in the phenomena under study.

In research that tests existing theory, phenomena in the social world are categorized prior to study into variables based on the theory. The investigator carefully searches the literature to assist in the operationalization of the theory into variables and their relationships, to examine methodological issues such as instruments, subjects, and settings in which the theory or phenomena has been previously studied, and to assist in research design decisions. Once the literature review is completed, the researcher is assured of the contribution of this study to the existing body of knowledge.

Grounded theory is based on a discovery model of theory development (see Artinian, chapter 2). The purpose of grounded theory is to account for or explain phenomena in the social world. In the discovery mode, the researcher first asks questions about what is happening. Immersion into the events under study allows the researcher to describe these events. Ongoing analysis leads to further questions for data collection, as well as more abstract analytic questions about concepts or categories and their relationships. The researcher proceeds from data collection to analysis to organize concepts and relationships into a theory.

In research aimed at theory generation, the literature is a source for data. The grounded theorist approaches the literature as data and raises questions about validity and reliability of the data as it is in the literature compared to the analytic concepts and relationships between concepts in the developing theory.

The grounded theorist maintains a cautious and skeptical attitude about the literature throughout the study. This is particularly important in the early stages of a project since at this point the researcher can unconsciously fall into accepting what is written. A concept or ordering of concepts may linger in the researcher's mind. The researcher can then categorize incoming data into the learned concepts and their relationships, thus closing off further analysis. Also, unconsciously or consciously, the researcher may look for those variables, concepts, and relationships identified in the literature. Further research in the discovery mode is fruitless, since the researcher has already closed off analysis and theory development (Glaser, 1978).

This does not mean that there is no literature reviewed in a grounded theory study. The reality of proposal writing for grants or academic purposes requires the investigator to demonstrate knowledge about the phenomena and methods for study. The question is not if the literature is reviewed or not, since it is essential to review literature to write a proposal, but how and for what purposes the review is done.

In a grounded theory study, literature is always approached as data in the form of written documents. The purposes of the review will change over the course of the study. Initially, the literature is reviewed to identify the scope, range, intent, and type of research that has been done. Other writings, such as case reports, are examined for the extent of what is known on the subject and the concerns of clinicians and others. Finally, the literature is used to establish the study's purpose, background, and significance.

For example, in the early stages of the "Nursing Interventions in a Methadone Maintenance Clinic," a literature review was done. This review of nursing and other health-related published work revealed six articles relating directly to the subject but no research studies on the topic. There were many peripheral articles on this treatment approach to opiate addiction. A gap of many years was found since any nursing article on the topic had been written. The relevant articles were then reviewed; the remainder were scanned for the scope and nature of the content addressed.

At this point, the researcher had a sufficient review to begin the study. However, there was not enough to support a research proposal. In order to generate a proposal, the following literature needed to be reviewed: (1) the development of and trends in methadone maintenance treatment (for example, numbers of clinics and clients treated, controversies around this form of treatment for addiction); (2) issues in methadone maintenance treatment (for example, what other treatment should be or is offered to opiate addicts); (3) research on staff in methadone maintenance programs; (4) evaluation research on methadone maintenance treatment; (5) information on staff-staff relationships and staff-client relationships in methadone maintenance programs; and (6) information on the roles of various disciplines in this treatment approach.

A basic research proposal such as that required for a review by an Institutional Review Board could be generated from the initial review. However, for academic settings and funding agencies, this would not be sufficient since the researcher would not be able to demonstrate an in-depth knowledge of the subject under study. If a full proposal is to be written, a complete review of the literature is conducted.

As the study proceeds, the danger of latching onto an idea, concept, or theory is decreased as data collection and analysis progresses. The richness and depth of qualitative data and the rigors of analysis foster the development of concepts and the ordering of concepts into categories.

Following the discovery model, the grounded theorist reviews the literature while the data collection and analysis go on. The review is specific and directed at each point. The purposes of this review are as follows: (1) to use literature as a source of data to verify and elaborate categories; (2) to elaborate on the structural conditions; (3) to learn more about the area's structural conditions (such as federal laws governing methadone clinics); and (4) to discover and learn about related subjects as they arise (such as the treatment of polysubstance abusers in methadone programs).

The literature in grounded theory is used to assist with the discovery process. Ongoing review assures that no data is overlooked. The researcher has an understanding of the social world under study and conditions under which the phenomena occur.

Finally, as the study is ending and the analysis is complete, the literature is again reviewed. The relationship of this analysis and its components to others is done. The theory is presented in the context of other work.

In the grounded theory study, the literature review is an ongoing process that is conducted to fulfill the needs of the analysis. Literature is conceived of as data and not viewed as inherently "true." At the end of the research project, the researcher will have a thorough knowledge of the literature and will be able to place the theory in context with existing theories and work on the subject.

THEORETICAL FRAMEWORK

Another common misconception about grounded theory is its atheoretical nature. This is a common misunderstanding and creates a problem for investigators with a research problem that can be addressed using this method. Investigators may be hesitant to use grounded theory methodology regardless of the fit between the method and problem because they need to have a conceptual framework to "guide the study." Often, researchers will use an unrelated framework that they then try to shape to fit the study.

This misconception is based on the assumptions which guide research for theory testing. Grounded theory research is directed at theory development. Hence, there is no attempt to operationalize concepts and relationships from theory. However, the research is guided by symbolic interactionist theory.

As Blumer notes,

> One can see the empirical world only through some scheme or image of it. The entire act of scientific study is oriented and shaped by the underlying picture of the empirical world that is used. The relationship between the research act and the theoretical framework is also critical. This picture sets the selection and formulation of problems, the determination of what are data, the means to be used in getting data, the kinds of relations sought between data and the forms in which propositions are cast (1969, p 25).

The entire research act is dependent upon the framework of the investigator or the investigator's initial picture of the empirical world. Grounded theorists espouse the symbolic interactionist perspective (Mead, 1934; Blumer, 1969). And grounded theory studies use this framework as a theoretical orientation.

From symbolic interaction, methodological principles guide the researcher using grounded theory. First, that the meaning of the event must be understood from the perspective of the participants. In order to accomplish this, the researcher must "take the role of other." Behavior must be understood at the symbolic and behavioral levels. Second, that meanings are derived through social interaction. Hence, to understand meaning, behavior must be observed in context. Research methods must be able to assist the researcher fulfill these methodological principles and capture process and change (Denzin, 1970). It is with this orientation that the grounded theorist approaches the problem under study. The use of symbolic interaction, however, is often implicit which fosters the misconception that grounded theory is atheoretical.

Further, since the purpose of grounded theory is to generate theory from research data, the use of symbolic interaction as an orientation is different from the use of theory in research that is aimed at theory testing.

CONCLUSION

In this chapter we have focused on the key elements in the early stages of the research process. We have specifically addressed the purpose, problem statement, review of the literature, and theoretical framework. Several misconceptions about grounded theory have been identified. Further chapters will pursue methods for data collection, analysis, and writing.

References

Blumer H: *Symbolic Interactionism: Perspective and Method.* Englewood Cliffs, New Jersey, Prentice-Hall, 1969.

Browne GB, Pallister RM: Introduction to the research process, in Williamson YM (ed): *Research Methodology and Its Application to Nursing.* New York, John Wiley and Sons, 1981, pp 43–63.

Denzin NK: *The Research Act.* Chicago, Aldine Publishing Co, 1970.

Dy AJ, Howard P, Kleber HD: The nurse in a methadone maintenance program: Expansions and transitions in role. *JPN and Mental Health Services* 1975; 13:17–20.

Glaser BG: 1978. *Theoretical Sensitivity.* Mill Valley, California, The Sociology Press, 1978.

Kerlinger FN: *Behavioral Research: A Conceptual Approach.* New York, Holt, Rinehart and Winston, 1979.

Mead GH: *Mind, Self and Society.* Chicago, University of Chicago Press, 1934.

Nelson K: The nurse in a methadone maintenance program. *Am J Nurs* 1973; 73:870–874.

Platt JJ, Labate C: *Heroin Addiction: Theory, Research and Treatment.* New York, John Wiley and Sons, 1976.

Rounsaville BJ, Glaser W, Wilber CH, Weissman MM, Kleber HD: Short term interpersonal psychotherapy in methadone maintained opiate addicts. *Arch Gen Psychiatry* 1983; 40:629–636.

Sweeney MA, Olivieri P: *An Introduction to Nursing Research.* Philadelphia, J.B. Lippincott Co, 1981.

5

Observation in Natural Settings

Marcella Z. Davis

This chapter is about the process of observation in natural settings. The focus is on how to observe, when to observe, and what to observe in the process of conducting field research sometimes referred to as *participant observation research*. As used here, natural settings refer to hospitals, clinics, and other health care agencies where most nurses practice. The term natural setting differentiates these settings from others, such as highly controlled environments like a laboratory or a specifically established room for testing. Therefore, this discussion is about direct observation of phenomena in their natural state and not about experimentally controlled observation.

Because the character of participant observation in natural settings, (eg, access to data sources, ease of movement throughout the institution, etc.) can be determined by the nature of the entrée effected, this chapter begins with a discussion on the process of gaining entrée to a setting for the purpose of conducting field research. This will be followed by a detailed discussion on the how, when, and what of observation in natural settings.

ENTRÉE

Entrée and Research Access

There is a difference between gaining entrée and what is commonly referred to as *research access*. All investigators irrespective of the kind of research they conduct (eg, biomedical or social science), negotiate with key persons in the institution they want to conduct their research for access to the institution's resources. On the other hand, gaining entrée as applied in field research departs and differs from the more general process of research access in a number of significant ways. Gaining entrée is integral to the conduct of the research process itself and continues throughout the data-gathering phase of the investigation. As is the case of research access, it is not a set of circumscribed steps that once accomplished can be set aside. These differences are anchored in the dissimilarities between the research strategies and basic logic underlying qualitative and quantitative-experimental research. The former is loosely circumscribed and emergent, thus maximizing discovery; the latter is highly circumscribed and controlled with an emphasis on prediction.

Very simply entrée consists of all those relationships and contacts made for the purpose of getting into the institution, as well as those for furthering research and insuring continuing access to places, persons, and documents within the institution. In short, entrée has to do with getting in, staying in, and getting what the researcher needs.

The following discussion on gaining entrée will address the situation of both nurses already inside the institution who wish to conduct field research, as well as nurses outside the institution who wish to gain entrée for the purpose of conducting field research.

Entrée from the outside   Identifying the institution in which you wish to conduct field research is a major step in and of itself. This point will not be discussed here other than to alert you to its importance. Locating a sponsor for your research is a step which goes hand-in-hand with the identification of an institution in which you wish to conduct your research. I will now comment briefly on sponsorship and its relationship to entrée. Should you know someone in the setting in which you wish to gain entrée, a useful approach is to have him or her make one or two preliminary contacts for you with key persons in the institution as a way of "breaking the ice." If the person whom you select is well thought of in the institution, all the better, for this tends to insure others of your trustworthiness. This person, in effect, serves as your sponsor. A professional society or organization (eg, the National Kidney Foundation, the American Heart Association), can also be a sponsor for your research. Nurse-investigators who have had these and other professional organizations sponsor their research are known to the professional organization through a long-standing relationship; their research interests are seen to be compatible with those of the organization. If you are a student, your sponsor and organizational affiliation is your school represented through your faculty advisor.

Frequently, the first person you see about entrée to the hospital or other agency may clue you in as to who else to contact in the institution. If the institution you are interested in has a nurse researcher on the staff, this individual would be a useful contact early in the entrée process to learn of other useful contacts and perhaps the sequential order of contact.

One should be prepared for possible delays in getting into an institution; therefore, it is wise to leave ample lead time. For example, nurse-researchers and others report that a wait six weeks or longer for an appointment to see various key persons is not uncommon. Prolonged delays could be for legitimate reasons; on the other hand, it may be a tactic to discourage you from pursuing your entrée to that institution in which case you had better rethink your strategy or take your study to another location.

A nurse-investigator who published an account of her first entrée experience comments:

> *"The best laid plans of nurse researchers are helpful but never entirely adequate. . . . Finding the setting can take much longer than you expect, even when you think you are familiar with the environment"* (Jacobson, 1978, p 372).

Since there are no firmly established rules governing how to contact an institution, investigators are frequently encouraged to be guided by their personal comfort when approaching an experience that may be new and different for them. For example, you may precede your phone call for an appointment with a letter identifying yourself, your sponsor or professional affiliation, and what you want from the institution. In the letter, state that a phone call to make an appointment to discuss your research in more detail will follow. Should you choose the route of a letter, it is best to keep the research statement general thus allowing you—should the opportunity arise in the course of the research—to take advantage of yet unforeseen data sources and data within the institution. An alternative to a letter might be to stop by the institution to make an appointment with the appropriate person.

The first appointment is the appropriate time for the investigator to mention his or her intention about providing feedback to the institution and what form the feedback might take, eg, written report or clinical conference.

Irrespective of your mode of initial contact for entrée—letter, phone call, or face-to-face contact—permission for entrée from these initial contacts conveys only that your presence in the institution has been legitimated. It does not mean you have access to all clinical sites, persons, and staff, but rather, that you are free to move about the institution, to contact persons and places, and to negotiate each step with whomever the appropriate persons may be. These negotiations are not confined only to persons in the higher echelon; rather, they are with staff members at all levels depending, of course, on the focus of your research. Your clinical background may be useful in pointing out who might be appropriate to contact as you move into your study.

Entrée from the inside   This section concerns someone with entrée to the institution by virtue of being employed by the institution.

As one example, I'll begin with my own experience as the research nurse at a research and teaching acute care hospital. I had been in the position less than 1 year when I began a field research study of the patient as a participant in the continuity of care. Since I had been a research nurse for a number of years prior to taking this research position, I did not have the problem of shedding the trappings of a clinical identity which is frequently the case for nurse clinicians who become engaged in research (Davis, 1968). But there were other kinds of identity issues which centered on the fact that the nurse researcher position conferred an administrative status as well as that of research. Even though the administrative component was minor, it nontheless formally aligned me with nursing administration. A field researcher has problems enough, at least initially, about being seen as the "company spy" without the added liability of being formally aligned with the power structure. My concern was that the formal link with nursing administration might jeopardize getting nurses on the ward to feel comfortable enough with me so that I could observe them at work, interview them, be allowed to attend their meetings, and move about the ward freely. Fortunately, this formal administrative link existed more on paper than in reality. That is, my work did not naturally bring me into contact with the nursing administrative staff; consequently, distancing myself from nursing administration was not difficult. The supervisors were contacted only when I wanted entrée to clinical units over which they had nursing jurisdiction. By confining our discussion to research-related matters, I used these occasions to reinforce my research identity with the supervisors. The reasons for the concerns just mentioned are based on my own experience as well as those of field researchers in general. We have learned that until you have established some trust and are accepted by the persons in the setting, it is not uncommon for you and your purpose to be held suspect. No matter how well you have engineered your presentation of self and described your purpose, you will still be defined and perceived within the frame of reference of "the other." It is the wise investigator who recognizes and prepares for the fact that the definition of others about who you are and what you are doing rarely coincides with one's own (Byerly, 1976, p 159). Some examples may illustrate this point. A nurse whose field research was to investigate the stresses and coping strategies of neonatal intensive care nurses had the following to say about her entrée experience:

> *The groups (referring to the nurses) usually had some concern about how I had selected their particular unit for participation. . . . One group was concerned that I was somehow out to "axe" diploma nurses (their term). Many nurses needed repeated assurance that I was not secretly doing a psychiatric study (Jacobson, 1978, p 373).*

Another nurse field researcher comments:

> *Even though they (the nurses) were told that they were not being evaluated and that it was the patient in whom I was interested, they were often uncomfortable. They would*

glance at the bedside where I was sitting as if to ask, "Am I doing this procedure correctly?" (Jackson, 1975, p 553).

And last, the nurse field researcher was greeted with teasing behavior when she appeared on the ward: "Here comes the spy!" Other remarks revealed concern that the nurse observer was there to check on the staff's performance, "She (nurse researcher) is looking to see if we really can 'cut the mustard' " (Byerly, 1969, p 233). There were still other reasons that were based on methodological grounds for my not wanting to be affiliated with one specific group in the institution. Namely, all field researchers engaged in the study of the work and practice of an institution must be free of all affiliations within the institution in order to keep their physical movement within the setting and lines of communication between and among all groups open.

Most important of all, I proceeded with the assumption that while I had entrée to the institution by virtue of my position, I did not assume I had entrée to persons and events. In effect, I viewed my situation from the perspective of an outsider. I went through the process of seeking entrée to specific wards by first contacting the nursing supervisor, then contacting the head nurse who arranged a meeting for me with all the staff nurses on each shift. At this time, I explained the focus and purpose of my research and offered some comments on how I would be conducting it. I also informed nurses of their rights regarding my research, eg, they were free to refuse to participate or to not answer my questions. I encountered no problems with my entrée although some nurses were more receptive to my presence than were others. This made the six to eight weeks of observation and interviews on that particular ward a little pleasanter. The same introductory procedure was carried out with respect to all other professionals I observed and interviewed, eg, physicians, social workers, occupational therapists. Patients and their families were also informed of my presence on the ward and why I was there. When I wanted to speak with them, I went through a similar explanatory introduction.

Although the example of someone on the inside seeking entrée was a research nurse with prior research experience, it nonetheless contains elements that are common for most persons on the inside who seek entrée to conduct field research. For example, it illustrates the continuing efforts at clarification the investigator engages in regarding his or her research identity, purpose of the research, the rights of others regarding the research, as well as the ongoing process of entrée as the researcher moves throughout the institution.

For nurse clinicians temporarily in a research role who want to use some of the strategies of field research, there are specific topics to which to pay attention. Because the research will involve participant observation and interviewing, it is important—if not vital—to ensure the least amount of misunderstanding. Following are some guidelines to help you avoid misunderstandings.

Because you may be unfamiliar with the methodologies of field research, it would be prudent to prepare a brief explanation to offer those you may be observing and interviewing (especially nurses and other health professionals), as to why these methods were selected over more familiar approaches (eg, questionnaires). Also, have some examples of the kinds of data you are interested in, for instance, recurring patterns which occur under certain specific conditions of the ward, and how these kind of data can best be obtained through observation and interviewing. Offer those who will be involved some idea how you plan to use the data. Finally, make a plan with them to provide feedback from your data collection. Providing feedback to those who participate in your research, as well as to those who cleared the way for your entrée, can be a constructive way of establishing reciprocity. There are times when patients are interested in a study's findings; it is appropriate for the investigator to explore with patients ways for them to find out a study's outcome.

HOW, WHEN, AND WHAT TO OBSERVE

How to Observe

In this discussion on observation, the focus will be on the role of the known observer. That is, the observer is known to those who are being studied. There have been occasions when the observer role is not known (ie, the researcher's identity is concealed to those being observed). For instance, some investigators with the intent of furthering their research effort have taken a job in the institution in which they intend to study, eg, they have become aides in a hospital or nursing home or will join an organization such as Alcoholics Anonymous. On record there are instances of field researchers who, because they wanted to study a mental hospital, feigned mental illness and were thereby admitted to a psychiatric hospital (Caudill et al, 1952). In other instances, the researcher may be a legitimate patient as was the case for a social scientist who began his study of life in a tuberculosis hospital where he was a patient (Roth, 1963). There are, of course, ethical issues surrounding the role of the unknown observer, to say nothing of the methodological disadvantages. With respect to its disadvantages, the concealed identity role is very limited and does not allow for the wide scope of observation and interview that the known observer role offers (Lofland, 1971). Ethical issues related to the concealed identity role, as well as other topics, are dealt with in another section of this book.

Conduct of self in relation to others   There is a definite style or manner as to how you, as the observer, might conduct yourself in relation to others in the setting. Your manner is intended to insure the comfort of those being observed and to make your presence as unobtrusive as possible. For example, while it is a very good idea to carry a small notebook at all times to jot down occasional notes, it should be out of sight and not used in front of others except perhaps if you are at a meeting and everyone else is writing from time to time, or if you have received permission ahead of time from the individual or group you are observing. Make your note taking as unobtrusive as possible; do it in some secluded corner, a room nearby, a cafeteria, or lounge. If no room is available, the lavatory has been known to be used successfully in some situations (Olsen, Whittaker, 1968, p 16). These notes are brief statements and key words which will be expanded into field notes later that day or very soon thereafter. Having made the point to be as unobtrusive as possible in note taking, the following excerpt is an example of the opposite strategy by a nurse field researcher. Wilson writes the following about her observations in a community-based psychiatric setting:

> The decision to record and take notes in full view of the interactants was in part a consequence of the structure of the setting and in part a consequence of an attempt to avoid the sociopsychologic risks of secretive behavior on my part. Unlike a hospital, a 16 room house full of people offered little opportunity for slipping off to a cafeteria or restroom periodically to record from memory (1977, pp 107–108).

Therefore, Wilson's strategy for handling the situation was to write in full view of everyone; her explanation to anyone who asked about her actions was that she was writing a description of what was happening. She made her notes available to whomever was interested in reading them. Wilson remarks, "every staff member availed themselves of this offer and some responded jokingly with comments such as "Well, it's accurate but boring as hell" (1977, p 108).

Other considerations while observing   The activities of talking or informally interviewing and listening have been artificially separated here from observation for ease of presentation. In reality, observation is a complex process of interweaving the activities of looking, listening, and asking (Lofland, 1971). For example, seeing something and then asking a question about it is a normal activity for most of us and is not seen as strange behavior. Therefore, the field researcher uses this ordinary and acceptable activity for his or her research purposes.

However, there may be some exceptions. For example, it may be more prudent not to ask questions while observing an event (eg, a nurse passing out medications or giving a treatment, doctors' rounds) and to hold your questions for later. You will be able to discern these subtleties for yourself on the spot.

Where to position yourself to observe is still another consideration. Your location at any point in time will affect the kinds of information and events that will come within your line of observation. Your decision concerning your position is in large part dependent on where you are in the data collection and what you still need to know about the phenomena under study. For example, you may decide to follow an event involving a particular patient to its conclusion, eg, patient discharged, died, problem resolved. In that instance, locate yourself wherever you would maximize the data collection around the event. This particular observational strategy is referred to as following a "tracer" and in some respects is analogous to the use of tracers in biological research (Strauss et al, 1964). On the other hand, there are advantages in staying in one place for a period of time to make in-depth observations which could greatly increase your familiarity and knowledge of that situation. However, most field researchers are mobile and do assume a variety of locations for positioning themselves for observation (Schatzman, Strauss, 1973). Other issues about where to position yourself might concern such topics as your comfort as well as the comfort of the observed. There are so many variations in situations where field researchers may be conducting their research that to suggest precisely where to locate yourself in order to enhance the research, or for your comfort or that of the observed would be impractical. However, a rule of thumb to keep in mind would be that of conducting one's self in as unobtrusive a manner as possible, a suggestion offered earlier.

Active and passive observation   In some of the literature on observation in field research, the process of observation may be separated into two modes: active and passive. Further, some field researchers when reporting on their research have made a special point of describing the circumstances which led them to abandon a passive role and assume an active or participant observer role. For example, the sociologist, Renée Fox, who studied critically ill patients on an experimental ward in an acute care hospital explains her shift in observational style:

> *My decision to be a relatively active observer was also influenced by my inner need to do something more than just watch, listen and take notes in the presence of such urgent human situations as one finds in a hospital ward (1959, p 214).*

The participant-observer role   For purposes of this discussion, the role of observer is that of a participant-observer who is always more or less active, that is, asking questions, carrying on informal and formal conversations, and, in effect, interacting at strategic moments and around specific events with those being studied. While the participant-observer role may make for a more comfortable stance for the researcher to assume as we saw in the example, it is important to recognize that the primary purpose for the participant-observer role is methodological, ie, it is considered the method *par excellence* for collecting data for qualitative analysis.

An added dimension for a research nurse in the participant-observer role is that for the nurse, unlike for the non-nurse participant-observer, the situation may become more complex because the research nurse is sophisticated clinically and knows what may occur when something is not handled immediately. On the other hand, the non-nurse participant-observer may note that something is amiss with the patient and as one remarked "In that case, I just run and get the nurse!" Nurse field researchers are aware of this issue and some have written about it as a dilemma for clinical nurse field researchers. For example, Byerly writes:

> *The third major dilemma . . . is whether to intervene when she [the nurse as participant-observer] has information directly pertinent to the welfare of a patient. Occasions may arise when she feels forced to make a nursing judgment even though her primary goal in the study does not involve patient care. She may be placed in a position where she must make some response: a blank stare or noncommittal answer are seldom sufficient once the study group has become familiar with the observer (1969, pp 232–233).*

This of course raises the question of bias and subjectivity of field researchers in the participant-observer role. Most field researchers in the participant-observer role are aware that they do have some effect on the situation they are observing and on the data obtained. The question, therefore, is not whether the participant-observers have or do not have an effect on the situation being studied; rather, the question is, what do field researchers in the participant-observer role do (a) to diminish their effect on that being observed, (b) to exploit their subjectivity to the advantage of the research, and (c) to increase the objectivity of the data?

It is important to keep in mind that unlike other forms of research where the contact with subjects is diminished or nonexistent because of the use of various forms of instrumentation, the field researcher in the participant-observer role is the instrument. And as such, he or she must learn to use the self in interaction within the dynamic social context to the advantage of the research process.

Concerning the field researcher's effort to diminish the interference with what is observed, suggestions were made earlier about observing in an unobtrusive manner. The examples illustrated tactics which would draw less attention and suspicion to the presence of the field researcher by having him or her blend into the setting and action.

Concerning the dilemma faced by some field researchers in a participant-observation role that may involve him or her in a clinical intervention, the tactic I would suggest centers on increased self-awareness on the part of the investigator during the event. If you decide to intervene, be aware that you are intervening, why you are as well as noting what occurs as a result of your behavior. I have found at times that these "problematic" situations can also be the serendipitous event which opens up a new way of thinking about a situation and provides data not obtained heretofore. For example, while conducting field research on the nursing management of patient pain, Shizuko Fagerhaugh, a nurse researcher, relates the instance when she was observing on a medical ward and a patient asked her on several different occasions to tell the nurse that he wanted his pain medication. Fagerhaugh learned a great deal from the involvement by noting the nurse's response each time she reported that the patient wanted his pain medication. For example, the nurses would remark, "Oh my God, I forgot all about it!" or "I see now he's recruited you to ask." These spontaneous comments reveal the nurse's attitude toward the patient's pain and pain-relieving behavior, the relationship between the patient and the nurse, and the maneuvers the patient must engage in to get the care he/she believes is needed.

An example from my own research in the early 1960s is about the interviews conducted in the homes of persons with multiple sclerosis. As the study progressed, I had learned a great deal about community resources available to house bound patients. Once the interview was over, I would give the patient information I had about community services such as meals-on-wheels, recreational center programs for the disabled, transportation, etc, because it was evident from the interview that he/she did not know of any community-based services. When I did this, most patients responded, "Oh my goodness, my doctor never told me about that!"

Some found the information invaluable because it provided some respite for family members involved in their care. What I learned from my approach was that physicians did not inform patients of community-based resources, out of lack of information on them because the physician did not believe in them. Subsequently, after interviewing physicians in the community, I learned that my initial hunches were valid (Davis, 1970, 1973).

With regard to field researchers, exploiting the subjectivity inherent in the participant-observer role, refers to converting one's own biases, sensitivities, and inner conflicts into an asset for the research process. For example, most field researchers are fully cognizant of the fact that they must be attuned to themselves as observers in a complex social context. This involves making a conscious effort to identify one's biases and sensitivities about the subject matter under study. Further, by being attuned to one's self and inner dialogue, so to speak, it is even possible to exploit one's inner conflicts to the advantage of the research process. Some examples may illustrate this point. In the first example, Jeanne Quint discusses such an occasion when she interviewed student nurses about their first experience with death and dying when she was an investigator on the Death and Dying in Hospitals study. She observed:

> My greatest upset came following an interview with a nurse who had discovered the body of a patient who had committed suicide. I was disturbed because I thought the interviewee herself was ready to fall apart emotionally, with the interview serving as the triggering mechanism. . . . In a very personal way, I was reminded that nurses (or at least, I as a nurse) are supposed to prevent scenes, not to provoke them. This insight came to conscious awareness through my discussions with the project director and were useful in interpreting some of the data (Quint, 1967, p 270).

Another example concerns Renée Fox who observed macabre humor among the patients on a experimental medical unit. It was not until shortly after this initial observation when she caught herself in the act of making a macabre joke that she realized she had learned to speak to the men in the ward in the same way they spoke with each other. She comments:

> Long before this insight occurred, my field notes contained many examples of ward humor. But it was only by virtue of self-observation that I became aware of its prevalence to regard it as a phenomenon central to my study (Fox, 1959, p 231).

As for increasing the objectivity of the data, several procedures relate directly to it. The first of these procedures deals with the advantages to the research process from the interaction between members on a research team. Discussing one's observations with team members, as we saw in the example with Quint, increases the opportunity for others to point out possible biases and distortions. Also, it increases the opportunity to get information not noted by the observer because of personal sensitivity and/or bias. Discussing your research on a regular basis with one or two trusted colleagues is helpful; this may mean using the phone when face-to-face contact is not possible. Writing daily field notes is also very useful in establishing distance from the data as well as providing an opportunity to become increasingly reflexive and aware of one's own feelings and biases which may have been aroused by the observations and interviews.

The last approach to increasing objectivity deals with the unique opportunity provided the field researcher to check on verbal and written data with observational data. It is not unusual for persons to hold a view of their behavior that is not borne out in the empirical data; these discrepancies come to light through the field research process.

When to Observe

When to observe refers to all issues concerning time and its relationship to observation, for example, how long to remain in the field on a day-to-day basis, when to terminate the study, making a time plan for the conduct of the study and planning observations to maximize data collection. These and other issues will be discussed here.

How long to remain in the field on a day-to-day basis   Decisions about how long to remain in the field on a day-to-day basis are based upon considerations such as the following: (a) what is going on in the field and if it is relevant to the research; (b) how far into the study you may be (some events will be repeats and unless you are "tracking" some clues, you may not need to observe them); and (c) your own comfort and energy level. If you're fatigued, leave the field or remove yourself from the immediate observational site and go to the cafeteria or lounge to recuperate. Concern for the investigator's ease and comfort stems from the fact mentioned earlier, ie, that the self in field research is used as a tool in the collection of data (Quint, 1967). Therefore, field researchers do pay attention to insuring their alertness and comfort when in the field.

There will be times when you are in the field for as brief a time as 15 minutes; at other times it may be several hours for observations and interviews. If you are near your research site, you will be able to take advantage of brief forays into the field coupled with prolonged sustained periods. These brief forays are generally done to track down some data, check on some emerging formulation in the data, and to validate, negate, or expand it with more evidence.

Some field researchers have preset times when they are in the field, for example, three or four times a week for four- or five-hour periods. In the instance of a hospital or other institution where work continues on a 24-hour basis, it is recommended to include the observation on more than one, if not all work shifts.

Handling the time dimension   A plan for how you envision the unfolding of the entire study is useful as a guide whether your study entails data collection in one clinical site or multiple sites, the same institution or several institutions. Your plan should contain an approximation of how much time you need for data collection, the daily write-up of field notes, analysis of data, and final write-up of the research report. For example, in the patient participation study mentioned earlier, an overall temporal framework was developed to span a two-year period which included the three major phases of the research, ie, the data collection, analysis, and write-up of the research report. Within this framework, time was further broken down into smaller units, for example, four to six weeks allowed for observation in each clinical site which included observation on each shift. Time was built in each day for the write-up of field notes and memos. One day each week was reserved for reviewing field notes, memos, and for catching up. Your time frame should be flexible so as to not constrain your movement. For example, when the period planned for observation is officially over, make it known to a significant person on the ward, eg, the head nurse, that you may need to return in the near future to check out an observation. You may find that after you have written your field notes and memos you need to return to the ward to track down some clue or hunch for further clarification or expansion.

One learns how much can realistically be accomplished in a specific span of time from experience. In fact, some field researchers have actually calculated that for each hour of observation, there should be at least two to three pages of field notes. However, this does not take into account the memos from the field notes. For the novice field researcher, a brief informal consultation with an experienced investigator familiar with field research would be a useful strategy at the planning stage.

Beginning field researchers must be warned not to be seduced into thinking that all the important action is in the field. Each act of the research process is as important as the other and each is dependent on the other.

Plan your observations so that you see the site both when it is busy and when it is not. In the instance of a hospital, try to see the institution when the census is low and again, when it is at full capacity.

Inform others when you are temporarily leaving the field. There are no established protocols for this and each field researcher must work out a plan that suits his or her situation. For example, if you know you will be leaving the field for the remainder of the day or for more than one day, you might inform the head nurse. Some head nurses will appreciate knowing about your comings and goings on their unit while others will be indifferent.

When to leave a particular site and move on to another one is determined by the usefulness of the data: if the data coming in reveal nothing new, it is time to leave the particular observational site. In the language of *Grounded Theory,* one would say you are at a point in the data collection when you know that the theoretical categories you have been systematically developing from your incoming data and sampling are now complete or, to use the more technical term, they are saturated. The term saturation refers to the fact that no additional data are being found whereby the field researcher can develop new properties of the category (Glaser, Strauss, 1976).

Concerning terminating the study, frequently a study has a preestablished termination date; this date may be tied to funding constraints or the researcher may set a time limit for the study.

What to Observe

What to observe is based on a number of factors, some of which relate to the basic premise and underlying logic of field research as a strategy for collecting data. Other factors concern the field researcher's theoretical orientation, previous research in related areas, life experience in an area related to the research, as well as the formulations being made when the study is in progress and the data are coming in. Each of these factors will be briefly discussed.

Basic premise and underlying logic   The basic premise of the field method in the social sciences states that since the meaning that objects hold for people cannot be divorced from the settings in which the objects are experienced, it is vital to first gain an understanding of an object by studying it in its natural setting. In order to gain understanding of a problem as well as to arrive at any sound conclusions concerning the nature of the social and human situations being studied, one must first grasp how the world is perceived, understood, and experienced by those whose lives are part of it. Therefore, the field researcher observes and interviews the actors in the setting. By so doing, the field researcher is able to provide a representative, comprehensive, and accurate rendition of the situation.

Theoretical orientation of the investigator   Social scientists who use the field method of research generally are sociologists and anthropologists. The focus of a sociologist or researcher with a sociological orientation, therefore, will focus on such elements as the organization of the unit of observation, the hierarchy of power and power relationships, social control, organization of work, and so forth. Researchers with a social psychological orientation, such as symbolic interaction, would combine both the sociological components with those from symbolic interaction (Blumer, 1962). In this instance, the researcher's focus would also include such phenomena as interaction, expectations, perceptions, perspective of those in the situation. A theoretical orientation provides the field researcher with a framework which points the investigator in certain directions for observation, at least in the initial stages of the study. Direction can and does change as the data are coming in and the study progresses. Field researchers do not enter the field with a preformulated theory (for testing) and formally postulated hypotheses; rather, the theoretical framework serves as a lens through which the field researcher identifies the major observational parameters of the study to be undertaken.

Previous research in related areas: coming to the field with preliminary formulations
Prior to beginning observations in the field, the investigator will have done considerable thinking about both the general as well as the specific features of the research topic. Through this process you will discover that you already have hunches and ideas. That is, you may know some of the dimensions and properties and may have some ideas as to what and where to begin to observe. If you have done previous field research in a related area, this too will provide you with direction as

to what to observe and where. The following examples will illustrate this point. In the study, *Nursing Care and Management of Pain in Patients* conducted by Strauss et al, direction for the study stemmed in part from some unanswered questions in their earlier research, *Death and Dying in Hospitals.* Many of these unanswered questions concerned patient pain and its nursing and medical management. Various kinds of pain and pain-relieving schedules were brought to light which the investigators saw as having important consequences for ward routines and patient care. The pain study dealt with those unanswered questions of the earlier study to elucidate what those consequences were as well as answer other relevant questions pertaining to the nursing management of patient pain (Strauss, 1972).

Another example of a field researcher having done previous work in an area which suggested direction for future work is my own research on the patient as a participant in the continuity of care. The focus for that study had its roots in earlier research with persons with multiple sclerosis in their home and community settings (Davis, 1970, 1973). From the earlier study, it was readily apparent that some patients under certain circumstances take the initiative in furthering the continuity of their care, a continuity which otherwise might not be there. Interestingly, when some of the patients were admitted to acute settings, they lost this initiative and without their participation their care suffered. In the end, they created problems for the staff, as well. I never forgot that piece of datum for as soon as I assumed my present research position, in an acute care Veterans Administration hospital, I designed a study to examine what factors facilitated and/or hindered the chronically ill patient's participation in continuity of care.

Life experiences in research-related areas   There are any number of examples of investigators getting into a particular area of research because of some personal experiences. There is the example mentioned earlier of the social scientist who began his observations while he was a patient in a tuberculosis hospital and continued his study after he was released from the hospital. Another example is of Anselm Strauss and Barney Glaser, both of whom had experiences with the death of a family member prior to their initiation of the study of death and dying in hospitals. The significance of their early experiences to the subsequent research is noted by the investigators themselves in their book, *Awareness of Dying.* They state that the beginning formulations for their paradigm for the study of *awareness contexts* began to take shape several years prior to the actual study. It was simply a matter of the investigators bringing their personal experiences to mind for them to crystallize the study's focus and direction (Glaser, Strauss, 1965).

Observations based on in-coming data   The best way to discuss this last topic which influences what one observes is to give an example. The example is taken from the patient participation in continuity of care study previously mentioned. Because information about one's illness and its management is an important element in the question of one's participation in the continuity of care, a considerable amount of time was devoted to the topic of formal and informal teaching and information exchange between the patient and various health professionals. Based on the observations and interviews with the interns, residents, and an occasional attending physician, it became quite clear that doctors did very little patient teaching. Rather, doctors tended to give information but rarely checked to see if the information was understood by the patient or was useful. As for the registered nurse on the ward, informal teaching was done on an ad hoc basis. Most nurses checked to see if the patient understood the information but did not check to see if the information was useful to the patient or how he/she was to incorporate it into the ongoing living situation. While nurses expressed an awareness of the importance of discussing these topics with the patient, this was not done at the ward level on any systematic basis; rather, it was done more by chance than by professional prescription. Given these circumstances, other areas were searched for where patient teaching and information exchange might occur. This search led to the off-the-ward, regularly scheduled patient teaching classes. Observation of the off-the-ward classes were made and staff nurses were informally interviewed on the topic of the classes. These approaches revealed that the ward staff nurses were not aware of the content of the classes. Consequently, many nurses felt they were unable to adequately respond to the patients' unanswered questions from the class. This finding pointed observation in the direction of attempting to learn what links, if any, the off-the-ward classes had with the ward staff and ward life of the patient. Other data from the observation of the classes revealed that patients entered the class at different points in the series, and that it was the rare patient who attended the full series of classes. Also, no provision was made for rescheduling patients who missed classes. This information suggested further exploration which revealed that the patients were frequently discharged in the middle of a class series. This finding, in turn, suggested further investigation to see if there was any follow-up for those patients who were discharged without completing the class. This investigative check revealed that a visit from the public health nurse or hospital-based home care nurse was planned for some patients, but that these visits might not occur for one or two weeks after discharge. The procedure for referrals emerged as the next piece of information to track down. From that observation it was discovered that a "bottle neck" existed there as well. From this example, it should be apparent how one piece of information can lead to the searching out for more data on the question under investigation.

GETTING STARTED: SOME FIRST STEPS IN OBSERVATION

To begin, you will need some plan as to who to interview, what to observe, and in what temporal order to do this. These beginning steps in the field are called "mapping" (Schatzman, Strauss, 1973, p 34) and refer to the process in which the field researcher engages to quickly learn the spatial, social, and temporal dimensions of the observational site. The terms *spatial, social,* and *temporal* have specific meanings. For example, *spatial* refers to such information as learning where specific areas are located, where certain events and meetings occur; *social* refers to learning about who works in the observational site, who is here for purposes other than work, eg, as students; and *temporal* refers to information about the temporal ordering of events in the observational site. For example, in the instance of a large hospital ward, you would want to know the time of each work shift, the time when reports are presented, time for doctors' and nurses' rounds and so forth. Knowing these elements will help to establish some kind of observational plan, some priorities for observation, and will help to begin to delineate the relevant parameters of the study. The relevance or non-relevance of some of these early decisions about what specific activities and who to observe have yet to be discovered and can only be established as the study progresses.

We will continue with the patient participation study to illustrate how a field researcher proceeds to choose specific items to observe from a vast array of possibilities (Davis, 1979, 1980). The study was begun with a general idea, an understanding one might say, of continuity of care. For purposes of the research, continuity of care referred to the integration over time of staff and patient information and actions directed toward furthering the physical and social psychological rehabilitation of the patient, beginning in the hospital and continuing after discharge. With this understanding as a guide, initial observations were made on the ward: (1) to learn what events and activities of the staff and others occurred in relation to continuity and to delineate the natural history of these events as they occur; (2) to identify patterns in this activity, gaps and breaks in the interconnectedness of one activity to another; and (3) to locate where chronologically the patient is and how this relates to the possibilities for his/her involvement in care. Observations were also made as particular patients were followed longitudinally over their hospitalization, often spanning weeks or longer so that aspects of continuity and/or discontinuity of care could be observed as they occurred.

As the various kinds of staff meetings on the wards were identified at which patients were discussed, observations were made at them to learn which meetings had the most relevance for the issue of continuity. Most meetings where plans for a patient's discharge were made were referred to as discharge planning meetings. However, not all meetings where discharge planning occurred were so designated; hence all meetings had to be attended to discern their content. Some examples of what was observed and listened for at these meetings are as follows. First, a point was made to learn when these meetings occurred in relation to the patient's known discharge date. Other observations included who attended the meetings, who did not attend but was expected to, whose attendance was erratic, were cancelled meetings rescheduled, and if rescheduled how much time elapsed. Attention was directed to listening for information exchanged about the patient, who provided it, and what was done with it. It was noted if each member in the group participated and/or assumed equal responsibility for providing in-put and assisted in the decision making, and if one health professional assumed more responsibility over all others in the decision-making process and information exchange. If the latter occurred, further investigation was done to learn how this came about, eg, did others fail to assume their share of the responsibility, hence the task fell to one person? Also observed was when and if a family member(s) entered into the planning. If they were, when and how they were brought into the discharge process were noted. How the patient learned of the plan, when, how, and what aspects of the plan were shared with the patient was also investigated.

Observations were made of the social interaction between patient and staff (ie, nurse and patient, and doctor and patient) in order to learn: (a) what expectations about self-care and other health-related matters were conveyed explicitly and/or implicitly through their interaction, and (b) to see what kinds of patient behaviors were reinforced by nurses and doctors in their patient interactions.

Observations were made of organizational as well as social and cultural features of each clinical unit since the patient and staff behavior being observed took place in a social context. As mentioned earlier, the basic premise underlying field research is that there is an interconnectedness between the environment in which a phenomenon occurs and how that phenomenon is perceived and experienced by those in the environment. Therefore, it was of importance to the study to learn what consequences specific aspects of ward organization and social and cultural features may have had for the phenomena under study. For example, a ward organizational feature that was considered was the work rotation schedules of interns, residents, and nurses. Ward cultural features that were considered were the dominant care orientation of the ward, the predominant mix of professionals on the ward at any one time, the typical style of nurse-doctor interaction, and transactions on the ward and so forth.

CONCLUSION

While there is much more to be said on the topic of observation, it is my firm belief that the best way to learn how to observe in natural settings is to go out and do it. To be sure, it is wise to prepare oneself by reading widely on the subject of field research and qualitative analysis. However, no amount of reading can prepare one for the satisfactions, challenge, fun, agonies, anxieties, and embarrassments as does being out in the field collecting data.

References

Blumer H: Society as symbolic interaction, in Rose AM (ed): *Human Behavior and Social Processes.* Boston, Houghton Mifflin Co, 1962, pp 179–192.
Byerly EL: The nurse researcher as a participant observer in a nursing setting. *Nursing Research* 1969; 18:230–236.

Byerly EL: The nurse as a participant-observer in a nursing setting, in Brink PJ (ed): *Transcultural Nursing.* New York, Prentice-Hall, 1976, pp 230–236.

Caudill WF, Redlich FC, Gilmore HR, Brody EB: Social structure and interaction processes on a psychiatric ward. *Am J Orthopsychiatry* 1952; 22:314–334.

Davis MZ: Some problems in identity in becoming a nurse researcher. *Nurs Res* 1968; 17:166–168.

Davis MZ: Transition to a Devalued Status: The Case of Multiple Sclerosis, doctoral dissertation, University of California, San Francisco, 1970.

Davis MZ: *Living With Multiple Sclerosis: A Social Psychological Analysis.* Springfield, Illinois, Charles C. Thomas, Publishers, 1973.

Davis MZ: *Organizational Context of Patient Participation in Continuity of Care.* Veterans Administration Medical Center, San Diego (unpublished research report), 1979.

Davis MZ: The organizational, interactional and care oriented conditions for patient participation in continuity of care: A framework for staff intervention. *Soc Sci Med* 1980; 14A:39–47.

Fox RC: *Experiment Perilous.* Philadelphia, University of Pennsylvania Press, 1959.

Glaser BG, Strauss AL: *Awareness of Dying.* Chicago, Aldine Publishing Co, 1965.

Glaser BG, Strauss AL: *The Discovery of Grounded Theory: Strategies for Qualitative Research.* Chicago, Aldine Publishing Co, 1976.

Jackson BS: An experience in participant observation. *Nurs Outlook* 1975; 23:552–555.

Jacobson SF: An insider's guide to field research. *Nurs Outlook* 1978; 26:371–378.

Lofland J: *Analyzing Social Settings: A Guide to Qualitative Observation and Analysis.* Belmont, CA: Wadsworth Publishing Co, 1971.

Oleson V, Whittaker E: *The Silent Dialogue: A Study in the Social Psychology of Professional Socialization.* San Francisco, Jossey-Bass, 1968.

Quint JC: *The Nurse and the Dying Patient.* New York, The Macmillan Co, 1967.

Quint JC: The case for theories generated from empirical data. *Nurs Res* 1967; 16:109–114.

Roth JS: *Timetables.* New York, The Bobbs-Merrill Co, 1963.

Schatzman L, Strauss AL: *Field Research Strategies for a Natural Sociology.* Englewood Cliffs, New Jersey, Prentice-Hall, 1973.

Strauss AL, Schatzman L, Bucher R, Ehrlich D, Sabshin M: *Psychiatric Ideologies and Institutions.* Glencoe, Illinois, Free Press, 1964.

Strauss AL: *Nursing care and the management of pain in patients.* Grant Application, Public Health Service, Department of Health, Education and Welfare, 1972.

Wilson HS: Limiting intrusion-social control of outsiders in a healing community. *Nurs Res* 1977; 26:103–111.

6

The formal qualitative interview for grounded theory

Janice M. Swanson

The formal interview is carried out according to a prescribed plan of action. Formal interviews are conducted when a nurse researcher desires in-depth information that can best be obtained in a private setting and from respondents recruited from predetermined sites.

THE FORMAL INTERVIEW AND GROUNDED THEORY

Formal interviews are of two types: structured and unstructured. A structured interview uses an interview schedule and the interviewer does not deviate from the questions in sequence or wording. The interviewer conducting a structured interview uses minimal extraneous talk to ensure uniform responses which can be quantified. The unstructured interview has been referred to as an intensive, in-depth, or qualitative interview. Its purpose is to get information in the respondent's own words, to gain a description of situations, and to elicit detail (Lofland, 1971).

Unstructured interviews are most commonly used to collect qualitative data; they are the formal interviews used in grounded theory. Lofland notes: "A goal of intensive or qualitative interviewing is to construct records of action-in-process from a variety of people who have likely performed these actions time and time again" (1976, pp 8–9).

In the unstructured formal interview, one may use an interview guide containing a set of brief, general questions, a topical outline, or a major theme. The interview guide or topical outline may be used by the investigator new to this method of interviewing in order to clarify the general areas about which the respondent will be asked. Unlike the structured interview, use of the interview guide is not rigidly adhered to by the interviewer. A topical outline may contain several themes or develop one theme in depth, such as, "experience with contraception" or "perception of wellness." Since the formal interview is requested by the researcher, the guide or outline is useful to provide structure early in the encounter. The interviewer introduces a pertinent theme and questions are framed to pursue the development of the theme. The interviewer is ever mindful to follow the respondent's major concerns or viewpoint.

This chapter will focus on the unstructured formal interview and will cover the following topics: (1) preliminary concerns; (2) characteristics of the interviewer; (3) the nurse and the research role; (4) the formal grounded theory interview; (5) interviewing the natural unit; (6) structuring the interview; (7) the interview; (8) private topics; (9) mechanics and (10) closing the interview.

Preliminary Concerns

Preliminary concerns must be addressed prior to conducting any research project. Initially, a research proposal must be completed. The interview guide, topical outline, or interview theme(s) are included in the proposal; also included are copies of recruitment flyers, informed consent forms, and medical record release forms usually placed in the appendix.

Entrée to an agency or research site to conduct interviews is also necessary. This is formal activity and follows the same entrée procedures presented by Davis (chapter 5). It is often necessary to determine the number of possible respondents, practical considerations such as facilities available, rooms for interviewing individuals or groups, lines of communication in the agency and between agency officials and researcher, procedures for recruitment of subjects, content of patient/client flyers or posters, involvement of staff in recruitment, and specific concerns of the agency. It is customary to give the agency a copy of the proposal. The researcher may need a letter of confirmation from agency representatives called "letters of support of research" in which the use of the site is confirmed. It is not unusual to be asked to draft this letter for agency officials.

In the formal interview, the respondent's agreement to participate in the study is obtained through the use of written consent forms; the respondent's signature on the consent form represents his or her willingness to be interviewed. There may be specific circumstances in which waiver of the written consent form for formal interviews is requested by the researcher to the human research committee.

Characteristics of the Interviewer

The interviewer must have the information and skills necessary to gain access to respondents, gain their respect, and to understand the interview topic (Gorden, 1975). Nurses bring to the research arena prior skills in interviewing. Gorden (1975) uses scattered adjectives to describe the interviewer, noting that interviewers with these characteristics must be sought out: courteous, respectful, friendly, supportive, and genuinely interested. Schatzman (1973, p 74) states, "There is no more important tactic . . . than to communicate the idea that the informant's views are acceptable and important." This means that there are no "right" or "wrong" answers to a research interview. The interviewer must accept what is heard from the respondent (or informant) at face value and communicate that acceptance to the respondent. No judgment by the interviewer is made. In addition, the interviewer is not a therapist. Respondent(s) must be referred to other resources if follow-up is necessary.

The manner of dress must be appropriate to the site at which the interviews take place. For example, dress may differ in carrying out interviews with drug addicts in a community setting and interviews with patients in a coronary care unit. Manner of speech is also important in interviewing. Terms appropriate and meaningful to the respondent should be used. The interviewer should listen for and be sensitive to language used by the respondent, and should use these terms when appropriate during the interview. Medical terms, if they are necessary, should be defined.

Gorden (1975) lists three personality traits which are assets to the interviewer: flexibility, intelligence, and emotional security. Flexibility enables the interviewer to assume an active or passive role when necessary in order to facilitate communication. The interviewer keeps the interview on course, does not panic with silence, and does not suggest answers. The flexible interviewer can shorten or lengthen the interview, arrange to move to a quieter place, or to meet again, when necessary. The intelligent interviewer knows the objectives of the interview, can remember what was said, can probe appropriately, and can evaluate the information given, asking for clarification of inconsistencies. The emotionally secure interviewer is free from anxiety about his or her self, sincere, observes the respondent's emotional needs, empathizes with the respondent, communicates warmth, and puts the respondent at ease. Although the beginning interviewer may feel insecure at first, these characteristics usually develop with experience.

The Nurse and the Research Role

Wearing the nurse hat versus the research hat may be problematic to the beginning nurse-researcher conducting formal qualitative interviews. The respondent may well wonder, "What kind of person is asking me these questions?" When introduced as a "nurse," some of the role expectations and images of "this person" may be answered in the mind of the respondent. One major problem for nurses is the desire to make interventions. Unless the health of the respondent is threatened, the best way to deal with the need to make interventions is to carry them out at the end of the interview in order to avoid altering the respondent's response. It is necessary to consciously take off the hat of the researcher and put on the hat of the nurse. For example, questions about the contraceptive regimen, such as its frequency of duration have to be answered at the end of the interview. As a nurse, the researcher may also need to respond to misinformation or a misconception, for example, if a respondent is taking the wrong dosage of a medication. Stopping during the interview to give correct information could alter later answers or give the respondent the idea that he or she does not have correct information. The respondent's concerns may yield important data, however. A sensitive or non-judgmental query must be made by the interviewer. Other questions may need to be referred to a health practitioner on site. In some situations, subjects will make requests that must be referred to staff, for example, "Will you make a phone call for me?"

The Formal Grounded Theory Interview

The formal qualitative interview for generating grounded theory may differ from formal interviews for other types of research studies in the following ways:

1. It is recommended that the nurse-researcher be fresh to the clinical area. For example, if researchers know the clinical area too intimately or have worked for years in the area, they may overlook important aspects of the experience of the respondents, take information for granted, or analyze data from their own experience. On the other hand, the unstructured interview can allow for more freedom of expression by the researcher and hence, bias or ideological expression may occur. A researcher fresh to an area may be more inclined to be open to new phenomena and expressions of perceptions of that phenomena.

2. Formal interviewing is usually done in conjunction with participant observation and informal interviewing. Topics from these data collection methods that need clarification to elicit the range and variation of a category may require a formal interview. Additional time, a private space, or perspectives of a partner or family member may be needed.

3. Interviewers may need to see respondents over time in order to account for phases in a process (such as during pregnancy) or to check their perceptions of phenomena which arise later in the study.

4. In early interviews, topic control may be exerted by the inexperienced interviewer as noted previously. The experienced interviewer, however, exerts minimal topic control during the first interviews. Early interviews may be sketchier than later interviews as the interviewer, experienced or not, may not know how the respondents perceive the problem and what information is needed to understand how respondents address the problem.

5. Formal interviews may later become narrowed in focus for specific data as theoretical sampling commences; the interviewer may only need to check out a few points toward the end of the study when categories are saturated and theoretical completeness occurs.

6. Analysis of data commences with the first interviews; comparison of the first two interviews should yield basic codes and some initial categories indicating beginning range and variation of experience. Interviews become richer and fuller as analysis occurs consecutively with data gathering.

7. Demographic information may be best obtained at the end of the interview when a relationship is well established. An interrogative style to elicit age, marital status, etc, may be less intrusive as a conclusion to the interview.

   A face sheet should be attached to the top of each interview after it is transcribed to help retrieve demographic data and specific interview content. The face sheet should contain information such as the following: code number, date of the interview, interview site (coded also), age, sex, education, race/ethnic identity, income, occupation, religion, and other information pertinent to the research. The health needs of the underserved are of such magnitude in most countries that it is recommended that this information be obtained in a manner which could facilitate easy access should nurse-researchers be asked, for example, the comparative nature of their samples with those previously studied or at-risk. This may be valuable information to present in response to questions concerning health policy at a research conference where the nurse-researcher is presenting findings. Although a body of research is needed to support major shifts in nursing practice and health policy, the health of the population will be enhanced by researchers who value their contributions, as elementary as they may be, by keeping careful documentation of the nature of their respondent groups. This is particularly important for formal interviews, as such demographic information will not be elicited, as a rule, through participant observation and informal interviewing. Any key words or anecdotes (descriptive data, "tidbits") which would serve as "memory joggers" to the researcher should also be included on the face sheet.

8. Only 20 to 50 interviews are necessary to elicit major, repetitive themes of the topic under study; 100 to 200 interviews or statistically derived sample sizes are not appropriate if theoretical sampling, accounting for a range of variation, has been followed (Lofland, 1971; Glaser, Strauss, 1967). Negotiation may be necessary, however, with the researcher's sponsor; compromises may need to be made with particular attention paid to the number of respondents from each site, the span of time allotted for data-gathering, the "mix" of formal and informal interviews and participant observation, and arrangement for following respondents over time.

Interviewing the Natural Unit: Individual, Conjoint, and Group

Nurses often interview natural units in a variety of hospital and community settings in their daily practice. Also, the nurse-researcher interviews natural units which may vary from the individual to couples to the family or varying-sized groups. As multiple units are naturally encountered by nurses working in a variety of health care settings with the ill or the well, so too, multiple units may be encountered by nurse-researchers as natural units for interviewing to complete a research project.

Although both the scientific and medical models have traditionally broken up the natural unit to facilitate care and to conduct research, a trend exists to re-think this approach, one which has been used most consistently by social scientists (Card, 1978; Stycos, 1981). This approach has been noted most, perhaps, in fields such as family therapy, counseling, and parenting programs. The impact of the family and significant others on health-illness behavior should be carefully considered when designing the research study. The purpose and nature of the study will determine whether multiple units are included in the sample. Participant observation and informal interviewing often involve multiple units. Formal interviews for grounded theory are especially suitable for gathering data from the natural or multiple unit.

Many grounded theory studies by nurse researchers include interviews of multiple units: May (1980) interviewed expectant couples; Stern (1982) interviewed stepfather families; and Swanson and Corbin (1983) reported interviews of couples using contraception. As the nurse researcher is sensitized to the occurrence of natural multiple units in participant-observation and informal interviewing, so too, the nurse-researcher conducting formal interviews should be sensitive to the occurrence of such units and the need to interview them. Natural units may come to the attention of the researcher after the study has commenced.

Much can be gained by interviewing couples as a unit even though partners interviewed together have voiced fear of disclosing too much in front of the partner (Allan, 1980). First, two responses are obtained instead of one. The researcher cannot assume one partner can speak for the other, a basic assumption in many studies. One partner may clarify the other's perception of an event. Partners may add to or detract from, and at times, challenge recalled details of an event. Both verbal and non-verbal interaction may be noted, including verbal fluency and power in the relationship. The interviewer is able to observe processes-in-action as it occurs, rather than through second-hand "telling."

Some of these processes include teaching, negotiation, and coercion; at times arguments may break out and processes of resolution or co-optation may be noted. Consequences may be observed, and later telephone contact with each partner individually may yield additional data and dynamics of the couple, as well as the long-term effects on the couple. Private information may be disclosed as new topic areas evolve a degree of risk-taking on the part of each partner. At times, the interviewer may have to let the couple know that they do not have to disclose selected information. When interviewing couples as a unit, caution should be exercised concerning the need for follow-up referral to an agency for counseling. Referrals may be problematic, and resources and reimbursement constraints should be investigated in advance by the interviewer.

Perhaps the greatest advantage to interviewing multiple units is the rich data that may be obtained, giving range and variation of categories needed for grounded theory development.

Structuring the Interview

Time and place are explicit and prearranged in a formal interview.

Time   The time for the interview is arranged to economize the energy and time of the interviewer, the agency, and the respondent.

The interviewer must realize his/her own time constraints and plan accordingly. Whether an educator, clinician, or administrator is conducting research, reasonable blocks of time per week must be set aside from other activities for interviewing. Based on the author's experience, the following recommendations are made for the beginning interviewer. A minimum of 50 minutes to an hour should be allotted per interview. Extra time beyond an hour, if possible, may be allowed in case a respondent is late or an interview goes overtime. Crowded booking of interviews may cause the interviewer to unnecessarily hurry the process, conveying insincerity or inattention to the interview. Nothing is more frustrating than to have to terminate or reschedule time with a respondent who is just beginning to disclose important or private information to the interviewer. It is also recommended that the interviewer only schedule two formal interviews per day as it is easy to experience overload. Formal interviewing takes energy; it is necessary to be alert and responsive during the interview. In addition, there is the need to transcribe the tape or notes and begin to analyze the data shortly after the interview is conducted. The interviewer should realize that a one-hour interview may yield 20 or more pages of typed transcript. One additional caution is suggested: the interviewer should allow time for parking and changing traffic conditions at different times of the day. Putting money into a parking meter every 30 minutes during an interview is most disruptive. The interviewer should always be on time and allow sufficient time to set up, and check the tape recorder. These details of getting to the interview site on time may be critical factors in a successful interview.

Prudent use of the agency's time is also important. The interviewer must keep within the hours previously arranged with the agency. Running overtime with an interview may be disruptive to the agency. The interviewer may, on occasion, need to work around the respondent's appointment to see a clinician, for example. Patient/client load in an agency may also vary. An interview may be moved to an odd room, for example, if there is overload in the clinic.

The use of the subject's time is also an important consideration. Appointments and meeting sites should be arranged in advance. It is important for the interviewer to keep to the prearranged time and place. To conserve the energy of the respondent, the interviewer may try to make appointments for the interview that correspond with the subject's return appointments to the agency. This will also increase the likelihood that the appointment will be kept.

Place   In selecting the interview site, major considerations are the convenience of the site to the respondent, the interviewer, and the agency, the need for privacy and safety. Interviews should be carried out at the site designated in the research proposal, the procedures for contacting respondents, the recruitment flyers, and in the informed consent form. Interviews may take place in a variety of sites: in the home or office of the respondent or the interviewer, in a counseling, examination, or hospital room within the agency, or other designated space. The site should assure privacy and should be free from interruptions and distractions.

Normal safety precautions should be heeded when arranging extra-agency sites for the interview. If the interviewer feels uncertain about going into the home of an unknown respondent (for example, respondents who work during the day and must be interviewed in the evening or on weekends or in an area unfamiliar to the interviewer), arrangements should be made to meet in a public place or in an office of the agency, if possible. One alternative is to be accompanied by a colleague or student. This arrangement should be agreed to by the respondent before the interview. The effect of a third party on the interview should also be carefully weighed.

The Interview

The following section will cover aspects of introducing the interview and interviewing techniques. In the introduction to the interview, explain the sponsorship of the interviewer, the purpose of the study, and the confidential nature of research data. The informed consent form and access to medical record forms (if applicable) are read and signed. The subject should be encouraged to answer all questions freely and to ask questions as desired. The subject is assured during the interview that there are no "right" or "wrong" answers. The section on interviewing techniques covers verbal and non-verbal aspects of the interview, and specific techniques known as the funnel and inverted funnel approach to elicit types of information.

Verbal   Social talk, such as, "Did you have any trouble getting here?" should set the conversational tone for the interview. The opening question should introduce the major theme or several themes of the interview, for example, "What comes to your mind when you think of contraception?" A conversational tone should be continued throughout the interview. Although both the interviewer and the respondent, or one or the other, may be nervous and rigid at first, the tone should develop as the interview progresses. Gorden (1975) suggests a warm-up period in which the interviewer asks the subject to discuss related events occurring before the events the researcher is most interested in. For example, when the interest is the subject's experience in a self-help group, questions can be used to "loosen up" the subject before critical areas are broached. "How did you first hear about the group?" or "How did you get into the group?" are questions that accomplish this purpose.

A generality statement (Mims, Swenson, 1980) may be used to give the respondent assurance that his or her concerns are acceptable and may be the concerns of others: "Some people express concerns about———.What are your concerns in this area?"

Ubiquity statements (Green, 1975; Woods, 1979) assume that a range of behavior is possible. Statements such as "When did you—," "Where did you—," and "How did you—," open up the interview and elicit a greater response than statements such as "Did you—" which often lead to dead-end responses, such as "yes" or "no."

The use of probes to encourage the respondent to tell more of his or her experience is also helpful. Gorden (1975, p 422) suggests use of two types: the silent probe and the neutral probe. The silent probe, pausing and waiting for the respondent's response, allows the respondent to proceed along a path of his or her choosing. For the beginning interviewer, silence may be interpreted as embarrassing. Experience most often proves the benefit of the use of silence as a probing technique. The neutral probe, "ummm . . . ," "hmmm . . . ," and "I see . . . ," conveys to the respondent that he or she has been heard (Gorden, 1975, p 422). Schatzman and Strauss (1973) note four types of probes commonly used: "chronology (. . . and then?; When was that?), detail (Tell me more about that; That's very interesting), clarification (I don't quite understand?; But you said earlier . . .), and explanation (Why?; How come?)" (1973, p 74).

Non-verbal   Non-verbal cues given by the respondent should also be noted by the interviewer (Gorden, 1975). Non-verbal cues include visual cues such as facial expression, gestures, body position, and movement of the hands, feet, or head; and auditory cues, such as pace of speech, pitch, intensity, and volume level. Changes and inconsistencies should be noted in relationship to the content and situational context of the interview. If an inconsistency exists, the interviewer should probe until the matter is clarified, for the objectives of the interview.

Funnel/inverted funnel approach   Gorden (1975) suggests the funnel/inverted funnel approach to aid in eliciting specific information from respondents. In the funnel approach, the interviewer starts with a general question, and follows with more specific questions. For example, the interviewer asks, "What do you think are some of the most important health problems found by women in today's world?" A more specific question follows, "Of all those you mentioned, which one do you consider to be the most important to solve?" Yet a more specific question is asked, "Where have you received information about this problem?"

This approach is used when: (1) the interviewer wants to discover unanticipated responses, (2) the respondent is motivated to give detailed description of an event or situation, and (3) the interviewer wants to avoid imposing his/her frame of reference on the respondent.

The inverted funnel approach, in contrast, starts with specific questions and follows with more general questions. For example, the interviewer asks, "About how many staff members were on the unit when the power failed?" The following questions become more and more general: "How many additional staff came to the scene?" "How long did they have to wait until the emergency generator took over?" "Did anyone give emergency care on the unit?" "Did you?" "In general, how well do you think the emergency operations were carried out?" The use of the inverted funnel approach is helpful when: (1) the respondent is not motivated to speak spontaneously, (2) the respondent's experiences are not important to him/her, and (3) the interviewer desires a judgment and facts are known to the respondent and not to the interviewer. Use of this approach will stimulate respondents to respond wholeheartedly and to base their judgments on the facts reviewed, in contrast to presenting facts solely as a rationale for initial judgments.

Private Topics

Nursing practice often addresses health/illness concerns of patients and clients involving very personal or private areas of their lives. For example, some private areas in nursing include helping a newly diagnosed patient admit he/she has epilepsy to significant others or colleagues at work; taking a mental health history; talking about reproductive surgery or a sexually transmitted disease. Other private areas commonly encountered by nurses include aspects of chronic illness, particularly patients faced with a colostomy or those with ulcerative colitis or a developmental or other disability (visible or invisible), mental retardation, genetic concerns, or infertility. Clients may fear that disclosure of their disability or health problem may expose them to be seen as less than normal by others (Goffman, 1963).

Nurses also conduct research in private areas such as those mentioned previously. Often in research, private information and experience is sought. Virtually all formal interviewing generates private information—the respondent has information which the interviewer does not yet have. The informed consent procedure itself is designed to protect subjects from exploitation and revelation of identity which may be damaging. Nursing research in private areas is conducted to increase nursing knowledge regarding the experience of an aggregate of patients/clients who must live with interruptions of life, touching very personal areas. It is the responsibility of the researcher to guard against disclosure of the location of the site(s) where the research is carried out and the identity of respondents in research communications, presentations, and manuscripts prepared for publication.

Three major conditions are necessary to elicit private information from respondents in the formal interview: (1) the comfort of the interviewer with the topic area, (2) the giving of permission to respondents to speak of their concerns about private areas, (3) the assurance of a private place and sufficient time for an unhurried interview. In contrast to participant observation and informal interviewing which are more or less publicly carried out, the formal interview is perhaps the best vehicle for eliciting private or personal areas of concern to respondents. The three conditions will now be dealt with in more depth.

First, it is essential that the interviewer know himself or herself and feel comfortable interviewing in the topic area. For example, the nurse-researcher comfortable with families should feel comfortable interviewing families. On the other hand, if the nurse feels uncomfortable in intensive care units or has difficulty working with the bereaved, interviewing respondents about these areas may best be left to others or should occur at another time in the life/career of the nurse-researcher.

Interviewing in private areas must coincide with the career preparation of the interviewer. To carry out research in other than one's ''natural'' areas, it may be necessary for the researcher to take courses or workshops to develop the necessary degree of comfort with a selected topic area.

Second, in eliciting private information, it is important to give permission to the respondent to talk about private areas of concern. It is necessary for the interviewer to take the role of the other, to be supportive. Careful attention should be paid to language use and the use of generality and ubiquity statements described previously is most helpful. Letting the respondent know that others have similar concerns and that his or her concerns are valid is important. Use of "door openers" can be helpful in giving permission. For example, "It must be hard to go through what you've gone through; many people have had similar experiences. What was that experience like for you?"

Finally, the setting is also key to eliciting private concerns of respondents. A private setting assures freedom from eavesdropping and interruptions. Structural constraints of health care settings present a challenge to the interviewer. For example, a private room may not be readily or consistently available, and interruptions by the laboratory or x-ray personnel may occur. Strategies to deal with such constraints may involve trade-offs with staff such as securing the shower room, for example. Attention to the needs of staff, patient/client flow patterns, and the needs of respondents will prove helpful in meeting the challenge of these constraints.

Mechanics

Recording procedures should be as smooth as possible. Note-taking by hand is difficult to do while conducting an interview, formulating questions, and probes. Tape recording the interview is preferred. If this cannot be done, brief notes can be made and immediately following the interview session, full notes are recorded on tape or typed. Bozett (1980) notes that interviewers must know their recorders and should have their own if possible. The borrowed tape recorder which is expected to be in the closet of the agency or department may not be there and, if it is, it may not work. Extension cords, extra batteries, extra tapes, and a built-in microphone are recommended. Bozett (1980) suggests the interviewer listen to the tape after the session to assure the interview has been recorded. It is also necessary to check the typist's rendition of the transcript with the actual recording for omissions and misinterpretations of the tape.

Transcribing of the interviews should be done by the interviewer, if possible, and done shortly after the interview. Self-transcription stimulates analysis of the data; the interviewer then may capture fresh ideas in memos and write directives regarding further interviews. A large margin on either side of the text should be left for coding; the script should be double- or triple-spaced. Fees for professional transcription typing are high; it may require from three to 12 hours to type one interview, for example.

Several carbon or photocopied duplicates (six or more) of the transcription should be made. One should be kept at the interviewer's institutional base and one kept in the interviewer's home to prevent loss of valuable materials in case of fire, theft, or other catastrophe. Other copies of the transcription will be used in coding, cut and pasted for memos, research presentations, and manuscripts for publication.

Closing the Interview

The closure of the formal, unstructured interview should be tentative. Although the interviewer may not realize it until analysis is well under way, the interview may be incomplete and more information may be needed. For this reason, it is recommended that the end of the interview be handled as an interruption only, not a termination. Inform respondents that you may desire to see them again to do a follow-up interview, or that you may wish to contact them by phone at some time in the future. This leaves the door open to obtain additional information if needed. Any questions at the end of the interview should be answered, and respondents thanked for their time and willingness to participate in the study.

CONCLUSION

The unstructured, intensive or qualitative interview is the best vehicle for eliciting the personal and private concerns of respondents. In a grounded theory study formal interviewing is most often combined with participant observation and informal interviewing. The formal, qualitative interview requires a private setting and the recruitment of respondents specifically for the purpose of the interview.

In this chapter, information about and suggestions for a successful qualitative interview was presented. The beginning interviewer may find this information particularly useful. The experienced interviewer may find some of the information useful and may wish to compare the suggestions made here with his or her own techniques.

References

Allan G: A note on interviewing spouses together. *J Marr Fam* 1980; 42:205–210.

Bozett F: Practical suggestions for the use of the audio cassette tape recorder in nursing research. *West J Nurs Res* 1980; 2:602–605.

Card JJ: The correspondence of data gathered from husband and wife: Implications for family planning studies. *Soc Biol* 1978; 25:196–204.

Goffman E: *Stigma: Notes on the Management of Spoiled Identity.* Englewood Cliffs, New Jersey, Prentice-Hall, 1963.

Gorden RL: *Interviewing: Strategy, Techniques, and Tactics.* Homewood, Illinois, The Dorsey Press, 1975.

Green R (ed): *Human Sexuality—a Health Practitioner's Text.* Baltimore, Williams and Wilkins, 1975.

Lofland J: *Analyzing Social Settings: A Guide to Qualitative Observation and Analysis.* Belmont, California, Wadsworth Publishing Co, 1971.

Lofland J: *Doing Social Life.* New York, John Wiley, 1976.

May K: A typology of detachment/involvement styles adopted during pregnancy by first-time expectant father. *West J Nurs Res* 1980; 2:445–453.

Mims FH, Swenson M: *Sexuality: A Nursing Perspective.* New York; McGraw-Hill Book Co, 1980.

Schatzman L, Strauss A: *Field Research.* Englewood Cliffs, New Jersey, Prentice-Hall, 1973.

Stern P: Affiliating in stepfather families: Teachable strategies leading to stepfather-child friendship. *West J Nurs Res* 1982; 4:75–89.

Swanson J, Corbin J: The contraceptive context—a model for increasing nursing's involvement in family health. *Matern Child Nurs J* 1983; 12:169–183.

Stycos J: A critique of focus group and survey research: The machismo case. *Stud Fam Plann* 1981; 12:450–456.

Woods NF: *Human Sexuality in Health and Illness.* St. Louis, C. V. Mosby, 1979.

7

The informal interview

W. Carole Chenitz

The purpose of a grounded theory study is to understand the concerns, actions, and behaviors of a group and explain those patterns of behavior at a higher level of abstraction, a theory. To do this, the researcher engages in the world under study and attempts to "see" this world as the interactants see it. The researcher's task is to collect and analyze data from the natural world. Natural data are best collected by natural methods. The informal interview, which is like an everyday conversation, is a valuable method of data collection.

While all research interviews are "conversations with a purpose" (Bingham, Moore, 1959), the informal interview epitomizes this statement. The informal interview is the use of everyday conversations for the purpose of collecting and validating data. This method is characterized by natural speech and interaction between the researcher and respondent. Like everyday conversations, informal interviews have no particular meeting time, length, or place. They are surrounded by no formalities such as the use of interview guides. There is also no ceremony that highlights the interview such as the signing of consent forms. There are no predetermined and agreed upon theme(s) or topic(s) for the interview.

The informal interview appears to be an ordinary conversation typical to a group; however, it is conducted for the express purpose of collecting data. The researcher consciously and self-consciously uses self to conduct informal interviews.

In this chapter, we will examine the characteristics of this method and the researcher's personal characteristics, the advantages of informal interviews, informal interviewing and participant observation, recording notes, informed consent, nurses and informal interviewing, and validity in field methods.

CHARACTERISTICS OF THE INFORMAL
INTERVIEW AND THE RESEARCHER

The major characteristics of the informal interview are its social nature and similarity with natural conversation to the group under study. The basic rules that apply to all ordinary conversations apply to the informal interview. As Becker and Geer note: "In this kind of interview, the interviewer explores many facets of his interviewee's concerns, creating subjects as they come up in conversation, pursuing interesting leads, allowing his imagination and ingenuity full run as he tries to develop new hypotheses and test them in the course of the interview" (1969, p 323).

Schatzman and Strauss have pointed out that "brief, situational or incidental questioning or conversation is extremely effective throughout the research" (1973, p 71). For this reason, the researcher may want to use informal interviews in a grounded theory study. However, it would be inadvisable to use this method if the researcher does not possess the personal qualities which are required to make it work in the field. Conscious use of self and one's interpersonal skills facilitate engaging with informants. As with all techniques, experience with this method will increase self-confidence and ability.

The researcher who needs more structure may become frustrated with field methods especially informal interviewing. To create structure, the researcher may focus too early in the analysis. This could lead to more pointed and organized questioning in the field but could also lead to a theory that lacks depth and credibility. To lessen the danger of this premature focusing, the researcher is urged to "ride out" the learning process of this method. It is natural, particularly in the early stages, to feel self-conscious, nervous, uncomfortable, and even inadequate in the field. One can capitalize on these feelings by recording the early experiences and perceptions and later analyzing them to improve the use of the method. With guidance and experience, researchers can use their experiences and perceptions as data. For example, if entering an institution or group was being studied, the researcher could use his or her own early experiences about what it felt like to be a newcomer, how newcomers are treated, etc., as valuable data.

Since informal interviews are conversations, an essential requirement for the researcher is the ability to engage others in conversation. Social norms and rules of the group apply to the researcher and these must be learned by the researcher. Sensitivity to group customs, norms, and rules are needed by the researcher (Dean et al, 1969). For example, the nurse-researcher informally interviewing opiate addicts in a clinic will use language and customs natural for this group. The customs and language will be different from those used by the middle-class elders in a nursing home setting. Social skill and sensitivity to group customs are essential. The insensitive researcher will be unable to put informants at ease and will have distorted and inaccurate data.

Another characteristic of the informal interview is the lack of ceremony surrounding the interview and the conversational flow of the interview. An informal interview may last minutes (such as conversations while passing in the hall) or it may go on for an hour or more when the subject and researcher are in ''deep talk'' and neither wants to end it. An informal interview can be conducted anywhere: hallways, nurses' stations, patients' rooms, offices, homes, or wherever the nurse-researcher and informant are. The researcher, therefore, must also possess conversational skills and interpersonal grace. The more skillful the researcher is at engaging in talk with another person or group, putting them at ease and disengaging with grace, the better the interview. The better the interview, the better the data. Since it is often necessary to have many informal interviews with one subject, the researcher conducts the interview in such a way that the subject is willing to engage in these talks again and again (Strauss et al, 1969).

The lack of formality or ceremony surrounding the informal interview means the researcher also needs a tolerance for ambiguity and flexibility. Interview themes will range from broad social issues and ideologies of groups to the specifics of daily life of an individual. Specific topics change with each subject and interview. The questions asked and how they are asked will also change. The depth, theme, and questions of the interview are determined by a number of factors such as stage of the research project, questions from data analysis, the events happening in the site, as well as the subject-interviewer relationship.

In the formal interview, researchers are fairly sure that subjects will have minimal constraints on their time and are interested enough in the subject or topic to meet for the purpose of an interview. The interviewer using informal interviews has no such assurances. At some times, subjects will be rich with data and willing, even eager, to share it. At other times, there will not be the time or willingness for the subject to fully elaborate on a topic and questions must be filed for another time, another site, or another subject.

The researcher using informal interviews carefully joins and engages with the subjects, constantly assessing them for fatigue and disinterest. Questions are framed at the time while listening to responses. The interview is an emerging process dependent upon the skill of the researcher. Uncertainty in each interview and the products of each interview require tolerance and flexibility on the part of the researcher.

ADVANTAGES OF THE INFORMAL INTERVIEW

The lack of formality and ceremony surrounding informal interviews offer many advantages to the researcher. These interviews provide data that lead the researcher to formulate new ideas. In this way, the subjects guide you into their world, the world that you, the researcher, need to enter and examine. Once engaged with the people in this social world—whether a ward, unit, clinic, or a specific group—the researcher has access to a broad range of data from ideology of the group to personal information about each person. The flexibility of the informal interview allows the researcher maneuverability to focus in on a particular topic or to keep the focus broad.

The informal interview allows the researcher to engage with subjects in their customary way. This natural style permits the researcher to get to know the subjects as people, understand them and how they see their world, and finally, perceive the events the way they do.

When the researcher engages with subjects in this informal way, the interview is highly individualized with each subject and setting. Questions are asked that match the relationship between informants and researcher (Strauss et al, 1969).

The informal interview permits the researcher to have any number of interviews with subjects. This is particularly useful when the researcher is examining changes over time, remains in a site for prolonged periods of time, or when the researcher needs to return to a site. These advantages, however, can also be disadvantages if the researcher does not have the social skill and other characteristics noted earlier, or proves untrustworthy in the field.

INFORMAL INTERVIEWING AND PARTICIPANT OBSERVATION

Informal interviewing in a grounded theory study is used conjointly with participant observation. The conjoint use of participant observation and informal interviewing heighten the ability of the researcher to collect and validate data. This section will focus on the use of informal interviews with participant observation.

Informal interviewing is the backbone of participant observation. As a participant observer, the researcher never assumes the meaning in an action or interaction, nor does the researcher assume that meaning is shared by all participants. The informal interview provides the researcher with the opportunity to direct and focus data collection. As a participant observer, the researcher follows and records events. Certain events raise questions that cannot be answered unless the researcher actively pursues the topic. At other times, a specific event may be at the heart of the research question. Informally interviewing participants allows the researcher access to the topic via the event. The researcher moves consciously from a "passive" observer role into an "active" interviewer role and deliberately engages in conversations.

Timing is a critical element in informal interviews used with participant observation. Since the researcher is on site as a participant observer, he or she is privy to actions and events not usually seen by outsiders. When an event or series of events occur, the researcher makes the decision about when and who to interview. The best time to interview is often immediately after a situation has occurred. People often need to "rehash" or think out loud with another. The confidential ear of the researcher provides a safe place to disclose and think through a situation.

However, if the event is critical, life threatening, or physically demanding, the interviewer steps back and waits for the best time. For example, immediately after a patient is "taken down" (physically restrained) on a psychiatric unit or after a cardiac arrest in an intensive care unit may not be the most appropriate moment to initiate an informal interview. There will be a lull after these events and the researcher waits.

The researcher will then move back into the participant observer role, deliberately collecting data as it occurs. He or she moves back and forth between interviewer and observer. The use of either or both of these methods for data collection is deliberate, done self-consciously, and purposefully.

RECORDING THE INFORMAL INTERVIEW

If you were to take notes or start a tape recorder while talking with a friend during a staff meeting or while having coffee with a colleague, you would be asked "What are you doing?" and "Why?" The natural rapport between you and the other person would abruptly change and the conversation would stop until you provided an answer. This would also be the case if the researcher took notes or taped most informal interviews. Aside from the social impropriety of recording informal interviews, there is the practical problem of conducting the interview. Most people without a written interview schedule to follow will be unable to take notes while interviewing. Throughout the interview, the researcher does the following: (1) considering what is being meant in what is said; (2) considering how to best phrase what you will say next; (3) observing the general pattern of events being discussed; (4) observing the pattern of the interview; and (5) assessing the informant for signs of discomfort, disinterest, distress, or conversely for interest, excitement, etc (Sullivan, 1954).

Most people cannot attend to the interview itself while taking notes. The tape recorder would then be the obvious answer. Here too the researcher has problems of social appropriateness. Taping without the knowledge of subjects is unethical. To get permission to tape on a unit, a nurses' station, or clinic would require that you inform each person of the tape in progress and get his or her consent. The quality of the recording would be uneven and the process wearing.

This leaves the researcher with unrecorded data in the field. Recording immediately and while still on site can be done. In chapter 5, Davis gives suggestions about where and how to record field notes in the site. I have found that during the interview there will be one or two sentences that in the informant's words highlight a particular interview. These key sentences are valuable capsules which summarize the topics covered. The researcher, mindful of this, will watch for these clues and store them to be recorded immediately. The rest of the data is recorded in abbreviated form. As Schatzman and Strauss (1973) point out, these "notes will be very brief—mere words, phrases, possibly a drawing. Their purpose is to provide stimulation for recall done within a matter of hours" (1973, p 95). Both key sentences and abbreviated notes are used to trigger the researcher's memory when typing or taping full notes away from the site.

A word of caution is necessary here. In order to record events accurately, the sooner the notes are made, the better. The use of abbreviated notes is only to jog the mind and to store specific quotes and information. The notes made in the field notebook must be converted into written notes. The more specific and careful the notes, the more specific the data and hence, the analysis (Schatzman, Strauss, 1973).

In assuming the researcher role, the nurse-researcher will find that there are specific times and certain sites in which it is preferable to visibly take notes:

- Note taking is congruent with the research role. Visibly taking notes can reassure informants that the researcher is gathering data and reveal the kind of data the researcher is interested in.

- The researcher has a relationship with informants over time and wishes to record verbatim their responses. The researcher might comment, "I really want to get that down" and start jotting the response.

- The informal interview occurs while taking notes during participant observation. For example, the researcher is sitting in the nurses' station recording notes and a nurse enters and begins to talk about a subject of interest to the researcher. The researcher may comment, "That's really interesting, I don't want to miss this," or some other remark that indicates interest. The researcher then turns the page in the field notebook and records data while conducting the interview or listening to the informant.

One must be aware that taking notes openly in the field may cause others to be suspicious or guarded. One is always cautious of the content of notes taken in the field. Descriptions, key points to remember, or descriptions of the setting are relatively safe. In-depth notes or those about one's perception are best written off site where they can be carefully stored.

Researchers will find the type of field notebook that best suits them and their needs in a site. Some researchers prefer a small notebook while others use a legal pad. In my experience, a spiral bound book, 6 × 9 inches, with about 150 to 200 pages is ideal. The pages are large enough to encourage writing and can be easily seen by all. It is not too small so as to raise suspicion of a secretive operation, but is small enough not to be cumbersome and obvious. Loose paper is not recommended since it can be easily lost. These small notebooks can be filed by site or date for later reference.

INFORMED CONSENT

Since informal interviews are on-the-spot conversations, consent forms agreeing to the interview are not used. The principles of informed consent, however, are not ignored. Instead, the researcher's presence in the agency and purpose of the study are made known to all staff, patients, and visitors.

The specific techniques used to disseminate this information vary between sites and studies. There are several principles that guide the researcher for dissemination. The basic principles are: (1) the subject's right to understand the nature and purpose of the study, (2) voluntarily consent to be in the study, and (3) awareness of the risks and benefits (Spradley, 1979).

In the grounded theory project, informed consent is not a specific act but an ongoing process to fulfill the principles just noted. Techniques that have been used to disseminate information and gain participation in a site include attending meetings with all levels of staff to explain the study, wearing a name pin with your title, making newcomers aware of your identity, and posting notices about the study and researcher's presence in the facility on staff and patient bulletin boards and in newsletters. It is usual to use several of these techniques and any others that may be more appropriate to a setting.

NURSE-RESEARCHER AND THE INFORMAL INTERVIEW

Informal interviewing is an essential element in nursing practice and a central method for data collection in qualitative research. The focus of this section is on the nurse as informal interviewer in a research project.

Expert nurses are experts at the act of informal interviewing. Since most nurse-client interactions are brief, informal, yet have a purpose, nurses use informal interviewing techniques constantly. As a research method, informal interviewing is distinguished from clinical work since it is done to collect research data and is not used for the purpose of intervention. Researchers are consciously aware of their relationship to informants, the purpose of the interview, the context in which the interview is taking place, and other people in the situation. Unlike the clinical interview, the research interview is confidential; the content is not divulged to others in the setting.

The question of identity and role emerges early in a research project and is an important one for nurses. At times, the nurse-researcher may find that the nurse component of the role is stressed. At other times, the research component is stressed. The nurse-researcher strives for role clarity and a clear identity. Since others have a positive impression of nurses, the nurse image can be very useful to gain the confidence of informants. People identify nurses with a caring, nurturing role. Further, people will talk to nurses and reveal to them content that they may not be so willing to disclose to others. In this way, the nurse component of the researcher's identity can be an advantage. The trust subjects have in nurses and nursing can be transferred to a nurse in a research role.

There are also disadvantages and ethical issues to the nurse component of the role to which the researcher needs to be sensitive. Each time the nurse-researcher stresses or uses the nurse identity, there may be an implicit promise to intervene. Subjects expect that you, as a nurse, can and will intervene for them or with them. You must be careful whenever you use the nurse identity that you are not implying that you are there in your clinical role. When the nurse-researcher is aware that the nurse role is being used, it is helpful to ask oneself, "Am I uncomfortable as a researcher? What is happening that is making the research role uncomfortable?"

The researcher can avoid this role confusion by making clear arrangements with the agency at the time of entry about the research role. Other arrangements can be made if the researcher wishes to contribute something to the agency, staff, or patients. It is helpful to have an idea and be clear on what, when, and how you will do something for the agency. For example, the researcher may offer to conduct an in services education program after the research is completed.

The researcher is also aware that staff will test the role of researcher. They may suspect the researcher has a "hidden" mission or they may be curious about what the researcher is doing, why he/she is doing it, and the outcomes of the project. Clarity and clear distinction between a clinical and research role by the nurse-researcher can avoid confusion, false expectations, and implicit promises that cannot be fulfilled.

The researcher should also be aware that her opinions or actions as a nurse may be called for by the subject, staff, or administration about clinical issues. To give your opinion may be contrary to belief, attitude, value, or behavior of participants or you may be revealing information obtained as a researcher. For example, I was once asked by the nursing staff to give my opinion about the use of psychotropic medication for a woman who was a behavioral problem in a nursing home. I had interviewed this woman several times and was aware of why she was acting the way she was. Yet, she was a behavioral problem. In this situation, I had to frame a response to the question that was true to my understanding of the situation and would not reveal information given without the informant's consent. I could not condone the use of medications, since I did not think she needed them; however, the researcher role versus psychiatric nurse role were clearly being tested.

This is one of many such situations in which nurses, as qualitative researchers, will find themselves. These situations are certainly uncomfortable; therefore, while a clinical background and experience are advantages in this method, the researcher must assume a predominantly research role to maintain versatility and maneuverability.

Perhaps, the major disadvantage for the nurse as field researcher is the need to intervene. The following field notes illustrate my struggle with the nurse versus researcher role. It was written four months after conducting my first field work.

Since I am a nurse, it was difficult being in a service setting with nothing to do (participant observation). The old call to deliver service was being responded to in me. I seem to be constantly struggling with my own need to deliver something to those I am meeting and interviewing! Now, it is getting easier for me. I don't feel I must be constantly on guard against my own education and experience as a nurse. I am delivering service in another form. As people talk to me, they find a sympathetic other. Many people experiencing health crisis need this. So, in terms of real life nursing, "hands-on help," I am useless to anyone. Once I accepted this and considered that people within institutional life needed someone to talk to, then data collection became easier.

Aware of the advantages and disadvantages in the nurse component of the role, the nurse-researcher can be sensitive to potentially uncomfortable situations and maintain integrity while in the field.

VALIDITY AND FIELD METHODS

In social life, validity relates to one's belief about what is happening. Beliefs will vary with participants; hence, in everyday life, there are no fixed truths. The more one acts or behaves in a manner that is congruent with his or her belief, the more true it is for them (Dean et al, 1969; Dean, Whyte, 1969). It is the task of the researcher to unearth the relative truth in the situation, to discover the range in people's beliefs, and the congruence between belief and action. This is the validity for which the qualitative researcher strives.

As Davis points out in chapter 5, we are "deliberately and artificially distinguishing between participant observation, informal and formal interviewing, the standard methods for data collection for qualitative analysis." In order to fully describe and explain these methods, each one is presented separately. It is stressed, however, that this separation is artificial; these methods are used conjointly in the conduct of the grounded theory research project to assure validity in the data.

Participant Observation

Participant observation is acknowledged to be the backbone of these methods. Yet when used alone, this research method raises serious questions about the validity of data. While this point may appear to be obvious to the reader, it is a central issue in satisfying the question of validity. Often, the issue of validity is not clear and leads to misconceptions of the nature of qualitative data.

Let us examine the use of participant observation alone and then examine the use of interviewing alone. In the case of participant observation without informal interviewing, you the reader are asked to conjure up the feelings you would have while being observed on a unit during your practice as a nurse. Each attempt you make to draw the "mute bystander" into the conversation is rebuffed. Your discomfort increases and your behavior becomes more and more unnatural as your awareness of being watched heightens. Data collected by this bystander would lack validity since what he or she is observing is not necessarily the actions and activities which reflect the beliefs of those under study. In this situation, you as the subject, would be reacting to being observed. The presence of an observer would reflect in your behavior (Webb et al, 1966). The point here is that validity decreases with the reactivity of the subjects being observed. The use of observation with no informal interactions on the scene not only decreases validity but cannot be sustained for long by either party. First, the subjects would rebel and exclude the bystander whether by action or by formally revoking privilege to observe. The observer would be hard put to maintain a mute presence in the everyday life of the scene.

Informal and Formal Interviewing

Let us look at the other side of the coin, the use of informal or formal interviewing alone to collect data. In this situation, you the researcher are restricted to only using the data that is obtained in interviews with subjects. Your observations, as well as the action that goes on around you, are excluded from your use. You observe and overhear a nurse interacting with a dying patient who is in pain. You watch her leave the room, enter the nurses' station, throw down the chart, sit in a chair, and put her head down into her hands. Another nurse enters the nurses' station, they talk about this patient and the first nurse describes in detail to her peer how frustrated she is and about her feelings of failure that this patient's pain cannot be managed. You later interview this nurse, and during the interview she explains that pain management is difficult and describes the usual techniques to manage pain. Also, she explains the ideology of the unit. However, she avoids repeating her feelings of frustration and failure in the interview situation. You observed this nurse and you know she has many feelings that she is not telling you now. In this case, the reactivity of the subject is to the interview situation. Again, the validity of the data you collected by interview alone would be questionable.

Participant Observation and Informal/Formal Interviewing

The use of participant observation and informal and/or formal interviewing increases validity by decreasing reactivity of the subjects. The use of interviewing with participant observation increases validity since it assures that the truth in the observations is checked with the active questioning of the interview situation and vice versa.

A basic assumption in all interviews is that the respondents are "telling the truth" about themselves and their world, as well as speaking the truth about their beliefs and perceptions about their world. However, the interviewer is aware that people will place themselves in the best light possible and tell what they think the interviewer wants to hear. The interviewer's skill and sensitivity are used to allow the subject full expression without judgment (Sudman, Bradburn, 1982). Interviews alone do not satisfy the qualitative researcher that the data is valid. Participant observation is used to verify the relative "truth" or validity of the interview (Denzin, 1970).

Sites and Sources

Not only are these methods used conjointly, but data are checked by using other sites and sources. Sites will be chosen by the researcher based on the need to verify

data under different conditions, elaborate on certain data, and challenge the ongoing analysis, as well as test hypotheses from the analysis (Glaser, 1978).

Common sources used to check or verify or elaborate data include professional
journals, personal documents (such as journals, letters), institutional statements of
philosophy, policy, or procedures, novels, newspaper articles, and other published
or unpublished works (Glaser, 1978). These sources can alert the researcher to
conditions, contexts, or consequences that might not be apparent in the data collected in the field.

The use of these sources can direct the researcher to new sites for data collection or be used as additional verification and elaboration of the emerging theory.
Validity is established during the ongoing process of data collection and analysis by
using methods, sites, sources, and subjects that allow for the full range and variation of behavior of the phenomena under study to emerge.

CONCLUSIONS

In this chapter, we have examined informal interviewing as a method for collecting
data in a grounded theory study. Informal interviewing requires skill, sensitivity,
and interpersonal elegance on the part of the researcher. To make these "conversations" natural, the researcher is cautious to assume the norms for behaviors of the
group. Yet, the researcher is always aware of the research endeavor and the central
role of researcher. In field situations, the nurse-researcher has advantages and disadvantages as a result of being both a nurse and a researcher. Integrity is maintained by self-conscious awareness of specific uses of the nurse role, clear
arrangement with the agency, and behavior as a researcher in the site.

The issue of validity during data collection in a grounded theory study is a
critical issue and deserves greater attention and exploration. So much of what is
done in field research is related to increasing validity. Yet, the issue of validity is
often never clarified and this leads to the misconception that it is not addressed.

References

Becker HS, Greer B: Participant observation and interviewing: A comparison, in McCall GJ,
    Simmons JL (eds): *Issues in Participant Observation: A Text and Reader.* Reading, Massa-
    chusetts, Addison-Wesley Publishing Co, 1969.
Bingham WVD, Moore BV: *How to Interview,* ed 4. New York, Harper and Row, 1959.
Dean JP, Eichhorn L, Dean R. Fruitful informants for intensive interviewing, in McCall GJ,
    Simmons JL (eds): *Issues in Participant Observation: A Text and Reader.* Reading, Massa-
    chusetts, Addison-Wesley Publishing Co, 1969.

Dean JP, Whyte WF: How do you know if the informant is telling the truth? in McCall GJ, Simmons JL (eds): *Issues in Participant Observation: A Text and Reader.* Reading, Massachusetts, Addison-Wesley Publishing Co, 1969.

Denzin NK: *The Research Act.* Chicago, Aldine Publishing Co, 1970.

Glaser BG: *Theoretical Sensitivity.* Mill Valley, California, The Sociology Press, 1978.

Glaser BG, Strauss AL: *The Discovery of Grounded Theory: Strategies for Qualitative Work.* New York, Aldine Publishing Co, 1967.

Schatzman L, Strauss AL: *Field Research: Strategies for a Natural Sociology.* Englewood Cliffs, New Jersey, Prentice-Hall, 1973.

Spradley JP: *The Ethnographic Interview.* New York, Holt, Rinehart and Winston, 1979.

Strauss AL, Schatzman L, Bucher R, Ehrlich D, Sabshin M: Field tactics, in McCall GJ, Simmons JL (eds): *Issues in Participant Observation: A Text and Reader.* Reading, Massachusetts, Addison-Wesley Publishing Co, 1969.

Sudman S, Bradburn NM: *Asking Questions: A Practical Guide to Questionnaire Construction.* San Francisco, California, Jossey-Bass Publishers, 1982.

Sullivan S: *The Psychiatric Interview.* New York, W.W. Norton and Company, Inc, 1954.

Webb EJ, Campbell DT, Schwartz RD et al.: *Unobtrusive Measures: Non-reaction Research in the Social Sciences.* Chicago, Rand McNally College Publishing Co, 1966.

8

Qualitative data analysis for grounded theory

Julie Corbin

Data analysis is the "nitty-gritty" of qualitative research. While there are several approaches available for the analysis of qualitative data, the approach presented here is based upon the grounded theory method (Glaser, Strauss, 1967; Glaser, 1978; and Strauss, 1986). Grounded theory is a systematic method of research whose purpose is to generate rather than to test theory. The advantage it offers the nursing profession is that it allows nurses to capture the complexity of problems and the richness of everyday life which make up so much a part of their practice. Grounded theory is not a replacement for the more "quantitative" approaches to research. It does, however, offer an alternative or supplementary means for generating and exploring problems through the use of data which does not easily lend itself to quantification (eg, interviews, written documents, and observations). This chapter will present a general overview of analysis.

Analyzing data by the grounded theory method may be thought of as a process requiring a direct interaction between the analyst and the data. It takes place over time, moves through phases, and results in a "grounded theory." This chapter will examine the conditions that influence the analysis of data, detail the strategies involved in carrying out the basic operations, and explain the results one might expect once the process is carried out.

CONDITIONS INFLUENCING DATA ANALYSIS

The conditions that influence data analysis can be broken down into two main types: those that are related to the researcher and those that are related to the research process, that is, how it is carried out.

Conditions Relating to the Researcher

The first condition is training. While it is not necessary to have years of intensive training to do a grounded theory study, it does influence the type of theory that eventually evolves from the data. The theory's density, complexity, scope, and the degree to which the concepts are integrated, varies with the level of skill and training of the researcher. In general, the more extensive the training, the more integrated and dense the theory will be. However, even with minimal training, a nurse should be able to build a simple descriptive level grounded theory with a basic sense of logic, using a systematic approach, paying careful attention to detail, and by following the basic guidelines detailed in this and other methods books on this subject (Glaser, Strauss, 1967).

The second condition is experience. Every nurse comes to the research situation (whether it be a qualitative or quantitative study) with a degree of experience and knowledge gained from practice, from other people, or from reading the literature on the subject. This experience and knowledge provide the nurse-analyst with certain advantages which should be capitalized upon, rather than denied. Most importantly, it gives the analyst a background which sensitizes him or her to pick up on relevant phenomena; a less experienced analyst might overlook relevant information. Experience also provides a background from which to interpret what is seen, and serves as a basis for making case comparisons, finding variations, and sampling on theoretical grounds. At the same time, experience and knowledge can be detrimental if the analyst allows it to cloud his or her ability to ''see'' what is really happening in the situation under study. Experience can also be detrimental if the analyst lays an established framework on the data that either doesn't fit or that only partially explains what is going on. Analyzing data by the grounded theory method requires the nurse to free him or herself of nursing, medical, or psychologically oriented viewpoints (at least during the research process) so that he or she might open the senses to what else of relevance is happening.

The third condition relating to the research and data analysis is self-confidence. The analyst must have confidence in his or her ability to interpret what is seen in the data, and in the end to believe in the findings. While confidence naturally develops over time, the researcher can build confidence by grounding the theory in actual data and by verifying and reverifying hypotheses as they evolve.

The fourth condition is tolerance for ambiguity. It is not uncommon for the analyst to feel overwhelmed by the data, especially in the early phases of the research endeavor. This is normal, and the feeling passes as the research begins to take form and a coherent theory is developed. However, until such time, the analyst must be willing to live with that feeling and to trust that it will work out. It is very important throughout the whole research process, for the analyst to talk with colleagues and others who have similar research interests. Not only does their support help one through rough points, but talking with others stimulates thinking, provides further insight into the data, and offers the opportunity to validate one's ideas with others. While a single person can do a grounded theory study, the research itself cannot be done in a vacuum; it requires interaction with others, as well as interaction with the data.

Conditions Influencing the Research Process

The first of these conditions is the perspective used to approach the problem. It stands to reason that different professionals, and even nurses with different clinical expertise, will approach the data from different perspectives, that is, frame the problem from a different angle. For example, a psychiatric nurse may view transition to parenthood as a stressor, while a maternity nurse may view it as a set of tasks to be learned. Neither approach is wrong and both have something to contribute to the theoretical body of nursing knowledge. However, it does mean that the analyst must present the theory in a logical, coherent manner so that nurses and other professionals who might want to use the framework can follow it and see the same thing, or can use it as a basis for intervention, or even as a base from which to take off and build on to the theory from their own perspective.

Another condition has to do with the type and amount of data collected. Data may be gathered from a variety of sources: interviews, observations, written autobiographies, letters, and even newspapers. In fact, the more variety, the more rounded the data. The validity of that data, however, is extremely important. The researcher must take the time to verify the sources of data. Additional interviews and observations that allow for checking the informant's stories and the researcher's interpretations and observations are necessary. This type of verification requires time. In addition to verifying the data, one must also gather sufficient data. One or two cases do not make a grounded theory—they make a case study. There are no set rules to determine what is sufficient. The analyst can, however, feel confident that the field has been thoroughly explored when no further categories emerge from the data, the categories are dense and well developed, the same patterns are seen repeatedly, and there is variation.

The third condition that influences the research process has to do with inductive modes of thinking. In the grounded theory method, thinking must move from inductive to deductive and back again, as the researcher moves through the process. This means that the analyst derives statements of hypothetical relationships or hypotheses from the data, and then verifies them either through a careful review of field notes or by going back into the field. Hypotheses that do not hold up under this verification process must be discarded or modified and the process repeated. This thinking process is very similar to that used by nurses in the nursing process, and as such, should come readily to nurses once they master a few basic operational strategies.

A fourth condition is abstraction. The theory must be built on concepts or abstractions of ideas and not on the ideas themselves. Furthermore, the analyst should always be moving towards higher and higher levels of abstraction. The more general the theory, the wider its scope.

The final condition has to do with the type of analysis carried out. There is no way around a detailed analysis of the data if the theory is to be dense with concepts and well integrated. This means that observations and interviews must be carefully recorded, ideas consistently kept in the form of memos, and most importantly, the data is analyzed, first line by line, then paragraph by paragraph, especially in the early phases of the research. A detailed analysis also helps the analyst to uncover the micro, that is, those situations and detailed conditions in which an event takes place, and the macro conditions or the general structural or broader idealogical conditions which impact the situation under study.

With these conditions in mind, let us move into the basic operational strategies of grounded theory analysis.

BASIC OPERATIONAL STRATEGIES

Categories

Categories are abstractions of phenomena observed in the data. They form the major unit of analysis in the grounded theory method. The theory that evolves by this means consists of categories that have been linked together and arranged in a hierarchical fashion. The central or core category, usually a process, emerges late in the analysis and forms the pivot or main theme around which all of the other categories revolve. The major categories, which are further breakdowns of the central category, form the dimensions of that category. In turn, there are other categories to explain the properties of categories or how the categories are defined, the conditions that explain why and when they occur, the strategies or how the action in the situation takes place and the consequences, that is, the results of the action. Conditions, strategies, and consequences form the theoretical linkages by which the categories are related to each other and to the central category (see Swanson, chapter 10; Glaser, 1978).

The major task of the analyst then is to code the data into categories, and then to define, develop, and integrate them. But how does one accomplish this task? While the task is not an easy one, there are strategies to help the analyst through the process. These strategies change in type or focus as the analysis proceeds.

Discovering the categories   One strategy for discovering categories is asking questions. These are questions the analyst asks him or herself or of the data. Questioning begins at the inception of the research project and continues until the final draft of the manuscript is written. However, the nature of the questions asked changes in different phases of the research. The questions asked at the inception of the project are generated from nurses, clinical or personal experience in the area, from the literature, or from previous research. A nurse about to embark on a study of terminally ill patients might ask questions such as: What is there about my own experience that makes this area significant to me? What have I observed in patients I have worked with? Have I observed the stages of death as described by Kubler-Ross? What is it that makes people move from one stage to another? What else seems significant about this period? and so forth. After the first interview or observation, the nurse analyst might ask: What is going on here? What does it mean? Why is it happening? When? Who is doing it? How is it being done? What happens as a result?

Another strategy is breaking the data down into bits and pieces. Each bit and piece of data represents a specific incident or fact. Breaking it down is done by reading the data line by line and paragraph by paragraph, looking for incidents and facts. Each one is then coded as a concept or abstraction of the data. For instance, incidents from interviews with terminally ill persons such as "making out a will," "teaching my wife the ins and outs of the business," "explaining to my partner how the books are kept," "inviting my friends in for one last big bash," may be coded as the concept "closure act." Since several incidents are coded under this one concept, "closure act" becomes a category. In this case, the analyst coined a term which can be used to describe or explain a phenomenon observed in the data. However, sometimes the respondents or interviewees conceptualize their behavior for us or use a concept to explain their behavior in a particular situation. The analyst may use these concepts also. In fact, they often become very important categories in the research. For example, a respondent might say something such as, "I think that over the past year, I have been coming to terms with the thought of death," to explain what he felt he was doing over a period of time. "Coming to terms" is a very good way of conceptualizing this phenomenon and may be used by the analyst as a category to describe similar behavior in other people such as, "I've been thinking a lot about death since the doctor told me my disease might prove fatal," or "My wife and I have now reached a point where we are talking openly about death," or "I feel like I am now ready to die." However, a category remains no more than a conceptualization of several similar incidents until it is more fully developed and densified by discovering (through data analysis) its properties, the conditions under which it occurs, the strategies used for getting there, and the consequences of those actions for all involved.

Categories develop quickly during the early stages of the research and less quickly in later stages of the research. While the categories are still emerging, it is important to move into the second phase of the analysis, that is building, densifying, and saturating the categories. There are strategies to do this also. While still continuing with the strategies described previously, the analyst begins to add to his or her repertoire these new ones. Some of these strategies are overlapping ones, that is, they help discover categories as well as build them.

Questioning persists throughout the analysis. However, questioning now becomes more directed at building categories once they have been discovered. Questions of this direct type might be: What category does this incident indicate? Does it fit with this category or is a separate category needed? Does a category have to be revised to include it? What type of category, property, condition, strategy, or consequence is it?

Making comparisons is another important strategy for discovering initial categories as well as for building categories. Making comparisons means comparing two or more incidents or cases and looking for similarities and differences between them. It is a wonderful strategy to use initially and when the analyst appears to have reached a dead end or becomes stuck somewhere along the analytic process.

To make these comparisons, one might draw upon past experiences, literature on the subject, or other conceptually related situations. For example, to develop the category "coming to terms" and bring out new categories related to the dying process, the analyst might ask, "In what other situations do people suffer a loss?" One could come up with situations such as divorce, loss of a job, or loss of physical abilities after a stroke or spinal cord injury. Then based on knowledge of these situations, the analyst compares them—situation by situation—at the macro level or at the categorical level to the situation under study. To give another example of making comparisons, let us return to the earlier example of "closure acts." As the analyst continues to interview, suppose an interview is done that is noticeably absent in closure acts. This starts the analyst thinking. "Why are they absent?" To discover why, the analyst begins to compare this case against other cases asking generative-type questions of the data. For example, questions asked might include: What does it mean to make a closure act? When do they begin? With whom and with what does one make them? How are they made? Are they made all of the time or some of the time? With some persons or with all persons? What are the conditions for their being made? What happens when the dying person or others involved in the situation attempt to make closure acts and the other won't let them or won't respond to them? What in the interaction stops or prevents them? What happens if time runs out and they are not made? What happens if they are made? This type of questioning continues until the similarities and differences between cases is clear. Using questions such as these, the analyst is making comparisons at the categorical level. The subcategories of a category evolve, that is, the properties of that category. For example, the conditions under which closure acts occur or do not occur, the strategies by which they occur or are avoided, and the consequences of making closure acts or not making closure for all involved.

Theoretical sampling   Another strategy for building and densifying categories is theoretical sampling. This means that the analyst moves on to the next population or site for gathering data on the basis of the evolving theory. The questions that normally arise when it comes to theoretical sampling include: How do I know where to begin sampling? Where do I go from there? How long do I continue to sample from one group? When do I know I have sampled enough groups? The answer to the first question is simple. The analyst enters the field with a sampling group in mind based upon knowledge or experience in the area as one would with any other research method.

To give the researcher some idea of where to begin, consider the following example. A nurse working on a cancer unit decides that she wants to study how adults with acute leukemia make decisions regarding the treatment process. She defines her population as newly diagnosed male patients between the ages of 21 to 65. The site from which she has chosen to draw her population is a cancer clinic located in a large metropolitan academic medical center. These characteristics would define the boundaries of the sample at the beginning of the project. As such, the analyst would not draw subjects from a doctor's office down the street or interview sarcoma patients along with the leukemia patients, or teenagers along with the adults, or even females along with the males. The analyst, however, might think of these as comparative groups to elucidate the important properties of the group under study at a later point in the study.

After a few interviews, the nurse discovers that age keeps coming up as an important condition influencing decision making about treatment. At this point, the analyst designs a sampling plan based on age to explore this variable. This sampling plan will include sites that will allow for different age cohorts to be represented. The researcher will systematically sample based on the variable of age until it is discovered why, how, and with what consequences age influences decision making. Another way of questioning could be how is it the same or different for each of these age groups? Or, how does decision making change as one moves from one developmental level to the next? Sampling for age continues until further differences between the groups are found. It is important to note that the analyst is not counting numbers but looking for general patterns. While it is not important to document every possible variation or exception to those patterns, it is important to note that there are exceptions.

In addition, the analyst might sample for another category that evolves from the data as an important condition affecting decision making such as treatment philosophy. This would lead the analyst to look for another site from which to draw his or her subjects, a site in which the treatment philosophy would differ from the one under study. He or she would continue sampling on the basis of treatment philosophy until the point of saturation (ie, patterns are established and no more relevant differences are found among the dimensions of conditions, strategies, and consequences for these two groups). Sampling on theoretical grounds continues until all of the major variables that have evolved from the data are explored and the categories that pertain to them are saturated. Variables such as cultural background, race, marital status, and type of treatment, to name a few, are not controlled. These variables and others do not serve as a basis for sampling unless during the analytic process they too prove to be important. In some research situations, sampling along theoretical grounds could go on indefinitely. In this case, the analyst has to determine the limits of a project and the degree of depth that will be pursued. Sampling should be limited to those conditions that prove to be of major relevance to the developing theory.

Linking the categories   Making linkages among the categories is a means of putting conceptual order on the mass of data that has been accumulating during the research process. It begins to a lesser degree during the second phase of analysis but becomes the focus when most of the categories have emerged, are developed, and dense. Making linkages should not begin too soon because it tends to foreclose on category emergence and development. Early foreclosure of categories leads to a theory with a few weak concepts based on categories that are poorly developed.

One of the strategies for linking categories is moving a category from a lower to a higher level of abstraction. For example, with the category "closure acts," the analyst might ask at this phase, "What are closure acts? What are they indicative of?" After thinking about these questions, the analyst decides that closure acts may be conceived of as a type of work. This work called "closure work" must be completed if the individual is to come to terms with death. By raising the concept "closure acts" to a higher order concept "closure work," the two categories of closure acts and coming to terms are related.

Another way of making linkages is to pose questions about relationships or make hypotheses and test them. This strategy can be made clear by continuing with our example of closure work. Let us suppose that once having conceptualized closure acts as closure work, work made up of various types of closure actions, the analyst continues with the line of thought that closure work is a prerequisite for readiness to face death. A hypothesis is posed, such as individuals who complete closure work by performing a series of closure acts are more prepared to face death than individuals who do not. Armed with this hypothesis, the analyst goes into the field to test the hypothesis. If after repeated interviews and observations the hypothesis holds true, then it may stand as it is (A is equal to B).

However, the analyst may discover that the situation is more complicated than it appeared at first glance and the hypothesis has to be modified. The analyst may find that before the individual can begin to do closure work, he or she must first accept the possibility of dying. Accepting the possibility of dying is identified as the first stage in the process of coming to terms and, at the same time, a condition for beginning closure work. Thus, the hypothesis is modified and the categories are linked together in a new way. A (accepting the possibility of dying) leads to B (doing closure work) which, if it is completed, leads to C (being prepared to face death). Here, A and C are two stages of the same process and B is an intervening variable. The analyst continues making, testing, and revising or modifying hypotheses until all of the categories are linked together. For the beginning analyst, Glaser (1978) offers a theoretical coding schema, the 6-C's, to aid the process of linking categories (see Swanson, chapter 10).

Identifying the core category   Oncc the categories have been built and linked, it is time to pull the theory together around a central or core category. By this time, the analyst may have some idea what that central category is or might still be unsure which of the many categories is the central one. One way to differentiate the core category from the other categories is to return to the basic technique of questioning. Questions at this point might be: In all of these interviews or observations, what seems to be the main story line, the main pattern or theme that I see happening over and over again? Sometimes the analyst has to sort and sift through all the memos, talk over the data with others, review the field notes, and try out different story lines before he or she finds one that seems to be consistent with and best explains what is happening in all the cases under study. Another line of questioning is, what category do all the other categories seem to be leading up to or pointing to? Or, which category seems to be of a higher level of abstraction than the others? Or, which one could the others be subsumed under? To give an example, suppose that the analyst had the following list of categories but didn't know which of them was the core category:

Treatment work: seeking alternative treatments, undergoing treatment, discontinuing treatment.

Closure work: making acts of closure.

Exit, no exit: giving up bope, clinging to bope.

Coming to terms: accepting the possibility of death, readiness to face death.

Biographical protection devices: living life in the fast lane, retreating into an inner world.

To determine which one is the core category, the analyst could arrange all categories in various hierarchical orders. Using a diagram, these orders are changed until a scheme is found that seems right (ie, fits the data). This scheme includes a core category under which the other categories fit and to which they all relate. Then, reviewing case after case, the analyst would check out that scheme to see if it did indeed fit or explain the major action in the data. It is very important at this point that the analyst not jump to conclusions and arrive at the central category too early, a common mistake in the novice unused to dealing with ambiguity. Checking and rechecking the scheme against the data is also essential. One method used to verify a conceptual scheme is to return to the field and ask more pointed questions of the respondents. One can also try out the scheme on informants. Of course, informants often do not use the same language as the analyst and they may be confused by it. The researcher is careful in this regard to explain all terms in a clear, concise way. The general picture that informants paint, however, should be similar in basic structure to the one the analyst has generated.

Another technique for discovering the core category is to look in the data for the basic social or structural process. For an excellent description of this process see chapter 11 by Shizuko Fagerhaugh.

Refining the theory   While the analyst has come a long way and should take the time here to congratulate him or herself, it is not time to relax just yet. There is still a great deal of work to be done. Before going on with techniques that may be used to refine the theory, it must be noted that while the analysis has been broken down into phases for explanatory purposes, in the actual research process, the break-down is not so clear cut. While there is a major focus for each phase, the lines between them are not as distinct as in this presentation. The phases of the analytic process tend to overlap, that is, categories may still emerge, be developed, or even densified during the refining phase. In fact, part of refining is doing just that, discovering, building, and densifying categories. Refining continues into the writing phase. This is not meant to discourage the analyst, but to assure him or her that the theory will become even more coherent and tightly integrated right up to the writing phase.

The analyst now has a theory made up of a core category around which the other categories seem to fit. Usually at this point, the theory has many rough edges and needs refining. One strategy for refining is trimming. Here, the analyst carefully examines all of the categories, their relationship to each other, and to the core category. If a category or two does not fit with the others, the analyst has two options. First, try to determine if the category can be subsumed under a higher level category which is already woven into the theory. For example, "notifying family and friends" can be subsumed under the broader category of "informing." It really makes more sense to put it there rather than to leave it as a separate category. If a higher level category can't be found and the category does not fit or add anything to the theory, then it is dropped. Often the analyst hates to let go of a category that seems to be a very good way of conceptualizing something. However, these ideas may be used in a separate but related paper, even if they do not have a place in the overall theory.

Another option is to collapse categories into a category of a higher level of abstraction. This cuts down on the number of categories and helps to make the remaining ones more fully developed and denser.

Perhaps the most effective strategy for refining the theory is laying out the theory in the form of a diagram. This way the analyst can visually examine the theory for poorly developed categories, missed relationships, or incorrect relationships.

A category considered a major category but which has only one or two subcategories listed under it requires rethinking. The category may not be as important as the analyst first thought. It should be moved to another place in the theory. The category, however, may be well developed. In this case, the analyst needs to return to the field and gather the data necessary to fill the gap by means of theoretical sampling. Poorly defined relationships also do not hold up under close scrutiny and these are tightened while the analyst still has access to the field.

Overall Strategies

Through the phases of the analytical process, two strategies stand out as crosscutting each of them. They are writing memos and diagramming. Because of their importance, a separate chapter has been devoted to their explanation (see chapter 9). It is sufficient to say here that no analysis is complete without them. To attempt to do a grounded theory study without writing memos is like trying to swim without using your arms and legs. It is not very long before the analyst feels that he or she is drowning within a sea of data, with little hope of being saved.

Results

After carrying out all of the basic operational strategies, what should the researcher have to show for all of the work and effort put into the analytic endeavor? The end results of that work should be a "grounded theory" that explains the major action in the situation under study. It should consist of categories that are dense with concepts and saturated to the point that a range of variation can be accounted for, verified by hypothesis testing, and integrated, that is, woven together.

A theory thus built would fit the area from which the data was derived. The concepts in this theory were not laid on top of, but came out of, the actual area. The theory should be understandable by laymen and professionals because it is made up of concepts of a lower and higher order, and it should hold with their experience in the area. It should be flexible and general enough to be applicable to diverse situations. It should provide practitioners with a basis upon which to explain patient behavior and plan interventions that can be changed as the conditions change. When the analyst has such a theory, it is time to write it in order that it may be added to the theoretical body of nursing knowledge and more specifically, so that it may be used by nurses as a basis for intervention in the area.

References

Glaser B: *Theoretical Sensitivity*. Mill Valley, California, The Sociology Press, 1978.

Glaser B, Strauss AL: *The Discovery of Grounded Theory: Strategies for Qualitative Research*. Chicago, Aldine Publishing Co, 1967.

Strauss AL: *Qualitative Analysis*. Cambridge, England, Cambridge University Press, 1986.

9

Coding, writing memos, and diagramming

Julie Corbin

Analyzing data by the grounded theory method is an intricate process of reducing raw data into concepts that are designated to stand for categories. The categories are then developed and integrated into a theory. This is a very complicated process that is broken down into steps, each step building upon the other. Therefore, as the data is being analyzed, it must be ordered, recorded, and stored in a manner that makes it retrievable and usable. In order to retrieve information at a moment's notice, it is necessary that the analyst have a method for doing so. That method is coding data, writing memos, and diagramming.

The first step in analysis is coding the data and writing memos about concepts that recur in the data. Examples of coding and formulating memos are presented. Memo development guides the analysis which culminates in diagrams depicting the relationship between categories which were generated from the codes and developed in the memos.

CODING

At the beginning of a study, the analyst codes data in the margins of the field notes or interviews, rather than coding on a separate sheet of paper. In coding, the incidents and facts are marked in some way, either underscoring or circling, and are rewritten in an abstracted form (as a concept) in the margins.

Oftentimes, the novice is confused as to what can be considered as data, what constitutes a fact or an incident, or how one begins to take apart a piece of data and work with it. These are real concerns. This section of the chapter will address some of these concerns. It is meant to provide general guidelines for coding data.

In the following example, a nurse on a pediatric unit has continuously made the observation that children's response to hospitalization seems to be influenced by their interactions with their parents. The nurse, curious about this phenomenon, decides that she wants to do a grounded theory study. After the preliminary work, she begins collecting data. The following is an observation written as a field note. It is coded by underscoring in the text of the field note. The code is placed in the right-hand margin (Schatzman, Strauss, 1973).

Date, Observation 1	Code
Today a 4-year-old male child was hospitalized with possible pneumonia. This was his first hospitalization. The parents stayed holding and stroking the child during the admission procedures. They kept telling him what was happening to him. They stayed with the child until late evening, reading to him and just sitting by his bedside. Before leaving, the mother explained to him that they had to leave because there were other children at home and because daddy had to get up to go to work early in the morning. She promised that she would return as soon as the other children left for school the next morning. Both parents held and kissed the child, and told him that they loved him. The child started to cry. Again, the mother explained why she had to leave. She told him that the nurses would take care of him while she was gone, and that he would be safe in his crib. She emphasized that she would return in the morning, and in the meantime she would leave her scarf with him as a reminder. Then she kissed the child, gave him his favorite stuffed animal and blanket, and settled him into bed. Both parents walked off rather sadly, but smiled and waved back at the child as they walked out the door. The child cried for a short while then clutching his blanket, stuffed animal, and his mother's scarf, fell asleep.	preschooler, separation confined initial encounter support work (reassuring) the beginning information work support work (preparing) entertaining or distracting strategy alerting information work reassurance separation is temporary support work (reassuring) protesting more information work offering a substitute protected environment temporary parting a substitute and token of her promise more support work comfort work parents' response/fronting parting gesture child's response self-comfort work

This short observation constitutes a piece of data. It is not long, nor is it complete. Often, the first interviews or observations are not complete because the researcher is not quite sure what he or she is looking for or needs at this point. A few paragraphs of an anecdote, observation, or interview constitutes a piece of data. It need not be long or complicated.

The analysis begins with the first paragraph of the observation. It will focus on interactions because they are the focus of the research. It is very important to keep this focus in mind as the analysis proceeds. For instance, the issue here is not the hospital's policy on parents' visitation, though this may later prove an important variable and worth looking into. However, it should not be pursued at this time because it would detract the analyst from his or her focus on parent/child interactions.

The paragraph will be taken apart fact by fact, incident by incident. The way the author codes a fact or incident may not be the way the reader would have done so. Or, the reader may pick up on a fact or have an insight that the author missed. This is good. It is hoped that the reader will become involved in the analysis and add his or her coding to that done by the author. In reading the analysis which follows, notice how it proceeds step by step, and how from its inception the scheme can be seen as evolving and giving direction to the next step in the analytical process.

The process that will be used to analyze the data will be as follows: (1) each fact will be written in the first column; (2) the second column will contain the code or conceptual label applied to the fact or incident; and (3) the third column will contain a theoretical note which explains some of the thoughts and questions going through the analyst's mind as he/she codes.

Fact or Incident	Code	Theoretical Note
4-year-old child	preschooler	Thinking about the child as a preschooler tells me a lot about him, what he is capable of understanding and doing, how I might expect him to act. It also tells me that while he may attend nursery school, he has not yet made the big break that comes when children actually start school. I am not sure at this point how this bears upon the interaction, but I will keep my eyes open.
hospitalized	separation	By being hospitalized, the child is being separated from his home, family, friends. He is confronted with different people, sights, sounds, etc.
pneumonia	confined	Because of the child's diagnosis, he is not well enough, at least for the first few days, to be up and out of bed. This means that he can't go to the playroom to be entertained or play with other children. He doesn't have the op-

Fact or Incident	Code	Theoretical Note
		portunity to explore his setting, something 4-year-olds like to do. Being confined seems to set structure for the interaction. It may be permanent or temporary.
admission	the beginning	From the viewpoint of time, I think of admission as the beginning of separation. It marks the child's entry point into the new environment—an official entry. At the same time, it marks that he will stay overnight and maybe longer.
first hospitalization	initial encounter	This is a new situation for the child. It is a condition under which the interaction between parent and child is taking place. The child has no previous experience with hospitalization (good or bad) from which to draw upon.
stayed holding stroking	support work (reassuring)	All three of these types of supportive work are aimed at reassuring the child, letting him know that he is protected, cared for, that his fears are recognized, etc. They are nonverbal interactions aimed at reassuring, reducing fears.
telling	information work	This is verbal interaction aimed at reducing the child's fears, reassuring him.
stayed until late evening	support work (preparing)	"Late evening" tells me that now they have passed the initial encounter; the admission is over and they are still with the child. They are still in that period of transition from home to hospital, but in a different phase. This time they are sitting with the child during what might be termed a "get acquainted phase." The child is becoming acquainted to the people, routine, place, and the space he will occupy for the next couple of days. Again, it is not clear how the child was acting or what he was doing during this time.

Fact or Incident	Code	Theoretical Note
reading	entertaining or distracting strategy	I believe this is a strategy similar to sitting there, only this time they are actively involved with the child though we don't know how the child was responding to the story. The parents don't seem to expect much in the way of interaction from the child. It is all part of letting the child become acquainted with the new environment, letting him feel more secure.
before leaving explained	alerting	Here I see change. It's the beginning of a new phase of the interaction. The mother is telling the child or alerting him that the time for parting has come.
had to leave	information work	Verbal interaction occurs aimed at explaining the separation, why they must leave him at this time.
promise of return	reassurance separation is temporary	The separation is only temporary. A child of 4, who has been left with a sitter can surely comprehend that the parent will return. However, this situation is different. It is a new and probably frightening environment.
held and kissed and told him they loved him	support work (reassuring)	This is support work aimed at reassuring the child of their love and that they are not abandoning him.
child started to cry	protesting	The child is protesting the parting. At the same time, he is bringing the mother back into the interaction.
explaining again	more information work	Verbal communication occurs aimed at reemphasizing why the separation must take place at this time. The mother is responding to the child's interaction.
nurse takes care while gone	offering a substitute	Here the mother is preparing the child by telling him who will care for him in her absence.
safe in crib	protected environment	She gives him instruction about safety.
will return	temporary parting	She is preparing him for the separation. This is "preparatory work."

Fact or Incident	Code	Theoretical Note
		She is doing this to ease the separation—
leave her scarf	a substitute, but also a token of her promise	"easing the separation" by giving him a part of her.
kissed	more support work	This is aimed at reassuring.
gave stuffed animal and blanket, and settled him in bed	comfort work	She is giving the child something to hold on to while she is gone, but also something familiar—familiar toys, familiar gesture. It is also something more. In a way, it is finalizing the parting. It is a signal to the child that this is it, the end of the interaction. They are leaving him as they would at home when they put him to sleep.
parents walked off rather sadly	parents' response	This indicates that the parting has an impact on them too. Part of the preparation that was going on was as much for them as it was for the child. There are consequences to the parents as well
smiled, waved back	front/ing parting gesture	as to the child. They put on a bravery act in front of the child. To let him know how they really felt might evoke more response from the child, continue the interaction, and perhaps make all of them feel even worse.
cried for short while	child's response	The child feels sad at being left alone. This is a consequence of the separation.
clutching animal, scarf, blanket	self-comfort work	The child gives in to a natural body state. By this time, he is probably too tired to resist sleep. However, he falls asleep holding on to those objects that are familiar to him.
fell asleep		They ease the separation, make it more bearable for him, and in a way, so does the sleep.

WRITING MEMOS

After initial coding of the first interview or field note, memos should be written to capture ideas and document recurring themes noted in the data.

Memos are the analyst's written records of the analytical process. They show the theory developing step by step. They allow the analyst to keep a record of and to order the results of the analysis. They also enable the analyst to know where he or she has been, is now, and needs to go in the future of the research. It is in memos that hypotheses are recorded, compared, verified, modified, or changed as new data comes in. It is from memos, compiled and sorted, that the analyst derives the material to write up the final theory.

Though memo writing is often seen as tedious and time-consuming work, it is work that cannot be shortcut; neither can it be omitted. As with the analysis process itself, superficial work produces a superficial theory. Worse yet, an incorrect theory can be produced. There is no way other than memos for the analyst to keep an account of the developing theory and to compare and verify findings as he or she proceeds. But how, when, and what kinds of memos should the analyst write?

There are no hard and fast rules for writing memos. They are generally written *by* the analyst *for* the analyst. Since no one evaluates the final theory, or the analyst for that matter, on the basis of memos, the anxiety usually associated with writing should be eliminated. The content of memos should not be a concern, especially at first. The content tends to correspond to the phase of the analysis and therefore, reflects that process. Rest assured that the memos will grow in depth and integration as the theory grows. The analyst should simply let the ideas flow.

Memos may be handwritten, typewritten, or typed into a computer. If the memos are to be of service to the analyst, they should contain at least a few basic elements; they should be dated, titled, cross-referenced, and filed. If possible, memos should be duplicated for cross-referencing and one copy stored in a safe place. It is also helpful if the memo contains a summarizing statement of the anecdote that triggered the memo, along with the code number and page of the field note or interview from which it was taken. This will save time if, in the future, the analyst wants to return to the original source for reanalysis of the data or to use the quotation as an example in the final writing. And since "brilliant" ideas tend to come to the analyst at unexpected times and places, it is a good idea to carry around a small pad and pencil to jot down ideas as they occur (Glaser, 1978) which can later be expanded into memos. There is nothing more frustrating than an idea that has been lost because there was no place to record it.

An example of the first memo from the previous field note addresses admission as a transition period.

MEMO 1

Admission as a Transition Period

Taken from Observation 1, Paragraph 1

I stop here and ask myself, why are the parents doing what they are doing? What is going on here? Admission seems to be a transition period from home to hospital. Here the assurance is at the immediate level. Admission personnel are doing things to the child that he has never encountered before. The parents are saying, "Don't be afraid, it's okay. We are here to protect you, this is what they are going to do." But there is something else going on at another level. It is aimed at preparing the child for the inevitable separation that is going to follow. The child may know or suspect this separation. From the data, I don't know how the child feels or what he knows. I can only speculate.

We see the two modes of interaction, verbal and nonverbal, on the side of the parents. What we don't get from this observation is the child's response. I must be more tuned in on my next observation to such things as who initiates the first inter- action, what cues they are responding to, and how the other responds. I suppose in this case the parents' behavior was initiated by their believing that the child probably felt strange and fearful. But I don't know this unless I interview and ask them. I also did not pick up on how the child behaved. Were there some cues in his behavior to which they were responding? Did he cling or cry?

Here is an example of a later memo from the same field note which was written after the analysis was in progress. It addresses preparing the child for separation.

MEMO 2
Preparing for Separation
Taken from Observation 1, Paragraph 1

I ask myself, what is going on here? It has become clear that the parents are prepar- ing themselves and the child for separation. I see "preparing for separation" as my first real category. From my codes, I see that it can be broken down into stages. There is a transition stage and a parting stage. Both of these can be further broken down into phases (there are perhaps more stages and phases and this will come out as I do more interviews.)

Transition Stage

The first stage is the transition stage—at least according to the data I have here. What I don't know is whether or not the parents began preparing the child before they left home. I only know what I have observed; therefore, I will have to fill in this informa- tion through interview. When does this preparation begin and how is it done? In this case, the mother probably took the child to the doctor only to find out that he was ill and needed to be hospitalized. There was probably very little time for preparation. She was probably more concerned with the actual physical preparations that had to be made, like notifying the father, packing, making preparations for someone to take care of the other children. (This is only speculation again and I must ask her to verify this.) I would think that the child's condition on admission would affect this preparation, that it would be different, for example, if the child had come in for a tonsillectomy. (Here I want to make a note to myself to do a comparative memo noting the similarities and differences between a hospitalization in which there was time to prepare the child and one in which there was not. After this I may do some sampling to see if this time variable makes a difference in the child's adjustment.)

Phase One: Initial Encounter   *The transition stage begins with the admission, which is the first phase or the "initial encounter." The parents had certain interac- tional strategies for handling this encounter. These interactions were nonverbal and included staying with the child, holding, stroking, and all types of support work. There was also telling (a verbal strategy) for handling the situation. These are "types of preparatory work."*

Phase Two: Getting Acquainted with the Environment   *The second phase of transition is "getting acquainted with the environment." Without more information on the child's response to their interactions, I can't be sure of this phase. I will need further observations and interviews to find out what makes the move from one phase to the next, what enhances it, and what hinders it. During this stage, the parents also use interactional strategies to help the child and themselves through this phase. These strategies include staying with the child and reading to him. Again, the child's response to this is not known, nor was what cued the parents that he was ready for them to move on to the next stage of separation, the parting. It may not have been anything originating from the child, but simply time constraints. Here again, this is only speculation. To find out, I must ask the parents what prompted them to begin to make preparations to leave at this time.*

Parting Stage

I see "alerting" as a bridging strategy between transition and the parting stage. This parting strategy may be broken down into the preparatory phase and the finalizing phase.

Phase One: The Preparatory Phase   *Here the parents use the strategies of giving information (why they must go), reassuring the child that the separation is only temporary, and doing some support work aimed at reassuring him that they do love him. The child's response to the separation is to cry. He is protesting it. This brings the parents back into making more preparation which lengthens this phase. Again they explain, offer substitutes, a protected environment, reassure him that the separation is temporary and offer a token of that promise, as well as offer a substitute for the mother. All of these are strategies and types of preparatory work to "ease the parting." They kiss the child again, moving onto the final phase.*

Phase Two: The Finalizing Phase   *The finalizing phase is the one where the actual break in contact comes. Everything they have done has been leading up to this point. To bring this about, they use familiar gestures, gestures that they use at home and mean something similar at a conceptual level. At home, the gestures of giving the stuffed animal, blanket, and tucking indicate that it is time for him to go to bed, a temporary break in the interaction. The familiar objects they leave with him as well as the familiar gestures are comforting and at the same time finalizing. In leaving, they put on a brave front and wave, terminating the interaction.*

Consequences of the parting are sadness on both the parents' and child's part. Yet if one were to evaluate it in terms of the child's adjustment to hospitalization, one could say they did ease the child's adjustment by the way they handled the separation. The child cried only for a short time and did fall asleep.

All kinds of questions now come into my mind: How does preparing the child for separation fit into the child's overall adjustment to hospitalization? When does this preparation begin? What are the patterns of parents' strategies for doing this? What are patterns of the child's responses to this? What happens if the child is eased into this separation? What happens when the child is not? What conditions facilitate the preparation? What conditions hinder it?

What do I have at this point? I have the category "preparing for separation." This is a process category as it takes place over time and can be broken down into stages and phases of those stages. I would hypothesize that children who are prepared for the separation from home and family adjust better to hospitalization than chil-

dren who are not. But this remains a hypothesis only and must be verified over and over again against incoming data. I know that this category has stages, phases, and some interactional strategies used by the parents to "ease the separation." I also have some responses of the child to that interaction and how that response furthers the interaction. Where do I go from here? There is much work to be done, but now I have some direction. I would want to do more observations of parents and conduct interviews surrounding the first few hours of hospitalization and how they prepare the child for separation. I also will do some comparative memos about what happens in other situations where the parents and the child must separate temporarily. That is how is the separation handled? How is the child prepared for it? One place to begin is to think of how parents prepare a child for the first day at school. How about when the mother goes to the hospital to have a baby or the parents go away for a weekend?

As the reader can see, even one paragraph provides a great deal with which to work. Of course, in terms of the overall theory or answer to the question of how the parent-child interaction influences the child's adjustment to hospitalization, there is still very little information. All there is at this time is one category. To build the theory, this kind of analysis must continue for many more paragraphs of interviews and field notes in order to determine all the possible ways that the parent-child interaction influences adjustment. What needs to be looked at are the interactions around separation. Following this step, the analyst begins to look for patterns of interactions surrounding separations, the conditions under which separations occur, strategies for handling them and the consequences of the interaction that result not only to the child but also to the parents and staff.

MEMO DEVELOPMENT

To further demonstrate how memos evolve and illustrate their role in theory development, the next section of this chapter presents examples of memos written by the author. The topic discussed in the memos is pregnancy superimposed upon a chronic illness. The memos have been arranged according to the process of analysis and are designated by type. These memos are meant as examples only. Their format should not be taken as the "true" or "exact" way to write memos. To follow a form exactly would be too constraining for analysts who must try out and develop their own style. What is important to note is that they capture the analyst's ideas, they incorporate analytic strategies, and they grow in depth and integration over time.

Phase One: Discovering Categories

The first step in discovering categories occurs through the process of coding and recoding. It portrays original codes and recodes. In the initial code, the facts and incidents have been largely restated. This is very common for the novice. The same field notes were recoded at a later date, demonstrating the process of refining the codes. Recoding at a later date allows the analyst to further conceptualize the original codes. It is important to note, however, that the major themes of weighing (balancing), negotiating, and prioritizing carry through in both sets of coding.

INTERVIEW
First Interview, Second Trimester
Code 15

Interview Notes	Initial Code	Recode
S: No. I would take it, you know, without even thinking about it, because up in Chest we discussed it, and I've sort of made a preference that I'd like to keep the dosage as low as possible so I can still function, which is probably why it's down to 10 mgs, sometimes it would be 5. Because they would be taking 20 mgs a day sometimes. I thought that was a lot.	difference the pregnancy makes in taking medication

weighing cost | unqualified acceptance

qualified acceptance

balancing risk self/fetus |
| R: 20 mgs each time you took it, so that would have been 40 a day. | | |
| S: It would have been, but I sort of convinced them that I could manage on a lot less, but it's only because of the baby. That's the only thing it would do to me. | negotiating

definitely because of baby | renegotiating the regimen self-need fetal needs prioritizing fetus above self |
R: So you're not worried about the effects on yourself, but mainly for the baby that you're concerned	baby is major consideration	protecting the fetus
S: Yes		
R: So you're trying to maintain a level where you feel you can breathe and do what you need to do.		
S: Without endangering the baby	weighing decision-making	balancing the dosage, protecting the fetus
R: What danger do you see to the baby if you were not very well controlled, or not being able to breathe?		
S: Well, first of all when I cannot breathe, I just don't feel good, I feel very weak, I lose my appetite right away. I have difficulty breathing and . . .	illness not controlled	symptoms, cues to own health status . . .

The way that these interviews are coded is not the only way the fact or incident could have been coded. Someone else may have used a different conceptual label. The point of these illustrations is to demonstrate the conceptualization process.

The following is an example of a memo labeled a "category memo." Here the author was beginning to form the category of strategies. This memo contains a quotation from an interview along with an interpretation of what that fact or incident might mean. From this and other incidents, a category may be formed. By putting the quote and the interpretation into a memo, the analyst has a ready reference to that category and can also check it against incoming data.

CATEGORY MEMO
Strategies for Self-Control

"I don't worry too much about it. If I worry about it, I think I'll trigger it and perhaps it will get worse. So, I seriously consider what they say and realize that there is nothing I can do about it, but there's plenty I could do to make it worse, so I try not to do those things. Generally, I put it out of my mind rather than . . . well other than trying to keep a positive attitude at all times, since I know being depressed or unhappy could bring it on." (Code 07).

She demonstrates a strategy for self-control, namely, putting it out of her mind. She must maintain an even course. Worrying too much might cause illness, another strategy, to keep a positive attitude allows her a sense of control.

Phase Two: Building Categories

The next two memos show the building and densifying of some of the categories.

The next example is what may be called a "comparative memo." It builds upon the idea of disease experience and looks at it from the perspective of similarities and differences between three cases. In this memo, what it means to have or have not experienced is amplified.

COMPARATIVE MEMO EXPERIENCE

A comparison of similarities and differences between these cases. One woman was a diabetic controlled (supposedly) by diet, the other was a childhood diabetic, and the third woman had cardiac disease. The first seemed essentially normal, that is, her disease process was not significant. The second and third each had a significant disease process. I then started listing the differences between the three taken from the notes and codes. What struck me were the differences in the problems that the childhood diabetic and the woman with cardiac disease seemed to be having during pregnancy. The childhood diabetic seemed to have a much easier time. Besides obvious physiologic differences, it was obvious that the one (diabetic) had a history of coping with her disease—an illness career or past experience. The other woman (cardiac disease) was essentially symptom-free until the pregnancy except when occasionally mountain climbing at high altitudes and strenuous swimming. Looking at the data, I asked, "What differences does having past experience with a disease do for you?" With past experience, one has a knowledge of symptoms and signs of the disease and knows what will happen under different circumstances. Also one knows what is life threatening and what is not. There is a knowledge base for dealing with a disease. When the disease process is essentially a new one or if symptoms are new, then one doesn't know what to expect from a disease, what signs and symptoms are significant, what to do about them, or what might occur in the future. When a disease is unknown, one doesn't know if it is liveable.

A person without past experience of a disease can seek information about it, try various approaches to manage it and observe others in similar situations. Information can be found through books, through health professionals, other pregnant women, television, friends, or others with similar experiences.

Now what do I have? I have three things. (1) The woman has essentially no disease process and no changes to make after the pregnancy. (2) A woman with a disease process which is changed by the pregnancy but who has lived with the disease long enough and has experienced enough changes that she can cope and accommodate to change. She feels that she can handle it. (3) A woman who had some disease before but it did not cause any changes in her life. She doesn't know what signs and symptoms are significant. Her activity is restricted both by physicians and herself. She develops strategies to cope with her problems: lies down, doesn't go too far from home, walks slowly. Still, there is a difference between these last two women. One woman can manipulate her disease. She has the experience to know what happens under adverse conditions and she knows it is liveable. Unless something unexpected happens, this woman can handle her disease. The other is coping with the symptoms and has found ways to walk, sit, etc, but doesn't know which symptoms are significant or how to prevent major complications. She really doesn't have a grasp on her disease.

Is there a qualitative difference related to the degree to which the woman feels she either controls her disease or her pregnancy, or feels the illness controls her? At first I thought it was related to the severity of the illness, that is, how the process of adaptation goes, but I think it has more to do with past experience, control, and the weighing and decision-making process that goes on in the process of adaptation.

Is past experience with a disease or a one-illness career important? If it is, how? Now I need to look at an individual who did not have a disease until pregnancy to see if there is any difference.

The following memo is a memo of degree. It is short but it shows the analyst picking up on the idea of degree, that somehow there is a difference in the degree to which a person feels an illness should be kept under control between the pregnant and nonpregnant state. This directs the analyst to begin looking at control as a category of range which can vary from lose control to tight control.

MEMO OF DEGREE
Degree of Control

R: When you were pregnant, you didn't feel that way about control of your illness? S: No, it is the total completeness of it. I had it to a certain extent, but not the completeness of it. Like, right now, the control that I feel is good enough, but when I was pregnant, it wasn't good enough. (Code 02) (Theoretical note: Control is a matter of degree.) Because of the impact on the child, it is more important to have tight control over the illness when pregnant than when one is not. What is satisfactory when only the mother is involved is not satisfactory when there is another affected by your actions. In this case, the other is not capable of protecting himself, therefore, the mother takes on that responsibility. I wonder if this is always the case. Do they feel control must always be so tight? Also, I must not forget that even though one might have a tight control over one's illness by following the regimen, there are going to be times when the illness is not so controllable (eg, when one has the flu, one's diabetes becomes difficult to control). There are actions that one can take to minimize the risk to the fetus, but those actions do not always work. What then?

From here all kinds of questions come up: Under what conditions does a woman feel the illness should be kept under tight control? Under what conditions does she feel this control can be relaxed? What is the factor motivating this control? Who is responsible for the control? Under what conditions does this responsibility change? How is control maintained? What happens when control is maintained? Isn't maintained?

Phase Three: Linking Categories

In the following memo, called a *hypothesizing memo,* the researcher hypothesizes what the relationship might be between two categories. The memo shows how the hypothesis was derived and how it was recorded for comparison against incoming data. The hypotheses have been underlined for emphasis.

HYPOTHESIZING MEMO

Holding Back as a Strategy for Managing Fear

At first I though Code 22 said that she wanted this baby very much but wasn't making any preparations for it and tried not to think about it too much. But I notice now that she is getting more and more excited about the baby as the pregnancy progresses and the illness remains stable. She is now shopping for furnishings, fixing up the room, and buying clothes. She constantly says, "If only I make it to 28 weeks." Twenty-eight weeks is her magic number. From information at the clinic and elsewhere, she must have heard that 28 weeks is the age the baby at least has a chance for survival.

I would hypothesize that women hold back to protect themselves should something eventually happen to the baby. The child may not make it because the risks are great; the greater the chances of having a healthy baby, the less the holding back and the greater the involvement in the baby and its arrival.

I must now start checking this out with each interview: The greater the perceived risk, the greater the holding back. The smaller the perceived risk, the greater the involvement with the baby.

Phase Four: Identifying the Core Category

This section contains a storyline memo. This type of memo represents the analyst's attempt to pull together his or her previous memos and thoughts into a story aimed at identifying the central idea of the phenomenon under study. "Just what is it that is happening here?" "What are these women doing?" "Why?" "How?" "With what consequences?" This memo shows the analyst beginning to get some grasp on the situation. However, it is interesting to note that at the time the analyst thought the central category was "control," two other categories, "assessing" and "balancing," were seen throughout the data and also appeared to be of major importance. The analyst was confused about what to do with them; her focus on "control" tended to obscure their function.

STORYLINE MEMO

A high-risk pregnancy is one that creates many stresses physically, psychologically, and socially for the woman. In fact, not only is the woman profoundly affected, her immediate family is also (husband and other children if present). A woman involved in such a pregnancy does so at great personal cost to herself and at times to her family. Once a woman becomes committed to the pregnancy (whatever her reasoning), she focuses on the delivery of a healthy baby; everything else, including herself, becomes subordinate. The woman is willing to undergo many painful procedures, laboratory tests, changes in activity level and diet, hospitalizations, disruption of family life, and so forth, to ensure the well-being of her expected child. That is not to say that the mother's health is not important, but rather that she is willing to "sacrifice" her health and comfort for the baby.

To manage a complicated pregnancy, a woman uses many coping strategies. These coping strategies are aimed at the following: (1) having some level of control over the baby's welfare; (2) keeping the illness or condition under control or bringing it back under control; (3) managing her fears and anxieties; (4) having control and input into the pregnancy experience; (5) managing her social world; and (6) integrating this whole experience while maintaining her integrity through it all.

The woman retains her control as long as her life and that of the baby's is not threatened or a critical point in the illness or condition is not reached. In times of high risk, her ability to control goes down. At such times, the woman is willing to delegate some of her control to others (husband, health team, social worker). Actually, control is always a matter of degree. (Even in the normal pregnancy, a mother must at times delegate control.)

Not all women are equally affected by the impact of a high-risk pregnancy. There are conditions of high risk and some of low risk and variations and phases of these. The physiology of the pregnancy, the nature of the illness or condition, and the individual woman's response to this combination make it different for each person.

Some women come through this experience better than others. Some of the reasons for this include: (1) the severity of the illness or condition; (2) her support systems; (3) her previous experience with illness and pregnancy; (4) her trust in the health team; (5) her level of knowledge; (6) her cultural beliefs; (7) congruency between expected and actual experience; and (8) social situation.

Finally, through continued scrutiny of the data and more focused interviews, it became obvious that the three categories—controlling, assessing, and balancing—were interrelated processes. They were the concepts that explained the means by which a woman protected herself and her growing fetus from harm. This led to abstracting the concepts to a higher level that would incorporate all three categories at the same time. The core category, "protective governing," was identified. "Protective governing" means taking action to protect the self and fetus from harm by means of assessing the risk level, balancing the options, and controlling both the illness and pregnancy either directly or indirectly by delegating all or part of the responsibility to the health team (Corbin, 1980).

This example was used to show how one might become sidetracked by one's own bias and by focusing too early. It also shows that within the method are safeguards to this practice. However, in order for those safeguards to work, the operational strategies must be carried out phase by phase, and the theory must be systematically checked and rechecked against incoming data as it evolves. The example also points out why it is necessary to sample to the saturation point, that is, until all variation has been accounted for.

DIAGRAMMING

Diagrams are visual representations of one's analytical scheme in whole or in part. They are useful to the analyst at any stage of the analytical process. Like memos, they grow in depth and integration as the theory grows and they allow the analyst to obtain an overview of the theory. Diagrams are a visual representation of the categories and how they link together. Examination of a diagram can point out where the theory needs further development; they are especially useful when the analyst is overwhelmed with memos and needs an overview of the analysis. In a diagram, the scheme can be rearranged, added to, and subtracted from, allowing the analyst to manipulate the data in a way that is impossible with memos. Diagrams are also useful during the writing stage because they enable the analyst to visualize the logical flow of ideas and to determine if any vital points in the argument are missing.

Constructing diagrams is not difficult but does require some work if they are to serve their purpose. Since they are overviews and do not contain a lot of detail, for the most part they may be constructed from data in the analyst's head. After they have been constructed, the analyst might flip through memos to determine if any of the major categories have been overlooked. However, after working with the data for many months, it is unlikely that the analyst would overlook an important category.

The easiest way to construct a diagram is to ask oneself a series of questions that are pertinent to the phase of the analysis in which the diagram is being constructed. The answers to the questions can then be listed in a diagramatic form. For example, to determine how well a category has been developed, the analyst might ask the following questions: What is the name of this category? What are its properties? Under what conditions does it occur and under what conditions doesn't it occur? How does it happen or not happen? Who is involved and with what consequences?

To link the categories, the analyst might ask about the major categories, the ones that are coded repeatedly in the data. What are the categories that all others seem to relate to as properties, conditions, strategies, or consequences (Glaser, 1978)? Things like movement, steps, and progression can be shown on paper. Con-

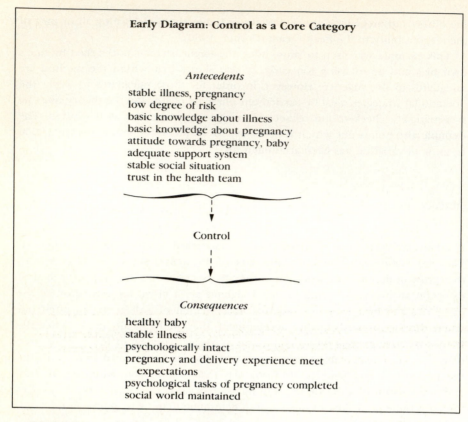

Early Diagram: Control as a Core Category

Antecedents

stable illness, pregnancy
low degree of risk
basic knowledge about illness
basic knowledge about pregnancy
attitude towards pregnancy, baby
adequate support system
stable social situation
trust in the health team

Control

Consequences

healthy baby
stable illness
psychologically intact
pregnancy and delivery experience meet
    expectations
psychological tasks of pregnancy completed
social world maintained

FIGURE 9–1.   In this early diagram the analyst thought "control" was the central category. "Assessing" and "balancing" were other central categories but the focus on "control" obscured their function.

sequences of one phase of a process often become conditions for the next phase. These become visible when laid out before the eyes of the analyst. Later, to identify the core category, the analyst might ask, "Which of these categories seems to explain the major action in the phenomenon under study?" If no category stands out or if two or three seem to be of equal importance, the analyst might ask the following questions: How do these categories relate to one another? Is there a higher level concept which might explain them all? How then do the other categories relate to it? Are they dimensions of that category? Then how do the other categories fit around them? Can they be explained as properties, conditions, strategies or consequences?

The analyst looks for holes in the logic. At this point, persistence is required to arrange and rearrange categories and continue asking questions until all the categories relate to one another. Finally, when it comes to trimming the theory, the

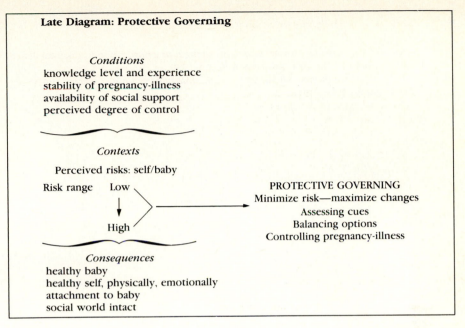

FIGURE 9–2.   In this late diagram the core category is named "protective governing" which consists of three interrelated processes; assessing, balancing and controlling.

analyst might ask such questions as, "Can any of these categories be moved to a higher level of abstraction?" "Can one concept be designated to stand for several of these categories?" "Does this category have a place in the scheme?"

Figures 1 and 2 are examples of two diagrams. These diagrams show the author's scheme of protective governing at different stages of its development. Compare the two stages and note the changes made over time.

CONCLUSION

Analyzing data by the grounded theory method is systematic, time consuming, and tedious work. However, the joy of discovery and the sense of accomplishment that comes from a grounded theory research project make that effort worthwhile.

There are no shortcuts in the analytic process, no quick schemes or fast routes through the grounded theory analysis. Each phase in the analysis builds up to the next; each phase is necessary to develop a grounded theory.

References

Corbin J: *Protective governing: Strategies for managing a pregnancy-illness,* doctoral dissertation. University of California, San Francisco, CA 1980.

Glaser B: *Theoretical sensitivity: Advances in methodology of grounded theory.* Mill Valley, CA, The Sociology Press, 1978.

10

Analyzing data for categories and description

Janice M. Swanson

This chapter will define categories, examine the development of categories, explore how to describe them, and give examples of how categories are reported in the nursing research literature.

Many reports of qualitative research using grounded theory in nursing describe categories derived from field data—largely participant observation and interviewing. These reports are valid and are needed as building blocks. From these initial building blocks, hypotheses may be generated that can lead to the eventual linking of categories and the generation of grounded theory. Even as a process or processes are generated, related articles may describe in detail related categories to add to the base of nursing knowledge.

DEFINITION OF A CATEGORY

Webster's Dictionary (1979, p 285) defines a category as, "in logic, any of the various basic concepts into which all knowledge can be classified. Aristotle made ten categories, viz., substance, quantity, quality, relation, action, passivity, time, place, position, and condition." A second definition from *Webster's Dictionary* states that a category is "a class or division in a scheme of classification; as, to put a person in the same *category* with another."

Categories are often generated in daily life. For example, a nurse who enters a nursing unit or a community agency may note educators, clinicians, and those in administrative positions on the scene. In doing so, the nurse has categorized people according to their job description. He/she may note the numbers of staff who are approximately 30 years of age or younger (the category of "age"). In addition, he/she may note that some staff are wearing uniforms while others (administrators or clerks) are dressed in street clothes (the category of "dress"). People, places, things, attitudes, behavior, etc, are constantly categorized often without conscious effort.

In order to define a category, it must be talked about, its characteristics listed, and comparisons with other categories made. The nurse from the previous example may relate to a colleague, that "compared to the educators and clinicians, the administrators were fewer in number, most were older than 30, dressed in business suits, and appeared to be more affluent." In relating this information, the nurse is giving the properties of the category. A property is a characteristic, trait, or attribute of a thing or a class of things.

According to Glaser (1978), categories and their characteristics (properties) are conceptual codes depicting the essential relationship between data and theory. Categories and their properties are mid-point indicators:

Data — Categories — Theory

They are building blocks to theory and are important for description and initial analysis of qualitative data.

DEVELOPMENT OF CATEGORIES

How are categories developed from data? The first step in developing categories is to make laundry lists (Fagerhaugh, personal communication, May, 1979) of substantive codes from the data (Table 10–1). In order to collapse these codes into manageable size, codes are grouped into clusters by similarities and differences. Finally, each cluster is labelled (Table 10–2). For example, in the author's study of men's role in family planning, the category called "contraceptive talk" (getting information about the difficulties regarding contraception and how to deal with them) was originally coded as "knowledge level," "information-seeking and gathering," and "getting the story." *"Contraceptive talk"* developed from grouping substantive codes into like clusters.

DESCRIPTION OF CATEGORIES

Once initial categories are identified, the researcher then takes on the task of fully describing them. This entails coding for the range (extremes) of the category and

TABLE 10-1.   Development of categories

"Laundry List" for Contraceptive Talk

Read newspapers
Read magazines
Heard radio
Watched TV
Talked with partner
Talked with mother
Talked with mother-in-law
Talked with friends
Talked to nurses
Talked to doctors
Talked to receptionists
Read pamphlets
Girls talked to mothers
Boys talked to mothers
Men talked to partners
Girls saw female films
Boys saw male films

---

variation in the category. An example of coding for the range or extremes of the category "contraceptive talk" follows.

Noted in the data were times when respondents talked about contraception with their partners ("talk") and times when they did not talk, but rather noticed or gave non-verbal cues ("non-talk"), as when a male respondent stated he assumed by his partner's exit into the bathroom shortly before they had sex that she had left to insert her diaphragm. The range in this category was represented by instances in the data when respondents reported they talked about contraception at one extreme, and by instances when they did not talk about it at the other extreme.

Coding for variation in the category is looking for instances of the category and comparing these instances with each other in order to note the similarities and differences that recur in the data. Some examples of the types of talk coded from field data are initial talk-later talk, forced talk-spontaneous talk, deliberate talk-chance talk, and individual talk-group talk. Each variation denotes characteristics or properties of talk. The researcher must ask of the data, "What property of a category does this incident have?" Properties of talk relate to timing, familiarity, comfort, privacy or degree of intrusion, and number of persons involved. Initially each person interviewed tells the researcher something new about the phenomena, as the meaning and experience for each varies. It is necessary to ask different questions in succeeding interviews, in order to elicit extremes and variation of the categories. Data is then reworked and categories adjusted. Also, it is necessary

TABLE 10–2.   Development of categories

Contraceptive Talk	
Laundry List	Label
Read newspapers Read magazines Heard radio Watched TV	Public talk
Talked with partner Talked with mother Talked with mother-in-law Talked with friends	Private talk
Talked to nurses Talked to doctors Talked to receptionists Read pamphlets	Professional talk
Girls talked to mothers	Same-sex talk
Boys talked to mothers Men talked to partners	Cross-sex talk
Girls saw female films Boys saw male films	Gender-specific talk

for the researcher to engage in theoretical sampling, actively seeking out respondents to gain data needed to complete or saturate a category or categories for theoretical completeness.

Theoretical Sampling

The nature of theoretical sampling will be explained through the use of two examples from the author's work. First, men, women, and couples spoke frequently during interviews about the "hassle" of using contraception (ie, learning about it, getting it, using it, how it affected their sex lives). An initial hypothesis was proposed that it was the technology of contraception that created the hassle. A sample of respondents who were using a method of contraception which did not involve technology was sought. The sample was a class of couples who were learning about fertility awareness, a natural method of family planning where basal body temperature and cervical mucus changes indicate time of ovulation. During participant observation in the class and formal interviews with couples taking the class or who had completed it, the author noted respondents' concerns about the hassle of fertility awareness (ie, taking one's temperature at the same time every morning, keeping records, dealing with time zone changes when making cross-country

TABLE 10–3.   A family of theoretical codes: The six c's

1. Causes	4. Consequences
2. Contexts	5. Covariances
3. Contingencies	6. Conditions

Glaser B: *Theoretical Sensitivity.* Mill Valley, California, The Sociology Press, 1978, p 74.

trips). The category "hassle" was expanded to include more than technology of contraception and management of such. During the fertility awareness classes, the author also noted that instructors engaging in "professional talk" at times had difficulty engaging the group in talk; often, "one-way talk" occurred. Another hypothesis was tentatively proposed: that respondents talked freely enough during formal interviews, but hesitated to engage in "group talk." One cause of this phenomenon was thought to be the presence of men in the fertility awareness classes. Did women engage in group talk when men were excluded from the group? To test this hypothesis, the author sought out a sample of women attending family planning group instruction in a traditional family planning clinic. During participant observation in the women's groups, the author again noted professional talk and a general lack of group talk even though the groups were entirely made up of women. When women were asked why they did not speak up in the group or ask questions, many stated they were embarrassed to ask something that "probably everyone else in the room knows." When asked who they went to for information, they replied, they sought information privately from their friends and family. Theoretical sampling thus enables the researcher to seek out relevant samples of respondents in order to fully describe developing categories, and eventually, to form links between categories which lead to theory generation.

THEORETICAL CODES

At this point in the research project, the nurse-researcher is very close to the data. He/she needs to step back from the data and begin to look at relationships between the categories. How is this done? Glaser (1978) lists 18 families of theoretical codes that enable beginning researchers to ask questions about their data (categories in the data). Theoretical codes allow the researchers to organize the categories, to clarify what each category is in relation to other categories, and thus, to develop theoretical links between the categories. These links will lead to the development of a process or processes and the generation of theory. One of these families will be used to illustrate this process—what Glaser refers to as the "6 C's" family of theoretical codes. He recommends this family for the beginning researcher and also for the researcher who, having conducted pilot interviews, must present a beginning theoretical scheme in a grant proposal for funding. The family of 6 Cs (Table 10–3) helps conceptualize how categories relate to each other and are integrated into the theory. Initially, each category developed from substantive codes is compared to each of the six theoretical codes. The following questions are asked of each substantive category: "Is this category a condition of some other category? Is it a cause, a context, or a contingency (bearing on another category)? Does this category co-vary with other categories?" In addition, Glaser and Strauss (1967) recommend that the beginning (and often advanced) researcher ask an additional question: "Is this category a strategy?" In other words, substantive categories are "matched" with theoretical codes. As with initial (substantive) category description, an important part of this process is to code for the range and variation of the theoretical codes, as one did for the substantive categories. For example, when one asks the question, "Is this category a condition of some other category?" the researcher must also ask, "Under what conditions is this category (contraceptive talk) maximized? Minimized?" The category "contraceptive talk" may be maximized when the couple is faced with instability and minimized during periods of stability.

An example of the development of theoretical codes is drawn from the author's grounded theory study. Although many substantive categories were grouped under each theoretical code, only one substantive category for each theoretical code will be presented here (Swanson, 1983). A good place for the new researcher to begin developing theoretical codes is to note the consequences of action or non-action.

The author went into the field to study contraception because of the defined research problem: Why, in the face of modern contraception and widespread family planning services, do unplanned and unwanted pregnancies and abortion persist? The *consequences* addressed were unplanned and unwanted pregnancies and abortion. Other consequences were later identified. The question that followed was, "What *causes* certain consequences?" One category that answered this question was the type of relationship of the couple: was it a long-term, comfortable relationship or was it tenuous and uncertain?

Another question followed, "Under what *conditions* does this cause (relationship) lead to this consequence (unwanted pregnancy)?" Talking about contraception was identified as a major condition. For example, "deliberate talk" may lead to management of contraception and no pregnancy may occur; whereas "non-talk" may lead to mismanagement and assumptions about a partner's use of contraception and an unwanted pregnancy may occur.

The next question was, "In what *context* does talk occur?" Degree of awareness, a property of privacy was a major context identified in the study, for example, awareness of where the other partner was in the relationship, of different methods of contraception and their use, and how these methods were affected by sexual practices.

Contingencies was also important to identify. A couple's use of contraception may be contingent upon, for example, a change in health/illness status (Swanson, Corbin, 1983). One woman respondent contracted a sexually transmitted disease (STD) which precluded her use of her method of contraception, the intrauterine device (IUD). Her partner did not know she was no longer using the IUD and she became pregnant. The STD is a contingency that impacts the family planning process.

The last theoretical code in the 6-C's is *covariance*. Covariance occurs when one category changes with the changes in another category. For example, talk covaries with coordinating management of contraceptive options; if a couple talks they can better share known contingencies. If talk diminishes, the discovery of contingencies and options becomes more private.

The final process in category description involves the saturation of categories, the identification of a core explanatory category, and identification of a theoretical process. These final steps go beyond the scope of this chapter; they are the next steps in generating theory (see Fagerhaugh, chapter 11). These aspects of the process (category generation and description) do not occur in limbo. One may, however, stop at this level and report one category or several related categories in a paper as many beginning grounded theorists have done. Or one may report a theoretical process or processes as others have done.

PRECAUTIONS IN DEVELOPING AND DESCRIBING CATEGORIES

The following suggestions to beginning nurse-researchers are drawn from the literature on the subject and from the author's experience.

It is recommended that category generation be carried out as a group process with other researchers. It is easier to get a handle on other people's data at first than to work solely with your own; it is difficult to pull away from the details of one's own data, and think conceptually, especially for clinicians. For example, it is easier to categorize nurse administrators than to review interviews with couples about contraception when you have recently completed several of the interviews. Glaser and Strauss (1967) caution not to extensively read other literature and theory in your field before you begin data analysis. Doing so tends to cause confusion and may yield preconceived categories. "Round categories won't fit in square category holes . . . similarities and convergences with the literature can be established after the analytic core of categories has emerged" (Glaser, Strauss, 1967, p 37). Lower level categories come early and quickly. Higher level categories (overriding, integrating, conceptualizations) and properties that elaborate them, come later. Glaser and Strauss caution that although the initial substantive theory will account for the majority of changes over time, more studies are needed in different sites with different populations; this process will not destroy the original grounded theory:

> Once a category or property is conceived, a change in the evidence that indicated it will not necessarily alter, clarify or destroy it. . . . it takes much more evidence—the creation of a better category to alter it. . . . conceptual categories and properties have a life apart from the evidence that gave rise to them (Glaser, Strauss, 1967, p 36).

TABLE 10–4.   Reporting of categories

Initial categories evolving from analysis
Categories from coding families
   A type family
   A strategy family
   The 6 C's
   Process
Multiple Processes

For example, categories and properties are concepts indicated by the data; they are not the data. Contraception stories vary, but the category, "privatized discovery," stands. It is not time and unit bound. The process of privatized discovery—how people find contraceptive options—accounts for changes over time. In most of the family planning literature, one or more variables are studied as discrete units; indeed, sex and the type of relationship have a bearing on successful use of contraception. The grounded theory study, however, generates these variables and others from the words of the respondents themselves and analyzes how they are linked, the major contribution of this research method. In addition, privatized discovery may apply to other contexts, such as patients' disclosure of mental illness or disfiguring surgery such as mastectomy. The theory is not limited to the contraceptive context.

REPORTING OF CATEGORIES

Categories generated from grounded theory studies are valid building blocks of research studies and may be reported in the literature. Categories may be reported a variety of ways: (1) an initial substantive category evolving from one's nearly completed study; (2) a category from a coding family, or a basic process which has been identified; or (3) multiple processes (Table 10–4). Reporting of a category is a way of organizing the world of nursing from one's data; it is a way of describing that world, generating hypotheses for further study, and of developing basic building blocks for research. The following examples are reports of categories by nurses who have conducted grounded theory research.

Initial categories evolving from an analysis of student nurses' accounts of learning the nursing world were reported by Melia (1982) (Table 10–5). The author defines six basic categories generated from the study, and reports one in full. This category, "Nursing in the dark," describes the initial problems student nurses have when initiating talk with patients.

Categories from a coding family are reported by May (1980) (Table 10–6). The author reports a type family (behavior, not people), a typology of styles adopted by first-time expectant fathers. The types—observer styles, expressive styles, instrumental styles—indicate variations in the way first-time fathers adapt to pregnancy.

TABLE 10-5.   Initial category evolving from analysis

Focus	Sources	Categories
Student nurses' accounts of their experience of being learners of nursing	Informal interviews of 40 student nurses	1. Learning and working (college v hospital approach to nursing) 2. Getting the work done (description of work on the wards) 3. Learning the rules ("on the job" socialization) 4. Nursing in the dark (difficulty talking to patients due to lack of information about them). Subcategories: Nursing in the dark; Coping with the dark; Fobbing off the patient; and Awareness contexts 5. Just passing through (transient training experience) 6. Nursing and being professional (what constitutes nursing and being a professional)

Melia K: "Tell it as it is"—qualitative methodology and nursing research: Understanding the student nurse's world. *J Adv Nurs* 1982;7:327–335.

Categories from the strategy family are reported by Stern (1982) (Table 10–7). The author reports 10 strategies of affiliating that stepfathers and children use to overcome friendship barriers. Any of the 6-C's may also be reported in a category paper, for example, conditions for men becoming involved in family planning (Swanson, 1980).

A process (also a coding family) may also be reported when a study reports two or more stages that refer to getting something done over time; stages, phases, or sub-processes may be reported. Wilson (1977) reported a basic social process (limiting intrusion) which insulates an experimental treatment community for schizophrenics from external mandates, regulations, rules, expectations, and values, preserving some degree of autonomy (Table 10–8).

Multiple processes are reported by Fagerhaugh and Strauss (1977) (Table 10–9). The authors reported seven processes, the result of interactions between staff and patients which are important to the management of pain.

In each of the examples it is important to note the variation in methods of data collection; some authors engaged in participant observation, formal and informal interviewing in multiple sites over time. One author conducted only informal interviews, several reviewed documents, while one reviewed letters, poetry, popular journals, and personal journals. Some authors were limited to only one site; time spent in participant observation varied. The need for various methods of data

TABLE 10–6.   A type family

Focus	Source	Categories (Styles)
A typology of detachment/ involvement styles adopted by first-time expectant fathers	20 first-time expectant couples Cross-sectional and longitudinal unstructured formal, taped interviews 100 hours of informal interviewing in waiting rooms of pre-natal clinics and maternity units Participant observation of two series of prepared childbirth education classes Anecdotal materials pertaining to expectant fatherhood (popular articles, personal journals, letters, poetry)	1. Observer styles (emotionally distant from pregnancy; a bystander) 2. Expressive styles (highly emotional response; a full partner) 3. Instrumental styles (emphasizes tasks to be accomplished; a caretaker or manager)

May K: A typology of detachment/involvement styles adopted during pregnancy by first-time expectant fathers. *West J Nurs Res* 1980;2:445–453.

TABLE 10–7.   A strategy family

Focus	Source	Categories (Strategies)
Strategies of affiliating that stepfathers and children used to overcome friendship barriers	Interview and observational data from 30 stepfather families	1. Avoiding *v* spending time 2. Poor timing *v* timing 3. Stinting *v* spending money 4. Poor role modeling *v* good role modeling 5. Close supervision *v* teaching skills 6. Failing *v* coming through 7. Doubting *v* trusting 8. Rejecting *v* accepting 9. Disliking *v* liking 10. Concealing *v* leveling

Stern P: Affiliating in stepfather families: Teachable strategies leading to stepfather-child friendship. *West J Nurs Res* 1982;4:75–89.

TABLE 10-8.   Process

Focus	Source	Process (Limiting Intrusion)
A basic social process insulates an experimental treatment community for schizophrenics from external mandates, regulations, rules, expectations, and values, preserving some degree of autonomy	200 hr participant observation, 11 interviews, documents	1. Minimizing approachability 2. Deflecting 3. Disengaging

Wilson H: Limiting intrusion—social control of outsiders in a healing community: An illustration of qualitative comparative analysis. *Nurs Res* 1977;26:103–111.

TABLE 10-9.   Multiple processes

Focus	Source	Processes (Politics of Pain Management)
Interactions between staff and patients which are important to the management of pain	Two years of fieldwork (participant observation, formal and informal interviewing) in two clinics, approx 20 wards, and nine hospitals	1. Assessing 2. Legitimating 3. Relieving 4. Minimizing 5. Enduring 6. Balancing 7. Controlling

Fagerhaugh S, Strauss A: *Politics of Pain Management: Staff-Patient Interaction.* Menlo Park, California, Addison-Wesley, 1977.

collection will vary, as will the time involved and the number of sites necessary for theoretical sampling. The important thing is to be open to flexible methods of data collection so that full description of categories and their links may occur. Reporting of categories too soon in the study or ending a study before saturation of categories may yield thin categories and an incomplete theory. The theory may not hold up when tested in further studies and will not be valuable to practitioners for whom the research is conducted.

References

Fagerhaugh S, Strauss A: *The Politics of Pain Management: Staff-Patient Interaction.* Menlo Park, California, Addison-Wesley, 1977.

Glaser B: *Theoretical Sensitivity.* Mill Valley, California, The Sociology Press, 1978.

Glaser B, Strauss A: *The Discovery of Grounded Theory: Strategies for Qualitative Research.* Chicago, Aldine Publishing Co, 1967.

May K: A typology of detachment/involvement styles adopted during pregnancy by first-time expectant fathers. *West J Nurs Res* 1980;2:445–453.

Melia K: "Tell it as it is"—qualitative methodology and nursing research: Understanding the student nurse's world. *J Adv Nurs* 1982;7:327–335.

Stern P: Affiliating in stepfather families: Teachable strategies leading to stepfather-child friendship. *West J Nurs Res* 1982;4:75–89.

Swanson J: Privatized discovery: The process of finding contraceptive options. Presented at Sigma Theta Tau Tri-Chapter Conference: "Nursing Research, the Bridge to Excellence in Practice," San Francisco, April 22, 1983.

Swanson J: Knowledge, knowledge, who's got the knowledge? The male contraceptive career. *J Sex Educ Ther* 1980;6:51–57.

Swanson J, Corbin J: The contraceptive context—A model for increasing nursing's involvement in family health. *Maternal-Child Nurs J* 1983;12:169–183.

Webster N: *Webster's Deluxe Unabridged Dictionary.* (Second ed) New York, Simon and Schuster, 1979.

Wilson H: Limiting intrusion—social control of outsiders in a healing community: An illustration of qualitative comparative analysis. *Nurs Res* 1977;26:103–111.

11

Analyzing data for basic social processes

Shizuko Y. Fagerhaugh

Process analysis serves as a central analytic approach to the development of sub-stantive theory (Glaser, 1978). The ultimate goal of analyzing qualitative data for process is to account for change in the social phenomenon being studied over time. Process analysis is often the most difficult level of analysis for the novice researcher handling qualitative data because it involves ordering and linking the hundreds of bits of loosely formulated categories into a logical whole. Process analysis provides direction and order.

This chapter will introduce the reader to the main elements of process analysis, and through the illustration of the author's own research, provide some notion of the analytic operations. First, a brief discussion of what is meant by "basic social process," its comparison to a core category, and its usefulness as an integrative analytic approach for substantive theory development will be presented. This will be followed by illustration of the analytic operations in developing process used by the author in her research of how patients with advanced emphysema manage mobilization.

BASIC SOCIAL PROCESS

An analytic focus on process serves to integrate the who, what, where, when, and why questions of the research problem. A process analysis tends to have much explanatory power because it integrates the multiple parts of the problem under study into a logical and understandable whole. A physical phenomenon familiar to nursing may make the point clearer. For a nurse to understand a specific kind of hemorrhage, it is insufficient to know the causes of the hemorrhage. Added understandings are required: the various blood elements, the complex biochemical and other physiological processes and sub-processes which occur sequentially and simultaneously in the bleeding-clotting process, the body's strategies for dealing with hemorrhage, and the various factors that disrupt the processes. So too is the case for understanding social phenomena. For example, if one were to understand how facially disfigured persons manage face-to-face interactions with others, the discovery of what problems they encounter would have limited explanatory power. A more complete level of understanding would be how facially disfigured persons cope with face-to-face interactions. The focus is the process of coping with specific kinds of problematic face-to-face interactions.

Developing process analysis which yields theory is important for nurses. It is important because it allows the use of qualitative data in generating theory and does not limit the use of this rich data to description only. Process analysis is also important to nursing because it has explanatory power from the theory developed and can be applied to nursing practice. Nurses have used many theories in practice which are the result of process analysis of qualitative data.

The impact of Kubler-Ross' study on nursing stems primarily from the fact that she offers a specific outline of psychological phases through which people move as death approaches. The various stages of dying and the ways in which the stages are manifested by the dying persons are logically developed (Kubler-Ross, 1969). Likewise, Piaget's study on children's cognitive process (Piaget, 1952) has had impact on nursing, again because of the focus on process. In recent years there have been many nursing studies related to coping, adapting, parenting, and so on.

A question is probably raised by the reader: "How basic is a basic social process?" It will, of course, depend upon the degree of generalizability. For example, one can undertake a grand study to understand the process(es) involved in enduring the unendurable and coming to terms with it. This could encompass excruciating pain, extreme psychological distress, death, or massive destruction (such as an atomic bomb explosion). Undoubtedly, there are some similar processes involved in all conditions cited. Most researchers must limit their inquiry to a manageable scope because of time and money constraints. Process has a time dimension, stages, and turning points. A given process may have subprocesses and may be linked with other processes. The extent to which all these elements of a process can be adequately integrated, the greater is its generalizability and explanatory power.

To understand a basic social process (BSP), it is helpful to first view it as a core category. Glaser states, "the goal of grounded theory is to generate a theory that accounts for a pattern of behavior which is relevant and problematic for those involved" (1978, p 93). The problematic behavior in this study was how patients with severe emphysema mobilized. The theory is explained by a core category, one which solves or processes the problem addressed, explains as much variation in behavior as possible, and uses the fewest number of concepts possible. The core category which explains how emphysema patients get around in this study, is "routing." It explains a wide range of behavior engaged in by these patients with relatively few concepts, as will be shown.

A core category always exists in a grounded theory study. What follows are Glaser's guidelines (1978) to developing a core category, or what he at times calls a core variable. The researcher examines the categories developed in the study and looks for those that recur frequently in the data and for one that is central to the theory. The researcher names the category, even if it does not fit exactly, until a better name is found. In this study, "mobilizing" was later changed to "routing." Only those categories with meaningful connections with the core category are included in the analysis. There may be more than one core category in a study, however. For the beginning researcher, focusing on one core category is recommended. Reporting only one core category at a time is also recommended. In their study of death and dying, Glaser and Strauss had more than one core category but they focused their writing on one core category at a time (*Awareness of Dying,* 1965; *Time for Dying,* 1968). The core category is completely variable; a condition, for example, time, varies the category completely as seen in an instant death with no preparation or a long, lingering death with much time for preparation. According to Glaser (1978), a core category can be any theoretical code such as a cause, condition, or consequence from any family of theoretical codes such as process or strategies. Therefore, while process (a BSP) is always a core category, not all core categories are BSPs. In a grounded theory study, a core category always exists; however, a BSP may not. A BSP is *one type* of core category. The difference between BSPs and core categories are that BSPs account for process—change which occurs over time. A BSP is a gerund ("ing"); examples are "becoming," "limiting," or "routing." Gerunds suggest movement and change, or process, over time. Not all respondents in a study go through a process in the same way. Conditions change such as, available resources, lifestyle, or disease processes and can alter mobility. But the process "routing" is basic, occurs over time, and remains intact even when conditions vary it considerably. The determination of whether a process is central to the social phenomenon under study is based on two major criteria. The first criterion is if the core process discovered in the data can account for a large part of the variation in behaviors, be it varied in types or degrees. The second criterion is if the parts of the process are logically linked. That is, the causes, context, contingencies, consequences, covariance, and condition as discussed in chapter 10 are logically integrated.

PROCESS ANALYSIS OPERATION

In the following pages, the analytic operations for process will be discussed by using the study conducted by the author on the physical mobilization of patients in the advanced stages of emphysema, "Getting Around with Emphysema" (Fagerhaugh, 1973). The published article is found in chapter 17 along with a diagram of the process. This study was selected because of its brevity. Some of the major elements of the process are included. A central concern of the author was to develop a framework to understand the mobilizing process.

Data for the study were obtained through interviewing late-stage emphysema patients being treated in a public respiratory clinic. The sample included 22 subjects; most of them were male, indigent, divorced, single, or widowed, and of course, elderly. Patients were interviewed in their home by using a semi-structured, open-ended interview. Aside from gathering the usual demographic information, patients were queried about how their illness altered their lifestyle and mobility needs over the years, how the medical regimen assisted or disrupted their mobility, who were the mobility agents and how they were used, and their current daily and weekly mobility needs. They were also asked to provide a detailed description of how they handled mobility.

The analytic operations are an extension of those discussed in chapter 10. There is a constant effort to integrate the loosely integrated categories into more generalized ones, and to link the categories. This integration is usually accomplished by reanalyzing analytic memos and always working toward higher levels of abstraction. In the process of analyzing memos, it may be necessary to reexamine selected data related to the emerging categories, or it may be necessary to gather more data to fill in the gaps.

The illustrative materials are selected memos written during the research process and diagrams of the relationships of the categories. Memos are used instead of the raw data because the integrative process is usually at the stage where much of the data has been initially coded and there is an accumulation of analytic memos. This chapter will therefore present memos from varying stages of developing the process supplemented with diagrams, rather than starting with interviews and initial coding. The reader is encouraged to read "Getting Around with Emphysema" (chapter 17) in Part II of this text and to note the two case presentations of patients with emphysema. During the analysis, it will also be helpful for the reader to recall previous or current patients' situations with emphysema, chronic, obstructive, pulmonary disease or other chronic illness for purposes of comparison. The reader will note that memos are titled. This makes for ease in sorting and locating.

In the process of analysis, memos are constantly reanalyzed. This paper will give basic excerpts from that process. Memos depicting major strategies of analysis include identifying categories and their properties, making hypotheses and identifying links between categories, identifying theoretical codes, looking for range and variation, change over time, and diagrams of the relationships between the categories.

The memos are numbered in order of the writing during the research. Commentaries will be added to elucidate the analytic process for categories, basic process, and sub-processes.

The author's files contain many memos; memos of major categories and their development may be followed by examining Figure 11–2, which links major categories in a manner which depicts the evolution of the mobility process. Numbers 1 through 6 in the diagram reflect the order of linkages made between major categories; they do not reflect numbers of the memos in the text.

Memo 1 was written early in the research process after two interviews. The purpose of the memo was to identify the major properties or characteristics of emphysema mobilization. The memo starts with the problem central to the study: mobility—how patients with chronic disease generally get around. This is the first major category. Here one identifies characteristics or properties of mobility. Note the progression in the memo from mobility in chronic disease in general, to mobility in emphysema in particular, then the initial comparison of "normal lungers" versus those with emphysema.

MEMO 1

Mobility Problems of Chronic Diseases in General and Emphysema in Particular

When I think about physiological sources of mobility problems in chronic diseases in general there are a variety of <u>causes</u>: (1) skeletal structural changes or loss of skeletal parts concerned with mobilization (amputation, arthritis, etc); (2) loss of sensory and motor control (neurological disorders); (3) lack of energy either by (a) disruption of getting source of energy, (b) disruption in energy delivery system, or (c) disruption in energy combustion and utilization; and (4) deterioration of all of the above causes is associated with the aging process. In some diseases there might be various combinations of the above causes.

Quality of mobility problem

When one thinks of mobility problems in chronic illness, the quality of a mobility problem must be considered. It can be painful, clumsy, poorly coordinated, involve equipment, etc. All of these pose different kinds of mobility problems.

Emphysema

Mobility problems in emphysema stem primarily from an inability to get enough air to produce energy. A certain basal amount of oxygen is necessary just to keep the body alive, and a reserve is needed for physical activity. Depending upon the activity, more or less oxygen is necessary. The problem of emphysema patients is there is little air reserve. Moreover, it takes these patients longer to "recoup" their air reserve, and they require more frequent "recouping" compared to normal lungers. These patients must "gauge" the amount of oxygen reserve required for various activities. This is extremely important because of the consequences of misgauging.

Normal lungers v emphysema

Normal lungers carry on activities with fluidity and can do multiple activities simultaneously. When normal lungers are short of breath, they pant a bit and continue, no worse for wear. Emphysema patients don't have this fluidity of action. They must chop-up actions into smaller units. Emphysema patients also have difficulty carrying on multiple activities, like walking and talking at same time.

In the reanalysis of the memo, it was noted that gauging of air as associated with recoupability was frequently mentioned by patients ("gauging" and "recouping" were coded terms used by respondents from the raw data). Thus, a proposition or hypothesis was posed that gauging was a process involved in mobilizing. Gauging involved estimating air need with recoupability and anticipating the consequences of misgauging. Chopping-up action into small recoupable units (such as stopping to rest frequently when taking a walk) was a mobility strategy.

In the reanalysis of memos, the same operations occur as when analyzing raw data (underlining key words, writing questions to oneself). For example, one might ask the question, "Under what conditions are patients unable to chop-up action into recoupable units, as when one forgets his prescription, the pharmacy is closing, and he is out of breath?" Note initial identification of theoretical codes, causes, conditions, strategies, and consequences depicted in this memo and in the discussion of it.

Memo 2 was written a few weeks after memo 1 and after several more patients were interviewed. The purpose of this memo was to locate the subjects, most particularly the male subjects. The central point here is that process must be seen in terms of the general overall mobilization phase across the life cycle. After reading the memo, compare the memo with each of the case presentations in the article.

MEMO 2
Emphysema and Life Cycle and Life Style:
Sources and Process of Change Over Time

Life cycle and life styles change for single, divorced, or widowed older males on welfare in late stages of emphysema. Sources of changes in life style include: (1) life cycle of patient; (2) stage of disease and degree of physiological disruption; and (3) degree and kinds of social disruptions either from disease itself or regimen. Process of changes over time include: (1) marital wipe out (daily needs become sole responsibility of patient); (2) financial and work wipe out (savings eaten up, can no longer work, finances get replaced with welfare); (3) friendship and sociability dwindles from lack of money and lack of energy; and (4) properties of life style at late stages of emphysema: present orientation; always standing at some relationship with the medical world; and conserving energy.

Here the author looked for range and variation in change in life style over time, or the life cycle, which became evident when examining the examples of patients in the article.

Memo 3 was written shortly after memo 2 and represents a major breakthrough. It names the three resources—time, energy, and money—that all persons, ill or well, balance to be mobile. These resources were later coded basic structural conditions.

MEMO 3
Time, Energy, Money: Mobility

Time, energy, and money are three resources that all people juggle and balance to be mobile. Depending upon the patient's life style, life situations, and the disability, there are varying kinds of mobility needs. There are varying amounts of time, energy, and money the patients can draw upon and juggle around. If the patient has money, he can save his own time and energy by buying other people's time and energy (having someone else clean house, hire taxis, etc). If he has no money but has family or a network of friends, time, money, and energy of others can be begged, manipulated, or negotiated. Yet, family and friends have their own storehouse of time, energy, and money. The degree to which a patient can save his time, energy, and money is dependent upon the numbers and reliability of mobility agents. Characteristics of aged, single, widowed, or divorced, indigent advanced patients include: (1) paucity of money; (2) paucity of energy; (3) paucity of other people's time, energy, and money; and (4) lots of time. Patients therefore tend to balance and juggle their ample time with paucity of air. What they tend to do is dole out small amounts of air over long periods of time. The other option is to expend air only on certain activities, or curtail or dole certain activities. These are major strategies.

"Time, energy, and money" was recoded from mobility resources to basic mobility resources (BMRs). This term has more conceptual grab and is linked to mobilization. Thus the major linkage between categories, BMRs, and mobilization occurred.

Memo 4 is a general memo outlining properties of the treatment regimen and consequences on life style and mobility.

MEMO 4
Treatment Regimen: Properties of and Consequences for Mobility and Life Style

The long term medical regimen for these patients is primarily to hold the line and compensate for the irreversible lung damage. The regimen includes: (1) prevention of further lung deterioration by treatment and prevention of acute respiratory infections, and (2) compensation for the decreased oxygen reserve by inhalation therapy, postural drainage, drugs to keep the air passage patent, and exercises for more efficient breathing. Regimen may be in combinations of one or more to all of them. The quality of regimen may be simple like taking a pill, or more difficult like postural drainage which often requires another person's help which these patients often don't have. Treatment may also involve equipment such as respirators or oxygen.

Regimen consequences on life style and mobility include the following:

Where patients have to take daily treks to clinic for inhalation therapy they may have to cut out other mobility needs (see patient interviews 6, 9, 10).

If inhalation therapy is done at home, patient may be confined to room in order to avoid difficult terrain, like maneuvering stairs (see patient interviews 9, 11, 12).

Drugs such as bronchiodilators often used as energizers, but where activity requires extended oxygen expenditures, these may be used for added energy spurt to complete an activity. Thus, the <u>consequence</u> can be overdose, even though patients warned of dangers of overdose (see patient interviews 3, 6, 9, 11).

(See Caplin I, Hames J: Complications of aerosol therapy in asthma. Ann Allergy 1969; 27:65–69, and Eisenstaadt WS: Some observations on new syndrome: Respiratory mendacamenthoses. Ann Allergy 1969; 27:118–190).

Memo 5 deals with residential features, life style, and mobility.

MEMO 5
Life Style Residence: Mobility

Each person makes decisions about his or her residence location on the basis of his life style and the time, energy, and money available. A residence location is chosen in terms of work, family, social life. Decisions to live in the suburb versus city are based on advantages and disadvantages of quality of school, rental costs, prestige, time and cost of commuting, etc. Anyway, there are plenty of variations.

Given paucity of air the patient's residence location is very important to save energy. Time, energy, and money availability and life style determine priorities of residential features: terrain of residence (flat or hilly), terrain of residence itself (first, second floor, elevator or no elevator, both down hall or in apartment, etc), distance and terrain to and from public transportation, and distance and terrain to grocery stores, cafe, bank, etc.

The majority of patients are unable to find residence and locations which meet air-saving specifications because of lack of money. Moreover, they do not have enough air to engage in extended residence hunting. For these two reasons, they have to settle for what meets their needs halfway. More often than not, it is a bad compromise at best. (See patient interviews 4 and 10 regarding comparison of how residential features and life style determine mobility priorities.)

Residential features was later found to be a social structural condition affecting mobilization.

Memo 6 is a major memo integrating previous memos. This memo shows linkages and interaction between the categories and is diagrammed.

MEMO 6
Mobility Priorities: Life Style and Social Situation,
Basic Mobility Resources (BMR), and Disease

A person's available basic mobility resources (3) are determined by his health status and life style and social situation (Figure 11–1).

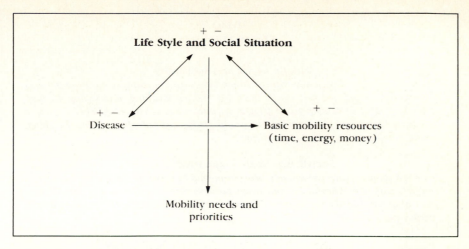

FIGURE 11-1.   Life style and social situation, basic mobility resources (BMR), disease: mobility needs and priorities.

When disease is imposed, depending upon the nature and quality of a mobility problem, there will be differential effects upon both life style and BMR status. Also, the nature and quality of the treatment regimen (effectiveness of therapy in increasing energy status, and the amount of time, energy, and cost involved in carrying out the therapy) will have varying negative or positive effects upon both the life style and BMRs. In turn, the way in which the disease and the treatment regimen impinge on the patient's life style, together with his particular social situation (residential location and features of, numbers and kinds of mobility agents), will determine how the patient does or does not comply to the medical regimen. This in turn will affect the disease course and subsequently influence his BMR status. This in turn will influence his life style. In other words, there is a constant interaction between the three parts of the structural conditions. A change in one part may affect changes in the other.

The <u>interaction</u> of these three parts will shape the patient's mobility needs and priorities. There is a constant fluidity so that mobility needs and priorities constantly change.

The central point here is that life style and social situation, disease (status and quality of regimen), and basic mobility resources are basic *social structural conditions* (Glaser, 1978). For the subjects studied there is a steady deterioration. Regardless of disease status, all emphysema patients are influenced by these basic social structural conditions which change over time: the disease fluctuates and the regimen is altered, life style and social conditions change, and BMRs also change.

Memo 7 is a collection of short memos. These were written at different periods of the study. They are listed here in order to illustrate how these somewhat related but unconnected memos eventually get integrated into the framework.

MEMO 7
Short Memos

Paucity of Air and Sociability

When air reserve is drastically reduced in the later stages of emphysema, these patients do not have enough air reserve for extended talking, laughing, and crying. In fact, extended talking or laughing can trigger off paroxysms of coughing. This is quite a contrast with normal lungers who take use of air for granted when talking, laughing, crying, singing, raising the voice, yelling, etc.

Socializing: Anxiety and Paucity of Air

Social situations which are anxiety provoking tend to bring on attacks of dyspnea. A characteristic of emphysema is that when patients become anxious they become very short of breath which brings on more anxiety. This is a vicious cycle. In other words, anxiety dissipates air.

Normative Aspects of Recouping Air

Patients concerned with recouping air in a manner which does not draw undue attention to others or make a public scene eg, having to sit on sidewalk.

Memo 8 is a central process memo dealing with gauging and routing. In reanalyzing the memos and selected data, mobilizing was recoded to routing (a BSP). These terms seemed more apt to the getting around process since routing is a process used by all persons whether ill or well. Thus, routing became a core process for physical mobility. At the same time gauging was a necessary process before and during the routing.

MEMO 8
Gauging and Routing: Two Stages of Process

Physical mobility of emphysema patients achieved by processes including:
1. *Calculating the availability of basic mobility resources—time, energy and money.*
2. *Gauging energy (oxygen) requirement in relation to the physical and psychological consequences of misgauging.*
3. *Making choices and setting priorities about when to be mobile which are determined by life styles and social situations.*
4. *Developing routing strategies for mobilization which take into account calculating basic mobility resources, physical and psychosocial consequences of misgauging energy requirement, and recoupability of energy.*
5. *Weighing whether to follow or disregard the medical regimen in terms of how the regimen impinges on life styles.*
The process of routing includes the following sub-processes: anticipation of numbers and types of activities; making judgments of where to condense, delete, or reduce activities; sequential ordering of activities; anticipating obstacles; and daily and cyclical routing.

The gauging and routing process is then added to the diagram of Memo 6, seen in a completed diagram (Figure 11–2). Once the two processes were identified the linking and ordering of the categories was greatly facilitated. For example, recouping of air is subsumed under obstacles both anticipated and unanticipated. This also gets

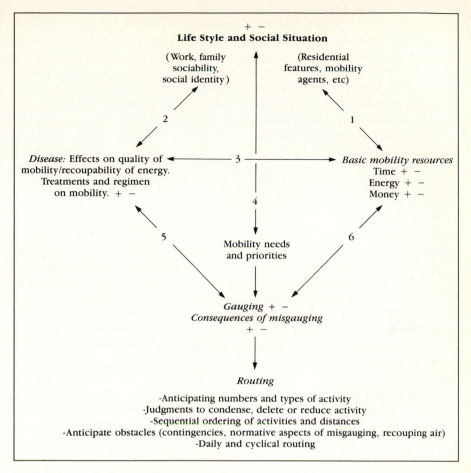

+ −
Life Style and Social Situation

(Work, family sociability, social identity)   (Residential features, mobility agents, etc)

2   1

Disease: Effects on quality of mobility/recoupability of energy. Treatments and regimen on mobility. + −   3   *Basic mobility resources*
Time + −
Energy + −
Money + −

4

5   6

Mobility needs and priorities

Gauging + −
Consequences of misgauging
+ −

Routing
-Anticipating numbers and types of activity
-Judgments to condense, delete or reduce activity
-Sequential ordering of activities and distances
-Anticipate obstacles (contingencies, normative aspects of misgauging, recouping air)
-Daily and cyclical routing

FIGURE 11–2.   General framework: Process in mobility.

linked with strategies of recouping air. Recouping is a subprocess involved in routing now shown in Figure 11–2.

Major turning points, at times called *contingencies* or *critical junctures*, affect the process (such as loss of money, home, or friends), which initiate movement or change over time. The patient then must carry out the basic social process over again from recalculating to rerouting with alternative sources of money, new friends, on a different terrain which must be regauged.

Numerous memos were written that consolidated the scattered categories into the process. Some of the titles included "Treatment regimens and their disruption of BMRs and life style," "Misuses and abuses of regimen," and "Gauging and misgauging."

Finally, once the framework and the process were developed, the framework was examined for its applicability to other diseases or generalizability. Selected cardiac patients were interviewed to see if the framework was workable and if it would account for variations. Also, colleagues studying ulcerative colitis and multiple sclerosis patients were interviewed to see how their data fit into the framework.

The reader will note that the completed article (chapter 17) is consistent with the memos. Process analysis together with extensive memo writing and rewriting greatly facilitates the final writing of a paper for publication. As a note of comparison, there are two versions of the article "Getting Around with Emphysema," one in *The American Journal of Nursing* and another version in *Chronic Illness and the Quality of Life* (Glaser, Strauss, 1975). One is written with a nursing orientation, the other is with a sociological orientation. Chapter 17 was written for practitioners. There are different forms of writing frameworks or theories. All process is written conceptually. Data are used to illustrate the meaning of a concept by giving an example.

It may appear that the process analysis and integrative process occurred rapidly and in an orderly fashion. Actually there were many days of pondering the data. A helpful factor was that the author had the advantage of a qualitative analysis class where the class discussed and critiqued each other's data, coding, and memos.

One final point needs to be made regarding basic social process analysis and its relationship to generalizability. Basic social process analysis helps to expand the process beyond the particular unit being studied (persons, groups, organizations, statuses, etc) so that greater generalizations can be made. Thus, although the study subjects were primarily in the late stages of emphysema and treated in a public health facility, the process developed tried to take into account a process that was less unit determined and which would explain variations across settings. This is not to say that had the author interviewed a larger sample of patients in different illness status and life styles that the process might have been denser. In the grounded theory approach by the use of constant comparative method and theoretical sampling (Glaser, Strauss, 1967) wherein the process being studied is constantly compared and analyzed under different sets of unit properties, greater generalizations can be made. Hence, theory is generated.

CONCLUSION

In closing, a suggestion is made to sensitize the reader to process analysis. Analyze studies and articles which report a process, for example, studies related to adapting, burning out, coping, etc. Try diagramming the process(es), their stages, and turning points. Are the basic social structural conditions and processes logically linked to the basic process? In other words, are the who, what, where, when, why, and how questions logically linked? The reader will find that process often gets mixed-up with outcome. Or, what are purported to be stages of a process are indeed different patterns of a process but do not explain the process for the differences in pattern.

Analysis of data for process enables the analyst to order categories into a logical whole. Analysis can focus on a basic social process or multiple processes that account for change in social phenomena over time. Analysis may be difficult since process serves to integrate the who, what, where, when and why of the problem under study. However, analysis for process has explanatory power and is the central analytic approach used in the development of grounded theory.

References

Fagerhaugh S: Getting around with emphysema. *Am J Nurs* 1973;73:94–99.
Fagerhaugh S: Getting around with emphysema, in Strauss A (ed): *Chronic Illness and Quality of Life*. St Louis, CV Mosby, 1975, pp 99–107.
Glaser B: *Theoretical Sensitivity: Advances in the Methodology of Grounded Theory*. Mill Valley, California, The Sociology Press, 1978.
Glaser BG, Strauss AL: *Awareness of Dying*. Chicago, Aldine Publishing Co, 1965.
Glaser BG, Strauss AL: *The Discovery of Grounded Theory: Strategies for Qualitative Research*. Chicago, Aldine Publishing Co, 1967.
Glaser BG, Strauss AL: *Time for Dying*. Chicago, Aldine Publishing Co, 1968.
Kubler-Ross E: *On Death and Dying*. New York, Macmillan Publishing, 1969.
Piaget J: *The Origin of Intelligence in Children*. New York, International University Press, 1952.

12

Writing and evaluating the grounded theory research report

Katharyn Antle May

Regardless of the style or subject of a research project, the process of research is not truly completed until findings have been compiled and communicated in a way that will advance the pursuit of knowledge. For most researchers, the last step involves writing the research report for publication either as a monograph or as an article or series of articles. Since most research that nurses and other health professionals are familiar with involves hypothesis-testing and statistical analysis, researchers learning to use qualitative methods, specifically grounded theory methodology, are often confused about how to write the research report and how to evaluate them. This chapter will begin with an overview of the writing process in grounded research and will discuss ways in which the preparation of the report is similar to and different from others. The second section of this chapter will be devoted to a discussion of evaluating and critiquing grounded theory research reports.

WRITING THE RESEARCH REPORT

Many of the challenges involved in writing grounded theory research are similar to those in any scientific writing project. The researcher must think out what is to be communicated and in what order. The researcher should have a specific audience in mind from the beginning and tailor the writing to that audience. Scientific writing requires solid fundamental writing skills, discipline, organization, and a willingness to seek out and profit from constructive criticism. However, there are some aspects of the writing process in grounded theory research that are relatively unique. Several of these aspects will be discussed in detail.

Continuous v Advance Writing

In many hypothesis-testing projects, much of the writing is done before data are collected (the presentation of the research question, the hypotheses, conceptual framework, literature review, and methodology). Often, even the tables in which the statistical findings will be presented are written in advance. Thus, only the presentation and discussion of the findings remain to be written in the final stages of the project. However, the researcher using grounded theory methodology must be writing continuously.

Data must be continually coded, sorted, and written up in field notes or memos. Later, memos must be combined and reintegrated into major memos which must then be organized into a framework or integrative outline explaining the theoretical connections between concepts. Finally, the theory itself must be written so that others unfamiliar with the field can understand it. Perhaps the most important process in grounded theory methodology is the writing that occurs throughout the analysis. If the researcher has kept up with that aspect of the process, the writing of the final research report tends to be relatively quick.

Large Volume of Data

One rather unique aspect of writing up grounded theory research is the fact that almost any project generates huge amounts of data, and usually the researcher alone writes it up. In other styles of research, there may be large data sets but they are summarized through computer analysis, and usually a statistician or associate could write up the findings given the research proposal and the computer output. On a grounded theory project, no one knows the data as well as the investigator who collected and analyzed it. Others may be able to take notes and memos on a certain theme and write them up, but the researcher is usually the only one who has worked out the overall scheme, can find specific data or memos easily, and can write up early drafts of the report.

Another characteristic of writing up grounded theory research is the tendency for the researcher to occasionally be overwhelmed by the sheer volume of data to be summarized. Probably the best strategy in this situation is to plunge in by writing a one- or two-page summary of the theoretical scheme. This summary can then serve as a ''map'' for the development of the research report. Sections with more detail and scope can be added and corrections made as the need arises.

Coining Terms v Inventing Jargon

Since the aim of grounded theory research is to generate theory about basic social processes, there are occasions when the researcher must come up with a name for a process or property reflected in the data. There is a delicate balance between coining terms that will be meaningful to others and inventing jargon that confuses more than enlightens. There are no quick solutions to this problem; the conscientious researcher will constantly ask colleagues to review and critique drafts of the research report, and may specifically ask for feedback about the usefulness and descriptive power of terms given to parts of the theoretical scheme.

Presenting Theory v Pure Description

A point that is sometimes troublesome in reporting grounded theory research is knowing what exactly are findings. In strict terms, the findings are the theory itself, ie, a set of concepts and propositions which link them. To present the findings, one must present the theoretical scheme. However, usually in grounded theory research, the researcher also has a wealth of detailed descriptive data (eg, how frequently a particular theme came up in interviews, recorded observations or behaviors which are clinically interesting but play a minor role in the scheme). There is always a tendency to lapse into pure description and present these data in detail because they are "too good to throw away." The grounded theory researcher must know the difference between the two types of reporting because each has a different power. If well constructed, the theory should be general enough to test and apply to a broader population than the one studied, that is, the theory should generalize well. However, the specific details in the data (eg, frequencies of events, characteristics of subjects and their actions, their interpretations of events) may or may not be generalizable to other groups, depending on how broad-based the sample was and how many different sources of data were tapped. This kind of data is descriptive, and its generalizability should be viewed as limited until there is evidence to the contrary. There is great value in descriptive research and most areas could benefit from more of it. However, the researcher must be clear about the difference between it and grounded theory.

Getting Started on the Report

The researcher in grounded theory writes from the very beginning. But at some point—either when the theoretical scheme seems to explain the phenomena under study or when the researcher needs to regroup and decide where to go next—the researcher will begin to consolidate shorter memos on related parts of the scheme into larger major memos. The next step is usually to write an outline that integrates all of the major memos and shows the theoretical scheme in skeleton form. The writing of the final report usually proceeds from this integrative outline, with the researcher going back to minor memos or actual pages of data to give examples and write in depth.

Undoubtedly the best way to learn to write research is to read it. The more familiar the researcher is with various ways of presenting research findings, the easier it will be to write final reports. However, there are several ways in which reports of grounded theory research differ from more common forms of research. The next section will discuss some of these differences.

Structure of the Report

The structure of a grounded theory research report differs in several ways from reports of hypothetico-deductive (hypothesis-testing) research. First, the original *research question* in a grounded theory project will probably be very broad, and will have changed several times during data collection and analysis as the research focus sharpened. This may or may not be apparent in the research report itself. However, it is often useful for the reader to have a brief statement about how the research question changed as the study evolved. The major research question should be clearly stated and key terms should be defined.

The *literature review section* presents the pertinent literature in the area. This section allows the reader to see the area from the researcher's perspective as the project was begun. The literature review in a grounded theory project neither provides key concepts nor suggests hypotheses as it does in hypothetico-deductive research. A lengthy or uncritical literature review in a grounded theory study can, in fact, reflect overdependence on existing knowledge. However, a review of existing literature can show gaps or systematic bias in existing knowledge, thus provide the rationale for launching a grounded theory study. There is usually no conceptual or theoretical framework presented in a grounded theory research report for the simple reason that grounded theory research is designed to generate theory, not test it.

The *methodology section* can be troublesome to write because the processes of grounded theory research occur simultaneously rather than in a linear fashion. For this reason, it may be difficult to describe the analytic processes succinctly. The researcher must decide how much detail will be presented on the analytic processes as opposed to a description of subject recruitment and data collection procedures. A description of the sample and setting is given, if appropriate. There have been several papers published in the last few years in which grounded theory methodology was described within the length limit of a journal article (Wilson, 1977; Stern, 1980; May, 1982). The novice researcher may do well to use these as models for how to describe analytic processes. Paying close attention to outlining subject characteristics and data collection procedures which will be unique to the study are also helpful.

The *findings section* includes the presentation of the theoretical scheme. References from the literature may be used here to enrich and show outside support for concepts or propositions in the scheme. Segments of actual data, either vignettes or quotes, are used for explanatory power. Segments of data usually "hook" the reader and allow him/her to make independent judgments about how well the theoretical scheme is based on or grounded in the data. Use of data segments may also serve to increase the credibility of the research, as the reader can identify with or recognize phenomena from their own experience. There is not usually a separate *discussion section* as there is in most hypothetico-deductive studies, because in the course of presenting the theoretical scheme, findings are usually presented in sufficient detail. However, there should be a final section which discusses the relationship of the theoretical scheme to other existing knowledge, and the implications the theory may have for further inquiry or practice.

Most research reports will have these components more or less in this order. However, grounded theory research findings can also be reported at different levels of detail and abstraction, ranging from presentation of theory to explanation of selected propositions, to description of only one concept or category. One reports different "slices" of the findings for different purposes. For instance, the researcher may report the entire theoretical scheme in a research journal article. A shorter research article might be written which presents only selected propositions from the theory in a journal for an interdisciplinary audience. In addition, a brief article describing one category or concept (and presenting little or none of the theoretical scheme) might be written for clinicians in a practice-focused journal. These "spin-off" articles are best written after the full research report is written so the researcher can work as much as possible from the well-organized scheme presented in the full report. The decisions about how to slice the findings are primarily based on what the researcher wants to communicate to whom and how.

Who Will Publish It?

This question may not seem particularly pressing to those who are not expected to publish as part of their professional role. However, new knowledge is useless unless it is communicated in some way to others who can evaluate, use, and expand upon it. The most frequent form of this communication is publishing in professional journals. However, because grounded theory research is not based on the widely accepted view that statistical analysis is the only valid form of scientific evidence, sometimes researchers have a difficult time getting grounded theory research published in the most widely circulated journals. There are at least two ways to deal with this problem. The first is to do the best possible job on the writing. To ensure this, the researcher should ask for peer review on the draft throughout the writing process. If peers are not convinced of the evidence, others will not be either. Second, the researcher should be aware of journals which do and do not regularly publish qualitative research. If the journal publishes only hypothesis-testing research, the paper reported a grounded theory study will need to be truly outstanding in order to be accepted. Finally, other mechanisms may be just as effective in getting new knowledge out where others can use it. Journals which are not widely circulated but are indexed in health science indexes make research reports accessible to others who might be interested in new findings. Specialty organization newsletters are another way to let more people know that a project is underway or has been completed. Finally, take every opportunity to present or discuss findings with colleagues; one never knows when research findings will stimulate someone else and will contribute in a significant way to practice or further inquiry.

EVALUATING THE RESEARCH REPORT

As more nurses use grounded theory methodology in nursing research, grounded theory studies are being reported more frequently in the literature. However, readers are often at a loss as to how to evaluate and critique grounded theory research. Difficulty in evaluating and critiquing grounded theory research comes in part from the nature of the methodology itself. Grounded theory methodology does not rely on statistical models of probability, yet most nurses are familiar with research based on these models. They look for classical hallmarks of scientific rigor, such as randomly selected samples, strict adherence to preplanned research designs and data collection, and coding and analysis in precise order, all of which are inappropriate criteria by which to evaluate grounded theory research. They may misread the study in question as a purely descriptive one or as an interesting pilot study, thus missing the theory-generating aspect and power of the research. Or they may miss any actual weakness in the study which might limit its strength and usefulness. The next section will present some guidelines for the evaluation of grounded theory research in nursing.

Nature of the Research Question

One of the most important points upon which to evaluate a grounded theory is the nature of the original research question (if known), and the subsequent questions that were the focus of the study. The original question may not be included as such in a research report; however, if it is included, it should have been broad enough to allow a focus to develop as data are collected and analyzed. If the initial focus is quite narrow or comes directly from the literature, there is the possibility of strong researcher bias in the data collection, analysis, and theory construction. In grounded theory research, the original research question is amended and narrowed by what is happening in the social setting under study. Although it is often difficult to assess in a written report, the reader should be alert to this evolution of the research question. If no change occurs, the investigator may have been guilty of too much "armchair" theorizing, too little time spent in the field, or holding on to preconceived notions about the phenomena under study, even in the face of conflicting data.

The second aspect of the research question that should be evaluated is whether or not the question is able to be researched in a social setting. Grounded theory methodology is based in an interactionist perspective and is used appropriately when the phenomena of interest can be examined by examining social interaction. Thus, the question should logically lead to data collection strategies such as observation, interview, document analysis, or participant observation. Preferably, more than one data source should be used; data should always be collected from a range of people in the social setting, focusing on how they perceive themselves and others in the same situation. Thus, questions focusing on areas such as intrapsychic processes, solitary behavior, behaviors and perceptions of small children or individuals whose ability to communicate is impaired, are probably inappropriate choices for study using grounded theory methodology. The sources of data about interactions and perceptions will be quite limited.

Nature and Scope of the Literature Review

The literature review in a grounded theory research study serves a different purpose from that in hypothesis-testing research. The most important function of the literature review is to allow the reader to "see" the phenomenon of interest as the investigator did at the beginning of the grounded theory research project. The literature review does not dictate the focus of the research; the data as they are coded and analyzed do that. However, the literature review may suggest fruitful directions for the early field work, and may add power and depth to the theoretical scheme once it is developed. The literature should be treated with a healthy scepticism; over-reliance on previous findings may lead to researcher bias in which case the researcher goes into the field to find the "truth" reflected in the literature, rather than discovering naturally occurring patterns in the social setting under study.

Multiple Data Sources

Another point to consider in evaluating grounded theory research pertains to the data collection techniques used in the study. Although grounded theory research is often mislabelled "inductive research," grounded theory methodology in fact involves both induction and deduction, both hypothesis generating and hypothesis testing. In the construction of grounded theory, hypotheses are developed, tested, and accepted or rejected continuously as data are collected and analyzed. The "reliability and validity" checks in this process depend on use of more than one type of data and careful selection of subjects. Interview data should be backed up with observational data whenever possible. A wide range of subjects should be contacted to assure that the researcher is seeing as much diversity as possible in responses. These strategies contribute to a better set of data and enable the researcher to develop good working hypotheses that will eventually lead to the development of a more powerful and useful theory.

Evaluating the Theory Itself

Evaluating the theory itself is probably the most important step in the evaluation and critique of grounded theory research. First, is the theory dense and clear? Density of the theory refers to the integration and interrelatedness of the categories or concepts within the theory. In other words, do the concepts logically hang together as a whole? Are there concepts which do not seem to fit? Is there sufficient evidence for concepts and propositions? Density also refers to the specification of conditions under which variations occur and the relative absence of unexplained exceptions within the theory. The theory should be presented in such a way that states the propositions (hypotheses), how they are supported by data, and how they are related. How good the theory is depends on how well the relationships are shown, how often the limits of the propositions are defined, how clearly the categories and concepts are described, and how clearly the conditions under which certain interactions occur are specified.

The second question the reader must ask about grounded theory is whether it fits with what else is known, either in everyday experience or in other scientific findings. Probably the best test of a grounded theory's "fit" is the reaction of individuals in the setting under study. The theory should explain clearly what the subjects (sometimes called actors) take for granted as true in their social world. Unfortunately, often readers cannot talk to actors about their reactions, so the reader must rely on personal knowledge. If there are discrepancies between the grounded theory and what has been found in other research, these discrepancies should be explored. If the theory seems difficult to accept, it may reflect weaknesses in the theory itself.

Is the Theory Useful?

Finally, any grounded theory should lend new insight into the phenomenon under study. Minimally, it should suggest new directions for future inquiry and should generate more questions than it answers. Because of the demands of practice, a grounded theory study in nursing should also have direct relevance to clinical phenomena. This is not to say that grounded theory should immediately be used to determine practice; any theory should be evaluated and tested cautiously before it is used to dictate professional actions. However, grounded theories related to patient concerns may serve to widen the professional's perspective, and bring into focus areas that were ignored in the past. In some ways, grounded theory research in nursing may be analogous to basic research in the "hard" sciences: It may provide a springboard for additional research, and while application may not be immediately apparent, it may fill a gap in knowledge which may later make a substantial contribution to practice as the discipline evolves.

CONCLUSION

This chapter was intended to guide the reader in the writing and the evaluation of reports of grounded theory research. Grounded theory methodology holds great promise to disciplines like nursing, which must contend with complex social settings and even more complex interactions between individuals. As more nurses become expert consumers and producers of this style of research, the "payoff" in terms of more effective clinical practice will be significant. How significant that payoff is will depend on the skill, discipline, and scholarship of those nurse investigators who master the techniques of producing, writing, and evaluating qualitative research.

References

May KA: Three phases in the development of father involvement in pregnancy. *Nurs Res* 1982; 31:337–342.

Stern P: Grounded theory methodology: Its uses and processes. *Image* 1980; 12:20–23.

Wilson H: Limiting intrusion—social control of outsiders in a healing community: An illustration of qualitative comparative analysis. *Nurs Res* 1977; 26:103–111.

13

Ethical
issues in
qualitative research

Patricia Archbold

This chapter focuses on the ethical issues that arise when the nurse conducts qualitative research. The chapter is organized in five subsections related to steps in the research process: problem identification, investigator/sponsor relationship, investigator/subject relationship, data collection, and publication of results. Throughout the chapter, examples will be used from two of my qualitative investigations: "The Impact of Parentcaring on Women" (Archbold, 1982) and "The Use of Community-based or Institutional Services by Frail Elderly in a Rural Area" (Archbold, Hoeffer, unpublished data, 1983; Hoeffer, Archbold, 1983).

PROBLEM IDENTIFICATION

As early as the problem identification stage, the nurse-researcher is confronted with ethical issues related to his or her research. Specifically, two questions must be considered at this point: What are the values underlying the problem statement and how can one establish the significance of the qualitative research problem prior to the conduct of the study?

From a disciplinary perspective, a less individual concern emerges at this point. That is, given limited monetary resources for research and the limited number of nurses prepared to conduct research, should the profession set priorities for the distribution of resources? This question is beyond the scope of this chapter. However, it is of interest to nurse-researchers and calls for careful analysis.

Myth of Value-Free Research

Much of the research literature assumes that the conduct of science is value free. Convincing arguments suggest, however, that all research is, in fact, contaminated by the personal and political sympathies of the researcher (Becker, 1970; Deutscher, 1970). The definition of a problem, as well as the choice of methods and nature of analysis, represent inherently ethical decisions on the part of the researcher. An example from the study of service utilization by frail rural elderly will illustrate this point.

In 1980, I served on a scientific advisory board for a state project involving the waivering of Medicaid funds from institutional to community-based services in four rural counties. The state researchers defined the long-term care problem of providing services to frail elderly people in terms of the cost of overuse of nursing home beds. The assumption of the state investigators was that increasing the availability of funds for community-based, long-term care would lead to a reduction of the cost for nursing home care. The data collected by the state was macrosociological and included, for example, how much was spent on institutional care and the number of nursing home beds used. I hold a different assumption about service development; I believe it should be planned based on population needs. I defined the long-term care problem as the lack of a continuum of care to meet the needs of frail elderly. The impact of services (or lack of services) on the lives of older people and their families was focused on.

The state project developed and used a functional assessment instrument to determine placement for frail aged persons. Those persons determined to be severely functionally impaired were considered "eligible for nursing home placement." This label entitled the individual to a wide range of institutional or community-based services.

The functional assessment tool did not directly screen for cognitive impairment and this was problematic when screening for nursing home placement. Evidence exists that suggests that families care for frail older members as long as possible before seeking nursing home placement and that cognitive impairment presents the most difficult problem for family members. My concern about the state project was that decreasing nursing home use before the development of community-based services would place an added burden on families caring for frail elderly relatives. Consequently, the state undertook a qualitative study on the management and impact of family care of a sample of the people involved in the project.

As Becker states, it is not a question of whether to take sides when conducting research, but rather a question of whose side to take. His response is instructive.

The researcher must,

take sides as (his/her) personal and political commitments dictate, use theoretical and technical resources to avoid the distortions that might introduce into (his/her) work, limit (his/her) conclusions carefully, recognize the hierarchy of credibility for what it is, and field as best (he/she) can the accusations and doubts that surely will be (his/her) fate (Becker, 1970, p 28).

Predicting the Significance of Qualitative Research

The review of research proposals for the protection of human subjects calls for a calculation of the risk-benefit ratio. This calculation necessitates an estimate of the projected significance of the study under evaluation. This projection is particularly difficult with qualitative research.

The qualitative researcher develops and modifies the focus of the research throughout the project. Data analysis begins as soon as data collection begins. Results of ongoing analysis lead the researcher down paths that were not thought of at the project's inception. This characteristic is considered a strength of qualitative methodologies. However, it creates problems when attempting to predict a study's significance.

The study "The Impact of Parentcaring on Women" began by investigating the impact of the caregiving role on the lives of women caring for severely impaired parents. The literature up to that point discussed the caregiving role. While conducting the interviews with caregivers, however, it became clear that the women interviewed were engaged in different activities although all were giving care to their parent. Some of the women were providing direct care services to the parent (bathing, dressing, feeding, etc). Others were managing the direct service provided by others (hiring nurses' aides, contracting for day care, etc). The two caregiving roles have very different consequences for the lives of the women. Although this discovery was the most significant contribution of this research, it would have been impossible to predict this conceptualization of caregiving at the beginning of the project.

RELATIONSHIP OF THE INVESTIGATOR TO THE SPONSOR

Most research is supported, directly or indirectly, by a sponsor. The sponsor may be a funding agent, the administrator who permits the conduct of research in his or her facility, or the agency that provides subjects. In each case, the "sponsor" works in a relationship of authority with the researcher.

The attitude of the researcher to those in authority must be carefully negotiated at the time of entrance (Barnes, 1970). Specifically, a crucial issue is whether, in what form, and how extensively the data will be shared. The sponsor is usually in a position of power over the subjects. It is essential, therefore, to guarantee subject confidentiality in order to afford protection to participants in the study.

The guarantee of confidentiality is especially difficult in settings where nurses are likely to conduct qualitative research (eg, hospitals, nursing homes, small communities, schools). In small social systems where everyone knows everyone, even the slight cues of demographic descriptors (age, sex, number of children) may reveal a person's identity. In some cases, it may be necessary to discard or thoroughly disguise data to protect subjects.

I have had one successful and one unsuccessful negotiation with a sponsor. In both cases, the sponsor was a state agency from whom I wanted to obtain subjects. This first example from the successful negotiation concerns obtaining a subsample of frail rural elderly from the state's waiver project. In the negotiations, the state requested that I make individual data available to them. The state researchers were interested in my evaluations of functional status of individual subjects so that they could compare them to the caseworker's evaluation. The state researchers suspected that caseworkers were manipulating scoring of the functional assessment instrument in order to obtain services for ineligible clients. I negotiated to share only means and medians with the state agency.

In the same study, I also wished to obtain a sample of service providers to interview. In this case, the state researchers kept control of who could be interviewed and the state identified the service provider participants in our study. Because it would be impossible to publish service provider data without risking the violation of confidentiality, I had to discard all the provider data for which supporting data was not available from other sources.

INVESTIGATOR AND SUBJECT RELATIONSHIP

This section focuses on the nature of the investigator/subject relationship in qualitative research, an area that has recently drawn considerable attention in the literature. The ethical issues related to the subject/researcher relationship center on the presentation of the research to the subject, the power differential in the subject/researcher interaction, and strategies to equalize subject/investigator power.

Presentation of the Research to the Subject

Human subjects have the right to know what will happen to them if they decide to participate in an investigation—what procedures will be used, how much time will be involved, the potential risks and benefits. While this seems straightforward, in fact, implementing informed consent procedures is often difficult. Informed consent in qualitative research is particularly problematic for several reasons. For one thing, all qualitative research has "hidden" aspects. At the beginning of a project, the researcher does not know all that he or she is looking for. The project develops and changes with ongoing data analysis in the presentation of the research to the subject.

A second problem in the presentation of the research to the subject is that the researcher does not want to influence the subject's behavior or responses by explaining in detail what is being studied. This is a problem that confronts both quantitative and qualitative researchers. However, it is most problematic in qualitative research designs in which the management of investigator subjectivity is a crucial problem.

Finally, even precise, detailed explanations of research will be understood differently by the subject than the researcher. Gray (1975) found that despite signed consent, almost 40% of the subjects questioned did not know they were participating in a medical experiment. Issues such as these create a dilemma for the researcher. Specifically, the question that must be carefully considered is: When we are carrying out qualitative research involving the behavior of other people, what do we tell them under what circumstances?

Most of the discussions of "presentation" of research focus on overt and covert presentation as dichotomous variables. In reality, it is probably more useful to conceptualize overt/covert presentation as a continuum (Roth, 1970). The extremes—pure overt presentation, or pure covert presentation—probably do not exist. All research is to some degree secret, since it is impossible to tell the subject everything. The issue of presentation must be carefully thought through by investigators on a project-by-project basis.

Power Differential in the Subject/Investigator Relationship

Subjects in qualitative research are reported to have more power in the subject/investigator relationship than subjects in quantitative research. In fact, it is suggested that the term *subject* is inappropriate in the case of qualitative research and the term *actor* should be used in its place. Consent to participate in a qualitative study is negotiated as part of the ongoing interactions between the actor and the investigator. Actors (subjects) may at any time discontinue interaction and have the power to resist questioning (Tilden, 1980).

However, when nurses conduct qualitative research, the power distribution within the subject/investigator relationship is more ambiguous. When the role of nurse-researcher is not well understood by the subject, he or she may cast the nurse-researcher into the more familiar role of clinician (Davis, 1968). To the degree that the subject sees the nurse researcher as a therapist, he/she is unprepared to assume the important self-protective role in the research situation (May, 1979). If the nurse-researcher is also the nurse-clinician caring for the subject, the power differential is official. It is unlikely that voluntary participation or refusal is possible in this situation.

Strategies to Equalize the Subject/Investigator Power

Informed consent   The traditional method for equalizing the power between the investigator and the subject is the informed consent process. However, as noted earlier, it is impossible to predict the course of an interaction in qualitative research, and consequently, obtain before-the-fact consent from a subject. The informed consent process is further complicated by the ambiguities of the nurse/researcher/clinician role.

Post-hoc review   Wax (1977) proposed an alternative to the traditional informed consent strategy to equalize the power between the subject and investigator in qualitative research. In this method, the investigator would be required to submit a detailed accounting of his or her work at appointed intervals to a critical jury of academic and professional peers. This method of equalizing the power between the investigator and subject is sensitive to the unique nature of qualitative research. It is surprising that it has not been implemented in the review process of human experimentation committees.

Conducting qualitative research with non-clients   Given the power differential that always exists in the nurse/client relationship, it is probably safest for the nurse never to conduct qualitative research with his or her own clients. It is unlikely that a patient could refuse to participate in a study if consent were sought by his or her nurse.

DATA COLLECTION

Several problems stemming from the nurse/clinician dual role have already been described. During data collection, other problems emerge. Some result from the inherent contradictions in the clinician-researcher role. The nurse-clinician is empathetic, knowledgeable about a clinical area, and prone toward intervention. On the other hand, the nurse-researcher is interested in minimizing subjectivity, obtaining reliable and valid data, and not changing a phenomenon by intervening. With that background, let us look at the methods used in qualitative research, the times when intervention is necessary, and the termination of the subject/investigator relationship.

Methods

Certain qualitative methods, particularly participant observation and focused interview, are highly suggestive of clinical assessment and interventions. Both involve prolonged interaction with a subject centering on an aspect of his or her life and the interpretation of it. While some researchers identify these methods as a potential benefit for the subject (Cassell, 1978), the methods also present risks. The process of reflecting on a phenomenon with the guidance of a skilled interviewer may change the subject's view of the phenomenon.

For example, one woman who took care of her mother had never taken the time to think about her own situation. In a focused interview, she reflected on the impact that caring for her blind husband and aged mother had on her life. The situation was an objectively difficult one which the subject had tolerated well for seven years. Her reflections increased her awareness of the negative aspects of the situation and this was an unpredicted consequence of participation in the study. This kind of change in attitude toward a phenomenon may have far-reaching consequences for many people. The data collection is, in fact, an intervention.

Intervention by the Clinician/Researcher

Within the context of qualitative data collection, it is not infrequent for the nurse-researcher to be confronted with a subject situation demanding intervention. This may relate to a clinical situation involving a crisis or one in which the health care delivery system has not been responsive to client needs. At these times, the clinician role becomes salient.

An example of the need for intervention is taken from the study of frail rural elderly. When I approached the trailer of a potential subject, I found him actively hallucinating in a dangerously unhealthy environment. None of the usual attention-obtaining interactions (greeting, calling loudly by name while standing immediately in front of the subject, or touching his arm) was adequate to obtain a response. At this point, I called the subject's case worker directly.

In other instances, the need for intervention becomes apparent during the process of data collection. For example, in the process of interviewing a wife caring for her frail husband, I found that the wife had delayed surgery for glaucoma for more than a year because there was no one to care for her husband while she was in the hospital. Her vision was rapidly diminishing and soon she would be unable to continue caregiving because of blindness. In this case the intervention was to locate an adequate caregiving system for the husband.

Once the nurse has intervened, however, he or she is confronted with another set of problems: one a research problem, the other a clinical one. What should he or she do with the data from a client for whom he or she has intervened? And what is his or her obligation to follow-up on the intervention? These questions have no "pat" answers, but must be thought through by the clinician-researcher in the situation.

Termination of the Investigator/Subject Relationship

Termination of a prolonged relationship that is based on the sharing of personal perceptions and feelings is painful. The investigator/client relationship in qualitative research has the characteristic of an intimate friendship; its termination places both the subject and the investigator at risk. Nursing research is often directed toward the lives of vulnerable groups, persons with fewer social supports and opportunities for social contact. In this case, the problem becomes more acute. What is the nurse-researcher's obligation to these subjects? What are his or her personal as well as professional obligations?

PUBLICATION OF RESULTS

The purpose of research is to seek answers to questions and share the answers with others. Publication of results is an essential step in the research process. The sharing of the results is an obligation the researcher has, not only to the subjects who gave of their time and thoughts, but also to the society which has a "right to know."

However, there is an essential conflict between society's right to know and the individual's (subject's) right to privacy. Access to data must be given in a way that safeguards confidentiality. As noted earlier, the nurse conducting qualitative research often does so in small social settings. It is extremely difficult to mask individual responses in this situation. In addition, these social settings are characterized by hierarchical power relationships among human participants. It is conceivable that published information from a study could be used by those in power in order to control subjects in less powerful positions.

Several techniques have been developed to minimize the risk involved in publication. The first is to share the information with subjects to make sure they agree with what is being said and to obtain their permission to publish it. A second technique is to use pseudonyms and distort non-relevant case material.

Despite these techniques, publication of data may still be problematic. The nurse conducting qualitative research must carefully consider the following questions prior to publication: How can one write up controversial findings to minimize misinterpretation? To what audience does one address the findings? Does one raise the visibility of vulnerable groups who may wish to remain hidden? The related issues of how to calculate risk of publicity to a vulnerable group must also be dealt with. While there are no clear answers to these questions, the issues must be discussed thoroughly by researchers before publication of any study.

SUMMARY

This chapter briefly reviewed some of the ethical issues nurse-researchers confront when conducting qualitative research. Some issues are common to all researchers conducting either qualitative or quantitative studies (eg, the issues related to problem identification). Other issues are specific to qualitative research. Examples include those surrounding overt/covert observation and the termination of the investigator-subject relationship. Finally, some issues confronting the nurse conducting qualitative research are unique. These include the nature of the clinician-researcher/client relationship and the application of certain qualitative methodologies (eg, focused interview) by clinicians. It is hoped that future discussion on the role of nurse-researchers in qualitative research will clarify these important issues.

References

Archbold P: An analysis of parent caring by women. *Home Health Care Serv Quar* 1982; 3:5–26.

Barnes JA: Some ethical problems in modern fieldwork, in Filstead WJ (ed): *Qualitative Methodology*. Chicago, Markham Publishing Co, 1970, pp 235–251.

Becker HS: Whose side are we on? in Filstead WJ (ed): *Qualitative Methodology*. Chicago, Markham Publishing Co, 1970, pp 15–26.

Cassell J: Risk and benefit to subjects of fieldwork. *Am Sociologist* 1978 13:134–143.

Davis MZ: Some problems in identity in becoming a nurse researcher. *Nurs Res* 1968; 17:166–168.

Deutscher I: Words and deeds: Social science and social policy, in Filstead WJ (ed): *Qualitative Methodology*. Chicago, Markham Publishing Co, 1970, pp 27–51.

Gray BH: *Human Subjects in Medical Experiments: A Sociological Study of the Conduct and Regulation of Clinical Research*. New York, John Wiley & Sons, 1975.

Hoeffer B, Archbold P: Interfacing Qualitative and Quantitative Methods. *West J of Nurs Res* 1983; 5:254-257.

May KA: The nurse as researcher: Impediment to informed consent? *Nurs Outlook* 1979; 27:36–39.

Roth JA: Comments on "secret observation," in Filstead WJ (ed): *Qualitative Methodology*. Chicago, Markham Publishing Co, 1970, pp 278–280.

Tilden V: Ethical considerations in qualitative research: A new frontier for nursing, in Davis AJ, Krueger J (eds): *Patients, Nurses, Ethics*. New York, American Journal of Nursing, 1980.

Wax ML: On fieldworkers and those exposed to fieldwork: Federal regulations, moral issues, rights of inquiry. *Hum Organiz* 1977; 36: 321–328.

Part II

Examples of

Grounded Theory

Method

The chapters in Part II illustrate the different levels of analysis that are possible using grounded theory. The first level of analysis is description that can be seen as the systematic presentation of data. The next level of analysis is the generation of *categories* that organize this data. Linking categories together with a *core category* is a further analytical level, one that illustrates a basic social process or multiple processes that occur in the phenomena under study. The core category functions as a theory that explains and predicts a phenomenon in the empirical world. This substantive theory can further be linked to a formal theory, or one which is at a higher level of abstraction and therefore addresses a broader range of phenomena.

Stern's study, in chapter 14, of conflicting family culture identifies a single category and explains all its properties. The category of culture is important in helping to explain the family dynamics in the process of integration in stepfather families.

Both Wilson's study, chapter 15, on the treatment of the mentally ill in the community mental health system and Hutchinson's chapter 16 on nurses in a neonatal intensive care unit develop core categories that explain basic social processes. Wilson describes a basic social process called "dispatching" that explains staff decisions that affect a patient's placement in the community mental health system. Hutchinson describes how the basic social process of creating meaning— emotionally, rationally, and technically—is essential to the effective functioning of nurses working in the highly stressful environment of neonatal intensive care.

Developing analysis around a basic social process, as Wilson and Hutchinson do, involves focusing on the central theme or action in the data. Parts of the whole are described in the stages, phases, strategies, context, and conditions through which the process takes place. This type of analysis is particularly useful for the study of systems and policy, such as health policy and its effects on health care at multiple levels in society.

In studying people with emphysema, Fagerhaugh, chapter 17, presents not only a general process which she calls "routing," but also presents the multiple processes that are part of routing: calculating resources, gauging energy requirements, making choices, and setting priorities. Through identifying and describing multiple processes, the study shows the complexity of the world of the person with emphysema and the problems that must be faced to engage in the activities of daily life.

In chapter 18, Chenitz's study of patient entry into a nursing home not only identifies "passage" as the basic social process that explains the response of older adults to their nursing home admission, but links this process to status passage theory, a formal theory developed by Glaser and Strauss. Linking a substantive theory to a formal theory, as Chenitz has done, adds to the specificity of the formal theory and sets the study in the broader context of a more generalizable framework.

The final chapter, by Kus, is an illustration of how one researcher has applied research findings to clinical practice. In a study of how gay men accepted their sexual orientation, Kus describes the several stages of the basic social process of "coming out." He found that arresting an individual's development at an earlier stage can produce negative effects on the person's physical and emotional health. By applying the insights of the study to help gay men with health problems move through the coming out process, Kus argues, the clinician can make effective interventions regarding the client's health problem.

It seems appropriate that we conclude this book with Kus' application of a grounded theory study to clinical practice. Professional nursing is expected to apply new knowledge and theory in practice and to evaluate the effects of interventions based on new knowledge (ANA, 1980). We feel that grounded theory is particularly suited to practical application and testing because it derives from and is verified by both clinicians and clients. There is a need for further systematic application of grounded theory to clinical practice.

References

American Nurses' Association: *Nursing: A Social Policy Statement*. Kansas City, Missouri, American Nurses' Association, 1980.

Glaser BG, Strauss A: *Status Passage: A Formal Theory*. Chicago, Aldine Publishing, 1971.

14

Conflicting family culture: An impediment to integration in stepfather families

Phyllis Noerager Stern

A family may be considered a microcultural unit. In our society of separate nuclear families, social units have less impact on individual family norms than might be the case in a more stable, closely knit culture where a society's model is carefully taught to proteges (Maxwell, Maxwell, 1980). The concept of individual family culture, developed in research on stepfather families, was found to be the basis for most rules governing behavior and for modes of enforcing rules in these families. Although couples in first marriages experience some conflict over rules and enforcement, in stepfather families the situation is influenced by previous family configurations besides the families of origin. In first marriages it's his and hers. With stepfather families, it's his origin culture, her origin culture, and the child's culture from the original home, and possibly her first marriage culture, his first marriage culture, and the child's culture from a transition period. Since some cultural prescriptions are likely to conflict, the addition of a new spouse causes disequilibrium for the whole family.

Reprinted with permission from *Journal of Psychosocial Nursing and Mental Health Services,* volume 20, number 10. Copyright © 1982, Charles Slack, Inc.

There are more than 15 million children younger than 18 in age living in step-families in the United States (Roosevelt, Lofas, 1976). This represents about 13% of the total population according to the Population Reference Bureau (1977). At the present time, about 1,000,000 children and 5,000,000 adults become members of stepfamilies each year (Visher, Visher, 1979). In most cases, children live with a full-time stepfather rather than a stepmother because in nine out of ten divorces, the mother keeps the children. A recent study in San Diego (Bohannan, 1975) showed 9% of that city's population to be made up of stepfather families. When she remarries, a mother and her spouse may think they will merge immediately into a happy integrated family, but as health professionals working with families may know, this often is far from the case.

LITERATURE REVIEW AND METHODOLOGY

The literature concerning stepfathers and their families is relatively sparse. Conflicts over discipline and the role of the stepfather in childrearing have been recognized as a particular problem in these families. Fast and Cain (1966) found that stepfathers were confused about the role they should assume *vis-a-vis* the children. Keith (1977), in her study of childrearing attitudes of stepparents, found that stepparents were more likely to be less accepting of normal childhood behavior and more likely to avoid communication with the child than natural parents. Mowatt (1972), doing group therapy with three stepfathers and their wives, found that mothers asked stepfathers to discipline their children but then prevented them from doing so. Writing about therapy with stepfamilies, Visher and Visher reported that "Many times the mother is sending double messages to the stepfather. She wishes help with discipline and at the same time feels the need to protect her children" (1979). Messinger (1976) found in her work with remarried couples that they had underestimated the emotional upheaval involved in remarriage with children. She found that children resisted an attempt to force them to act toward the new parent as a "real" parent. In addition, the child may feel displaced by the stepparent as aspects of the relationship established with the biological parent during the transition from nuclear family to single parent family are relinquished. Ransom, Schlesinger, and Derdeyn (1979) describe this pattern as a complicating factor in the revolution of loss leading to a signification of the child as the target of parental anger or ambivalence toward the previous partner.

E. M. Rallings (1976), writing about the difficulties of "instant" fathers, cites the lack of "a model or models to pattern after" as particularly troublesome. He adds that the "ambiguous role expectations" of the stepfather in the family can be a "detriment to the family's mental health and happiness."

In general, however, studies suggest that the outlook for children in stepfather families is favorable. Bohannan and Erickson (1978) found that the mental health, school achievement, and self-esteem of children in stepfather families were equal to a comparison group of children in intact families. This finding supports a secondary analysis of two public opinion surveys (Wilson et al, 1975), which showed no difference in a comparison between adults from stepfather homes with those from intact homes. Medeiros (1977) found stepfamilies and first marriage families equally healthy in their styles of relating. In earlier studies, Bernard (1956) found that college students from both stepfather and stepmother homes did not differ significantly in studies of personality from those reared in intact homes. Goode (1964) concluded that the children of remarried women suffered no ill effects. In contrast, Langer and Michael (1963) found the effect of remarriage was worse for children than living in a broken or bereaved home. Nye (1957) reported that an unhappy home is more stressful than a broken home, but that children from lower-class homes are more stressed by remarriage. Messinger and Walker (1979) in viewing remarriage from the perspective of family boundaries and roles, differentiate the *ascribed* roles of the adult and child in the nuclear family from the *achieved* roles of the adult and child in the remarried family. This indicates that an achieved role must be filled through individual effort and competition.

Integration in both stepmother and stepfather families has been studied by Duberman (1973). Each spouse was asked to rate the family for closeness versus distance, and the investigator similarly rated the family through interview data and observation. Duberman found the adjustment between stepparent and child and between stepsiblings influenced integration scores, and that 45% of the 88 step-families so rated were highly integrated. Duberman's findings conflict with an earlier study by Bowerman and Irish (1962) who concluded that step-homes with teenagers were more likely to have stress, ambivalence, and low cohesiveness than a similar group of intact families. However, Palermo's study of 50 remarried couples in 1980 suggested that factors other than age influence stepfamily relationships. These include unresolved conflicts in the child and/or parents, the relationship of the natural parents, and of course, the child's relationship with one or both natural parents.

To date, the *process* of integration and the conditions which either enhance the process or impede it have not been studied. The concept of individual family culture as a problem in the integration of stepfamilies has not been introduced.

Data Collection

The proposal for this study was first approved by the Committee for Human Research, University of California, San Francisco. The use of fictitious names protects the anonymity of the participants.

Interview and observational data were collected from 30 stepfather families in 1975 and 1976. Subjects were referred to the investigator by other stepfamilies and by nurse colleagues. Data were collected by speaking with 62 persons in 85 hours of intensive interviews, covering a total of 132 persons from present and former marriages. The original intent was to interview whole families as a unit; however, because of family resistance, this was possible in only eight cases. The remaining interviews were conducted as follows: five couples, 12 grown stepchildren living out of the home, four mothers only, one stepfather only, and one aunt to children living in a stepfather home. Separate additional interviews were conducted with six stepfathers, ten mothers, and four stepchildren living in the home. The social class of the subjects ranged from blue collar to professional, with the majority in the middle range. Ethnic representation included 86% white, 6% black, and 8% other persons. Protestants predominated with 52%, 20% were Catholic, 18% Jewish, 3% other, and 7% had no religious affiliation. It should be noted that several families were of mixed religions. The majority of the children were born in California while most parents were born elsewhere. The ages of the 61 children at the time of the spouse union ranged from 2 to 19 years, with a fairly equal distribution of 31% pre-school, 38% grade school (age 6 to 12 years) and 31% teenage.

Analysis

Data were analyzed using the qualitative method of continuous comparison developed by Glaser and Strauss (1967) and Glaser (1979). According to Antle-May (1980), "Briefly, a grounded theory is a substantive theory, well grounded in data, that describes and in some cases predicts events or processes in a given social setting." In four overlapping processes (Maxwell, Maxwell, 1980), data were first coded for processes that occur during the course of observation or interview. Coded data were clustered into naturally related categories (Stern, 1980). Categories then were compared with one another and with new data to discover links among categories (Schatzman, Strauss, 1973; Wilson, 1977). Categories so related were reduced and once again checked against incoming data to assess their pivotal relationship to emerging hypotheses. Concepts not supported in the data were dropped and new categories formed. Once formed, concepts were connected and reduced once more for increased abstraction and generalizability. Finally, Antle-May (1980) notes, "This process continues until the researcher is satisfied that the theory describes a process in a social setting in such a way that is true to the data, and that stimulates new thought and inquiry."

FINDINGS

It was discovered in the research that the impact of individual and conflicting family cultures becomes apparent as spouses in a stepfather family begin to live together in the presence of the mother's children. Although individual family culture may be influential in all family life, difficulties surface when one culture comes in close proximity with another family culture, as in the case of remarriage with children. These cultural differences account for spouses' idiosyncratic ideas about proper and fitting behavior in family life, especially in the case of childrearing and discipline. Family cultural beliefs also account for the child's values, which may differ sharply from those of the stepfather.

Individual family cultural prescriptions guide the way rules are made, how the rules are transmitted, how they are enforced, and the acceptability of rules and rule makers. It is interesting to note that the disequilibrium over clashing cultures is temporally specific. All families in the present study reported that after one and a half to two years, "things settle down." Resolution of the conflict occurs through stepfather-child affiliation, or conversely through estrangement and separation.

Individual Family Cultural Rules

To the outsider, family cultural prescriptions may seem foreign because the observer is from another family culture. In the stepfamilies under study, for example, one family had a rule that dinner and dessert must be separated by an hour's wait. In another, children were forbidden to speak at the dinner table, and in a third, all members were required to turn their socks "right side out" before placing them in the laundry hamper. All of these rules seemed exotic to the investigator, a foreigner in the individual family cultural sense.

Family value systems are part of individual family culture, but the focus here is on the unconscious rules that dictate where the sugar bowl goes, the way to clean the stove, the time dinner is served, and the way members should behave. Family cultural norms may "go public" at important rituals such as weddings and funerals, but it is the trivial intimate behaviors that cause conflict in most stepfather homes. Enormous difficulties arise in stepfather families when members have entrenched and opposing ideas about what every child, every father, or every mother should do. Beliefs about fitting and proper behavior are internalized, and as such are held tenaciously.

Discipline, the making and enforcing of rules, is a necessary measure to insure that children's behaviors will agree with the family cultural beliefs of the parents. Problems in the stepfather assuming a co-management role usually are disagreements over incompatible family cultures. Will the stepfather be allowed to make rules; will he be allowed to enforce them? Interview data suggest that he will if his cultural rules and his cultural norm for enforcing rules do not depart dramatically from the cultural norms of the mother and child.

The child entering stepfamily living experiences family cultural shock as formerly right activities suddenly are wrong. Children in these homes have already been taught right from wrong and their mother has done at least some of the teaching. When a stepfather enters the scene with his cultural rules, the child's theoretical framework for behavior is threatened with drastic revision. As one stepchild reported, "My friend had a stepfather, and when I told her mom was going to marry Karl, she said "Look out, there's gonna be a lot of new rules.' "

Any two parents have trouble agreeing on the cultural norms of their disciplining. "The chances of spouses doing at least some things differently from one another are just about 100 percent, as neither was brought up the same way" (Satir, 1972). In stepfather families, all persons involved have their own cultural prescriptions or right way of doing things.

Family members cite a Platonic form or model of perfection or "right way" when they argue about family rules and rulemakers. Issues can be over small matters such as one that occurred in the data over bouncing a ball in the house.

"You know it isn't *right*," said the stepfather. The answer, cased in the mother's cultural model, was, "He's not hurting anything." Arguing for social-structural control in the household, the stepfather's rationale was based on his model, "You should let me make the rules because a child needs a father's hand." Family culture also is the rationale used on a social-psychological process level, that of rule making: "We should make this rule because it's not right to bounce a ball in the house." The cultural model is used to reinforce the mother's power base in these families: "They're my kids, my responsibility, and I want them to have the freedom of ball-bouncing in the house; I don't want them inhibited."

The substance of family cultural issues differed in stepfather families, but family cultural issues existed in all the families studied. As an example, newly married Brenda and Bruno were having trouble over Randy. Mother and stepfather had cultural prescriptions concerning Randy's behavior, and so did Randy. Randy's mother reported:

> Bruno says 'I don't see that Randy finishes his jobs, he does them half-way,' and I say, 'That's right, the way he's doing them is O.K. with me.' You see, he'll make up for not completing a job by doing something like the dishes which isn't his assignment—it's his way of complying, and still retaining some autonomy. Bruno can't accept that.

In this household, Bruno believed in thorough work. Brenda believed that Randy should be able to work out his own compromise, and Randy had his idea of how to manage: a half-finished job patched up by another job.

Perhaps the real issue here is the stepfather's desire to enforce his own family cultural prescriptions, and the mother's and child's perplexity over allowing or following rules that seem nonsensical, foreign, and mystifying to them. An interaction between George and Gloria which involved Gloria's 8-year-old son, Clint, illustrates this concept:

> We were in the family room, and suddenly George said, 'Why are you letting Clint do that?' Well, I couldn't see what George could be talking about, so I said, 'Do what?' So George said in this really indignant voice, 'Turn the television on and off like that.' Well, I knew that Clint just liked to see the little light go on and off—we have an old set—and I couldn't see what was wrong with that, so I said, 'What's wrong with that?' George gave me this look of sheer disgust, like I was out of my mind, and sort of sputtered and said, 'It'll wear the knob out!' Did you ever hear anything so off the wall?

From George's point of view, *everybody* knows what's wrong with turning the knob off and on, but George's belief didn't make sense to Gloria, because it wasn't part of her family culture.

Transmission and Acceptibility of Rules

Individual family cultural models exist for the proper form in which rules are issued, who issues them, and for the way in which they are accepted and enforced. Mothers in most of the families interviewed had spent some time alone with their children before remarriage. In the absence of adult companions, these mothers often fell into the habit of talking with their children on a relatively equal basis. Rules, instead of being issued as commands, were presented persuasively as suggestions. A majority of the stepfathers found such interactions unacceptable to their cultural beliefs, and demanded that the mother act like a "parent" rather than a companion. Virginia, a social worker, had lived alone with 10-year-old Essie for 8½ years when she married Gene, a psychologist. Virginia said:

> I was strict with Essie, but I talked to her adult to adult. If Essie did not think a rule was fair, she could question it. And you couldn't say, 'Because.' She wouldn't accept that. She would say, 'That's no reason.' But Gene feels that a parent-child interaction is appropriate—if you're familiar with transactional analysis.

Although there were exceptions, most stepfathers also spoke strongly about how rules, once issued, should be accepted. It may be sex-typical rather than cultural that stepfathers generally objected to "back talk" from stepchildren. Gene, in the example above, said that to give Essie a choice invited "back talk" from his stepdaughter. He explained that:

> Sometimes I think Essie is just confused by Virginia's wording. Virginia will say, 'Would you like to clear off the table?' Essie, being an honest kid, says, 'No, I wouldn't.' I just tell her to clear off the table.

In their clashes over family cultural prescriptions, couples occasionally cite references to support their point of view. Gene, in this example, agrees with Wood and Schwartz (1977), while Virginia holds with the democratic style advocated by Gordon (1970).

Guessing the Rules

Cultural prescriptions for families are so entrenched and at the same time so unconscious that members of stepfather families think their own family cultural model is universal. Therefore, they expect other members of the family to have been trained to observe the same "model importances" (Krassen-Maxwell, 1979). In other words, they expect the rules to be known without being spoken. Rules for chore performance represent a case in point. Stepfathers expect children to perform the chores they had been assigned in their own childhood, and furthermore, they expect the child to anticipate chore assignments without being issued explicit instruction. Mothers who have learned different family model importances often view new chore demands by stepfathers as a disparagement of their childrearing ability. One reason for this is that the stepfather's approach suggests that he thinks the child has been "spoiled," that the child is "lazy," or that the child "gets away with murder" because he or she doesn't assume the responsibilities which the stepfather expects. Emil was 7 when Harry married his mother Daisy. Harry criticized Emil on the ground that Emil was spoiled:

Daisy was at his beck and call for transportation, and he never did anything to help her. One time Daisy came home from the store loaded with groceries, and Emil didn't even make an effort to carry them in the house! I never saw such a lazy kid!

Daisy, for her part, said Emil had never been taught to carry in groceries:

About the groceries, well, you see, my first husband was a cripple, and he couldn't do anything. Emil didn't have his father for an example, and I don't know, I guess I just got used to doing everything. Anyway, how was Emil supposed to guess that Harry thought he should carry in the groceries?

Harry replied that "any kid should know enough to help his mother." According to Harry's family cultural model, children learned to help out. Apparently, Harry had learned this at so young an age that he was unable to recall the lesson. When asked about being taught to help out, he said, "I always knew that."

Criticism of the child's deportment is perceived by the mother as criticism of her parenting. When stepfathers rankle at incomplete chores or back talk, mothers answer defensively. Dorothy, the mother of 12-year-old Rose, admitted that her daughter argued with her about household duties and sometimes didn't complete her tasks before Dorothy and Karl were married, but her tone was angry when she said, "I just didn't have time to watch her like I should, but I saw to the *important* things!" Children most often complain and talk back about chore assignments, and at first, so do mothers.

Enforcing the Rules

Cultural prescriptions concerning the enforcement of rules vary widely and are generally a reflection of the enforcement style of the parents' families of origin. Stepfathers who used corporal punishment to enforce rules had been so punished themselves as children, although not all stepfathers who were beaten used this technique. Family cultural prescriptions can be altered, especially when they are identified as undesirable. Some stepfathers tried to make up for what they considered past wrong doings of their own parents: "My father was a brute," said one stepfather; "I'd never do that to a kid." In families where corporal punishment was used to enforce rules, the mother tended to accept the cultural prescription of male as head of household. Dale, a designing engineer who had been a stepfather for three years, used a belt to enforce rules issued to his stepsons, Ivan, 10 and Jack, 8 because, "That's the way my father did it. He always said taking his belt off and having us kids unbutton our pants gave him time to cool off." His wife, Gale, agreed with her husband's methods because, "My father was the boss in the house. I can't understand women who have trouble letting the stepfather discipline their kids. I just let Dale take over."

Once family culture agreement over an enforcement mode is reached by the spouses, the technique persists even though empirically, it proves ineffective. "Spanking doesn't work with Jack," said the mother above, "Nothing works. But we spanked the other one—you have to be fair."

Social and technological progress has some influence on family cultural prescriptions. Restricting television viewing time was far the most popular punishment in stepfather families.

The mother whose cultural prescriptions do not agree with the stepfather's disciplining style undermines his efforts. She does this by acting as go-between to stepfather and child.

Playing Go-between: A Natural Interim

Playing go-between is a natural role for the mother at the beginning of the stepfamily relationship. It is she who knows both spouse and child best, and it is necessary to the child's security that the mother maintain control over childrearing during the introductory period—the most intense time of family cultural shock for the child. Children feel left out in homes where the stepfather suddenly is allowed to take over a disciplinarian role, without the mother's mediation (Stern, 1976; Stern, 1980). These children, having lost the physical presence of their biological father, resent a stranger taking over the management of their lives. Occasionally, the child's need for gradual adjustment is sacrificed in the hope of a smooth marital relationship. The mother to one 4-year-old said to her son, "This is your new father. Do what he says." The child became frightened and bewildered and the incident ended in an uproar.

Consequences of Prolonged Go-Between Activity

Limiting the stepfather's role of rule maker and rule enforcer by acting as go-between acts as a distancing mechanism between stepfather and child. If this pattern continues, the stepparent and child are unable to talk with each other about their feelings, and thus become estranged. Satir (1972) writes about communication through a third person:

> *If the family habitually transacts business without all members present, and also has little pair time, then family members get to know each other through a third person. I call it* acquaintance by rumor. *The problem is that most people forget about the rumor part and treat whatever it is as fact.*

Going between has a cumulative effect, and in the present study where this social structural pattern was the rule, even benign communications between the child and stepfather were responded to by the mother. During interviews, the mother not only answered for the child to the stepfather, but to the interviewer. The mother in this situation gets in the way of all messages that come to the child or issue from the child. To a lesser degree, the mother, self-appointed censor, either answered for the stepfather or interpreted his response.

Most mothers provide a watchful presence only until they are confident that the stepfather is as concerned with the child's welfare as he is with obedience to rules. The stepfather must prove his good intentions before she can relax. This is a particularly difficult period for the stepfather. He is on trial. Left out of childrearing, the stepfather may retaliate with failing to befriend the child. By failing to treat the child in a sufficiently friendly manner, the stepfather protests being left out.

RESOLVING THE DISEQUILIBRIUM: AFFILIATION OR SEPARATION

Disequilibrium over conflicting family culture can be minimized by a degree of separation between stepfather and child with the mother continuing to act as go-between, or the family can become integrated through a process of stepfather-child affiliation. Although the process is reciprocal, the stepfather, by virtue of his years of experience, has at his disposal more practice in applying strategies that make him agreeable to other people, including a recalcitrant stepchild. Stepfathers in the present study made themselves valuable in the eyes of the child by teaching special skills to the stepchild, by assisting the child with homework, by sharing histories— telling the child about his own childhood, and listening to the child's history and family culture. Stepfathers enrolled their stepchildren in needed special schools, bought longed-for athletic equipment, and some paid the rent. One stepfather helped his hyperkinetic stepson with sports and supported the child while he weaned himself away from amphetamines. Another hired his stepsons to work around his printshop, giving the boys pocket money, a sense of responsibility, and a knowledge of the printing trade.

According to the data, the stepfather who is a friend to the child is more likely to be tolerant of the child's family cultural beliefs. He also is in a better position to enforce his own cultural prescriptions, because he has an affectional base to call upon with the child. Children, like most of us, are more willing to cooperate with a friend than an enemy.

Given time, a stepfather family begins to develop an individual family culture of its own. Friction continues to occur over rules and enforcement as the child progresses developmentally, but with time and shared experiences, the family gains a feeling of familiarity and a sense of observing its own model importances. They begin to believe their stepfather family's ways of doing things are right.

IMPLICATIONS OF INDIVIDUAL FAMILY CULTURE

The concept of individual family culture is important to the integration of stepfather families. Individual culture, discovered in the present study of stepfather families, seems to be a general phenomenon in Western families, seems to be a general phenomenon in Western families, but it becomes problematic during the joining together of two separate family cultural units as in the case of stepfather families. Unaware of their idiosyncratic view of family behaviors, spouses and children in these families have little tolerance or understanding of an invading culture. Made privy to the knowledge that there is a family cultural prescription for behaviors rather than a right or wrong way, stepfather families might attain increased tolerance for foreign family rules.

Stepfather-child affiliation is a vital process in alleviating family disequilibrium resulting from cultural differences. Befriending helps the child tolerate the cultural shock of a radically altered family system.

Health professionals who work therapeutically with such families or who offer preparedness classes for stepfamilies can help them understand the concepts of family culture and stepfather-child affiliation. Such classes can be beneficial to the adjustment of such families. Ineffective discipline is one of the areas of difficulty listed in a learning needs assessment geared toward teaching parenting skills that will promote maturity and autonomy of children (Perdue, Horowitz, and Herz, 1977). In fact, the authors stress that teaching these parenting skills is the key element of nursing intervention with families in general. Jacobsen (1980) refers to the educational approach to potential stepfamily members as a "rehearsal" for reality which will allow them to understand their own feelings and to anticipate and deal more effectively with any difficulties that may arise.

BROADER IMPLICATIONS

It is conceivable that many family interactional problems that involve in-laws are based in individual cultural norms. The daughter-in-law, for instance, who can't cook or who doesn't warm the plates before serving dinner may be following the prescriptions of her original family culture. The father-in-law who leaves the table while others are still eating may be modeling his behavior after his own father and may intend no insult. Once voiced as family cultural prescriptions, intolerable behaviors of in-laws may become possible to accept.

CULTURAL PRESCRIPTIONS: SENTIMENTAL ORDER

The concept of individual family culture has its roots in the theoretical construct of *sentimental order,* developed by Glaser and Strauss (1965) in their study of dying patients in hospitals. Sentimental order, according to the authors, is what hospital ward personnel consider to be fitting and proper behavior—the way it's *supposed* to be. It is not fitting and proper, for instance, for a patient to cry out and disturb the ward.

Health professionals impose their internalized cultural prescriptions on their charges without being aware that they are doing so. For example, restricting family visiting on a maternity ward may be tolerated by Anglo-Saxons, but may mean real deprivation for Filipino-Americans (Stern, Tilden, and Maxwell, 1980; Stern, 1980).

In advising parents on childrearing, individual family culture must be taken into account. Health professionals, in these instances, must be aware that their own individual family cultural prescriptions may be right for them just because of a feeling of familiarity, but may seem foreign to the client family, whether the client is from another ethnic group or not.

FURTHER STUDIES

Work is needed in the area of stepmother families to determine what problems individual family culture pose for this group. Future studies might be so directed.

The San Francisco Bay Area has an admittedly unstable population. America, a highly mobile society, is also a conglomerate of regional cultures. A study similar to the present one, conducted in a more stable society, might provide additional insights into the role of individual family cultures with implications for our own.

References

Bernard J: *Remarriage: A Study of Marriage*. New York, Dryden, 1956.

Bohannan PJ: Stepfathers and the mental health of their children, in *Final Report of NIMH*. Western Behavioral Science Institute, La Jolla, California, 1975.

Bohannan PJ, Erickson R: Stepping in. *Psychol Today* January 1978, 53–59.

Bowerman CE, Irish DP: Some relationships of stepchildren to their parents. *Marr Fam Living*, 1962;24:113–121.

Duberman L: Step-kin relationships. *J Marr Fam* 1973;35:283–292.

Fast I, Cain AC: The stepparent role: Potential for disturbances in family functioning. *Am J Orthopsychiatry*, 1966;36:485–491.

Glaser BG, Strauss AL: *Awareness of Dying*. Chicago, Aldine, 1965.

Glaser BG, Strauss AL: *The Discovery of Grounded Theory: Strategies for Qualitative Research*. Chicago, Aldine, 1967.

Glaser BG: Theoretical Sensitivity. Mill Valley, California, The Sociology Press, 1978.

Goode WJ: *The Family*. Englewood Cliffs, New Jersey, Prentice-Hall, 1964.

Gordon T: *P.E.T.: Parent effectiveness training*. New York, Plume, 1970.

Jacobson DS: Stepfamilies. *Child Today* 1980;9:2–6.

Keith J: *Child-Rearing Attitudes and Perceived Behavior Patterns of Natural Parents and Stepparents,* doctoral dissertation. North Texas State University, Denton, Texas, 1977.

Krassen-Maxwell E: *Modeling Life: A Qualitative Analysis of the Dynamic Relationship Between Elderly Models and Their Proteges,* doctoral dissertation. University of California, San Francisco, 1979.

Langner TS, Michael ST: *Life Stress and Mental Health*. New York, Free Press, 1963.

Maxwell EK, Maxwell RJ: Search and research in ethnology: Continuous comparative analysis. *Behav Sci Res* 1980;15:219–243.

May KA: A typology of detachment/involvement styles adopted during pregnancy by first time expectant fathers. *West J Nurs Res* 1980;2:445–453.

Medeiros J: *Relationship Styles and Family Environment of Stepfamilies*, doctoral dissertation. California School of Professional Psychology, San Francisco, 1977.

Messinger L: Remarriage between divorced people with children from previous marriages: A proposal for preparation for remarriage. *J Marr Fam Couns* 1976;2:193–200.

Messinger L, Walker K: Remarriage after divorce: Dissolution and reconstruction of family boundaries. *Fam Proc* 1979;18:185–192.

Mowatt MH: Group psychotherapy for stepfathers and their wives. *Psychother Theor Res Prac* 1972;9:328–331.

Nye FI: Child adjustment in broken and in unhappy unbroken homes. *Marr Fam Living* 1957;19:356–361.

Palermo E: Remarriage: Parental perceptions of steprelations with children and adolescents. *J Psychiatr Nurs Men Health Serv* 1980;18:9–13.

Perdue B, Horowitz J, Herz F: Mothering. *Nurs Clinics North America* 1977;12:491–501.

Population Reference Bureau. *New York Times*, November 27, 1977.

Rallings EM: The special role of the stepfather. *Fam Coord* 1976;25:445–449.

Ransom J, Schlesinger S, Derdeyn A: A stepfamily in formation. *Am J Orthopsychiatry* 1979;49:36–43.

Roosevelt R, Lofas J: *Living in Step*. New York, Stein & Day, 1976.

Satir V: *Peoplemaking*. Palo Alto, California, Science and Behavior Books, 1972.

Schatzman L, Strauss AL: *Field Research*. Englewood Cliffs, New Jersey, Prentice-Hall, 1973.

Stern PN: *Integrative Discipline in Stepfather Families*. doctoral dissertation. University of California, San Francisco, 1976.

Stern PN: Grounded theory methodology: Its uses and processes. *Image* 1980;12:20–33.

Stern PN, Tilden VP, Maxwell EK: Culturally induced stress during childbearing: The Filipino-American experience. *Iss Heath Care Women* 1980;2:129–143.

Stern PN: A comparison of culturally approved behaviors and beliefs between Filipino-immigrant women, American-born, dominant-culture women, and Western-female nurses: Religiosity of health care, in Leininger M (ed): *Proceedings of the 1980 Transcultural Nursing Conference*, vol 6. Salt Lake City, University of Utah Press, 1980.

Stern PN: Stepfather families: Integration around child discipline. *Iss Mental Health Nurs* 1978;1:50–56.

Visher EB, Visher JS: *Stepfamilies: A Guide to Working with Stepparents and Stepchildren*. New York, Brunner/Mazel, 1979.

Wilson HS: Limiting intrusion—Social control of outsiders in a healing community. *Nurs Res* 1977;26:103–111.

Wilson KL, Zurcher L, McAdams DC, et al: Stepfathers and stepchildren: An exploratory analysis from two national surveys. *J Marr Fam* 1975;37:526–536.

Wood P, Schwartz B: *How To Get Your Children To Do What You Want Them To Do*. Englewood Cliffs, New Jersey, Prentice-Hall, 1977.

15

Usual hospital treatment in the United States community mental health system: A dispatching process

Holly Skodol Wilson

Prior to the 1960s, conventional treatment for the mentally disordered in the United States took place behind the walls of large state mental hospitals that served as "warehouses" for society's troubled and troublesome individuals. Paradoxically, it was the reforming spirit of crusaders like Dorothea Dix that led to the development of these structures of the past. Our idyllic romance with them, however, came to an end with the sad realization that institutional care cannot eradicate mental illness and, further, that patients confined to institutions are often denied their human rights. These findings are well detailed in the works of Stanton and Schwartz (1954), Goffman (1961), Caudhill (1958), and others. These writers acknowledge that large state mental hospitals in the USA were clearly suited to custodial care and frequently had numerous deleterious effects on the patients who resided in them. Among these effects were incarceration with little attempt at adoption by the patient of behavior patterns dysfunctional to successful re-entry into the community.

When the community Mental Health Act was passed in 1963, heroic efforts got underway to do everything possible to avoid the evils of hospitalization.

The hospital is now seen as a launching pad or staging point. It is a place where people and forces are regrouped and retrained quickly to rejoin the struggle in society (Abroms, Greenfield, 1971, p 3).

Community programs as developed in the United States consisted of two essential features: (1) The establishment in the community of psychiatric services for the mentally ill which would have previously been part of the state hospital program. The emphasis is on brief hospitalization, the stabilization of acute crisis emergency situations, and the use of diverse community supports for the mentally ill person to limit and minimize the effects of his or her condition. (2) The establishment of services for those persons who formerly would not have been considered in need of psychiatric care. The emphasis is on indirect services and education in the hope of preventing major psychiatric "breakdowns" under the period of stress (*California Mental Health Services Act,* 1974).

During the period 1960 to 1975, the concept of community mental health became increasingly pervasive as an alternative to prolonged state hospital care. Institutions began vigorously competing with each other to report shorter and shorter hospital stays. Yet the contemporary system of psychiatric care has also become a highly prescriptive, elaborately formal structure of policies, regulations, and standards that require participating units to comply with multiple reviews, evaluations, and procedures to qualify for funds.

In effect, the state hospital "warehouse" has been replaced by a similarly "bureaucratized clearinghouse." Large numbers of highly diversified patients are held, medically screened, patched together, stamped with a label, sorted, and dispersed back into the community as quickly as possible and under the pressure of high demand for available beds. This process, termed variously as crisis intervention, evaluation and referral, triage, and administrative psychiatry, is conceptualized in this chapter as a *dispatching process.* The core analytical idea of dispatching explains most of the basic social processes that occur in day-to-day life in the study setting and others like it.

This chapter reports results of a qualitative case study of "usual psychiatric treatment" offered to patients in a community health center's locked wards. The intent of this research was to develop a conceptual explanation of basic processes of usual treatment in settings that share the conditions found in the study setting. The analysis is based on qualitative field data and was undertaken from a symbolic interactionist perspective. It includes comparisons with other settings possessing similar characteristics. The questions that guided this study included: (1) What are the basic social and psychological processes involved in "usual psychiatric treatment"? (2) What are the properties or characteristics of these processes? (3) Under what conditions do they occur and under what conditions do they vary? (4) What strategies are employed in their implementation and with what consequences?

This is a study designed to discover and conceptualize a relevant analytic explanation of the social psychology of a particular milieu. It was not intended primarily as an accurate and precise description of static or transitory features of single setting; nor was it geared to test any preconceived hypotheses deduced from existing theory. Through observations of behavior in its natural setting, this study provides a comprehensive and integrated rendition of "usual treatment" within the community mental health approach in the United States.

THE STUDY SETTING

The major setting that provided the data for this analysis was a psychiatric inpatient service near San Francisco, California. At the time of data collection, it comprised two locked units in a wing of a large community general hospital. Although located physically in a medical center hospital, the units are officially part of the California Community Mental Health System and *not* the hospital *per se*. The inpatient facility has a bed capacity of approximately 60 with a monthly admission rate ranging from 200 to 280 patients. Both units are staffed with psychiatrists, a psychologist (serving both wards), social workers, nurses, community workers, psychiatric technicians, and mental health workers with a staff-patient ratio of approximately 1:2.5 on the day shift. Almost all of the patients receive psychotropic medications. Physically, the wards appear like long, dreary hallways with a central nurses' station, staff or examining rooms, medication rooms and kitchens. Patient bedrooms, usually two to three person occupancy, line both sides on the halls. Both wards have a "day-room" type area with a TV set and furniture, but these are seldom used by the patients for congregating. Instead, patients lie on their beds or stand around the outside of the nurses' station.

DATA COLLECTION AND ANALYSIS

From January through June in the 1970s, data were collected on the two inpatient units approximately twice per month (120 hours) using field notes and interviews in accordance with conventions of field research used by anthropologists and sociologists (Schatzman, Strauss, 1973). Although most of the blocks of time spent in the settings took place during the day shift (7:00 AM to 4:00 PM), observations during the afternoon and night shifts occurred as well. The days of the week were alternated so as to capture as much of the variation in social patterns as seemed feasible. Field notes were recorded during the observation time in order to avoid relying on recall. Informal interviews with all levels of staff on both units were conducted. Reports, team meetings, group intake interviews, ward meetings for patients, occupational therapy activities, etc, were all observed. All documents available on the units including the Kardex, patients' charts, nursing worksheets, staffing work schedules, bulletin board notices, guidelines for medical coverage, manual on aftercare facilities, patients' rights statements, etc, were also analyzed. Observations were guided by the notion of theoretical sampling—a strategy for achieving saturation of conceptual categories by logically elaborating the comparative situations that might help to develop an emerging concept and then setting out to look for them. This sampling methodology has been referred to by sociologists Glaser and Strauss in *The Discovery of Grounded Theory* (Glaser, Strauss, 1967).

FINDINGS: THE DISPATCHING PROCESS

Original expectations for the community mental health movement may have been limited to making mental health care accessible, optional, and protective of the legal rights of patients. Certainly the codified rigidity of the old state hospital warehouse has not been solved by the new clearinghouse approach. Instead of storing the mentally ill, "usual psychiatric treatment" in the USA consists of an elaborate and complex process for dispatching them. Dispatching is a core analytic variable that encompasses the multiple operations, conditions, strategies, tactics, and consequences of processing patients through a clearinghouse (Wilson, Kneisl, 1983). Properties of the dispatching process include (1) a highly formalized and prescriptive set of procedures which govern and constrain its operation, (2) an intensely felt time pressure that derives from a number of sources including legal mandates concerning limits on involuntary confinement of psychiatric patients and the influx of new admissions constantly lining up for the limited bed space, (3) an ideological context that simultaneously advocates administrative efficiency and medical model theory and treatment, and (4) limited resources and options for dispersing patients back into community placements.

Each of the stages in the dispatching process that constitutes "usual psychiatric treatment" is reviewed in the following sections.

Piecing a Story Together

Proportionately speaking, most of the staff members' time and energy is devoted to the first stage of the dispatching process. Information-gathering and intelligence tactics consume the staff's focus during the first 72 hours (and sometimes longer) of a patient's confinement. A key focus during this phase is the interaction of staff members attempting to uncover information about a patient in order to engage in fate-making decisions while the patients are attempting to cover up what they believe to be damaging data about themselves.

Patients are generally viewed as wanting to "get out of here" and feeling that they are undergoing some sort of imprisonment. Consequently, patients tend to learn the scripts for getting out, or at least try to pick these scripts up. One patient asked me, "Does it go against you to be lying down for two hours in a row" (field note).

The major modalities for this interactive contact are the "group intake interview," where a newly admitted patient is confronted by a group of six to 12 staff members in an interview room and questioned in a mildly interrogative style, and the "second hand report," where bits and pieces of data are passed along from shift to shift verbally and on the patient's chart. These are used to make generalizations about the patient: "a little socialization," "somewhat reclusive," "superficially appropriate," "looks flat," "very poor insight," "high as a kite, may be hallucinating" (field note).

Often, the requirement to exchange such tidbits of information with each other is the only press to "get out there and talk to my patient so I have something to chart and report." It seems sufficient to have a comment to make without much concern about how representative that comment may be. Staff members tend to latch onto a tidbit for reporting purposes that later may become reified because of constant repetition in shift reports and charts without additional exploration.

On one occasion a concern was expressed about things people chose to tell in report because of the way things get "latched onto around here." For example, a patient may acquire a label as a homosexual or heroin addict because of revealing one experimental experience (field note).

Another characteristic of the information-gathering process is a correctness assumption. Frequently, staff members have decisions already made—that a patient will get medication even though the patient has expressly refused it, or that a patient will not be discharged at the end of 72 hours but will, indeed, be certified for 14 days. The contact with the patient is then used more to ferret out cues that enable the staff to justify a decision that had already been made.

In addition to a correctness assumption on the part of staff, there is a concomitant invalidation of the patient's point of view. A patient's statement that he or she does not want psychiatric help is often used as an indicator that he or she needs it. A patient's crying in the interview is viewed as a psychiatric symptom rather than a predictable response to the immediate social context of the interrogation, locked ward, involuntary confinement, etc.

One patient was reported as being very paranoid . . . delusional because he thinks we're trying to hypnotize him. The subsequent therapeutic decision was to "up" his medications. Another patient was described as "obsessive-compulsive" in her preoccupation about whether we'll evaluate her as crazy. We told her we only wanted to talk about how to help her stop worrying (field note).

In summary, piecing together a story emerges as having a somewhat preconceived quality, relying considerably on speculation that easily becomes truth, on second-hand information, and on some degree of trickery in an effort to "find things out" as quickly as possible.

The Holding Pattern

Following the piecing together of a story and patching together of symptoms within the first phase of dispatching, patients on 72-hour hold waiting for sorting and labeling are kept in a holding pattern where they spend most of their time asleep or otherwise unoccupied. Staff, in dramatic contrast, engage in activities resembling the hustle and bustle of a clearinghouse.

One of the consequences of a holding pattern period during the dispatching process is that structures are set up basically to provide for storage of people and their possessions. Staff spend considerable space in their log-like communication book focused on implementing these structures.

> *Remember, all packages brought in for patients are to be checked for sharps and meds. Let's be consistent. Patients' belongings belong in the closet in the staff room. Put cigarettes in top drawer of nurses' station (field notes).*

Another outcome of the holding pattern is the emergence of standard operating procedures that reflect codified, formalized approaches to patient care problems rather than individualized ones. There is not even any pretense at keeping up the "individualized" rhetoric.

> *The standard operating procedure for sleep medications is that the night nurse gives sleep medications at 12:45 AM. All patients are to try to sleep on their own before then (field note).*

Sorting and Stamping with a Label

While patients are stored in a holding pattern, their symptoms adequately patched up and the pieces of their story being fitted together, a third phase of the dispatching process takes place and occupies the time and energy of staff—that is, sorting patients into legal categories and stamping them with a diagnostic label.

Patients are sorted according to legal status, according to their salvageability, and, in a preliminary way, according to their likely diagnoses. California's mental health legislation provides the major criteria for sorting according to legal status. Admission criteria are the following: (1) dangerous to self, (2) dangerous to others, (3) unfit to care for self, eg, "gravely disabled." Involuntary admission automatically carries with it a 72-hour hold (not counting weekends) for the purpose of "observation and treatment." If staff "still don't know enough" to piece together a story and begin making distributing decisions, patients are certified for 14 days on the same grounds that warranted admission. The 14-day certification can be renewed for patients who are deemed suicidal. For patients deemed dangerous to others, this can be followed by a 90-day post certification. Finally, any patient who is gravely disabled as a result of mental disorder can be conserved for one year. This essentially means that the patient's rights are taken away. In many cases, staff have figured out ways to work this system to do what they want and need to do.

One patient whose 72-hour hold was up was certified as gravely disabled; but since she came in (admission) as suicidal, staff were urged to check that ground as well for the "added clout" (field note).

In many ways, the legal structure in California that limits residential treatment combined with the medical model approach promotes a revolving door pattern of utilization.

We're really limited by what is legal. A specific problem is the patient who is admitted here, put on phenothiazines. We decide to put him on a conservatorship just as he's getting put together due to the drugs. The patient decides to challenge in court. By the sixth day the patient looks pretty together, the judge lets him go, three weeks later the medicine wears off and he's back in again (field note).

Sorting according to who can be helped is a form of triage based on "salvage-ables." Salvageables are distributed differently from those who are not.

This ward is like a managerial triage thing where you have to decide where to put your resources. For the grossly psychotic, you basically have no community options so just push meds to get cognition and affect under control (field note).

Sorting decisions with fateful consequences for patients are based on the non-credibility assumption. The fact that a patient has gotten himself into the hospital is used as evidence that the patient is not managing. The likelihood that his or her story will be received as credible is very slim; particularly if conflicting stories must be considered in the sorting process. There is irony in a system designed to promote revolving door patterns of hospitalization, when the actual use of the community mental health facility becomes grounds for losing one's rights.

There is a range of sentiment about the revolving door patients, from agreement that the hospital facility is an "OK" place to come for a recharging, to the following quote:

There has developed a certain professionalism among the utilizers of the system who have made patientism a career. Such individuals have long given up efforts to establish an adequate adaptive outside coping system. Instead, they have joined in a collusion with psychiatric professionals established to perpetuate maladaptive behavior (field note).

With revolving door patients who are frequent users of the system or patients who have comparatively longer stays, scripts and cues are learned to influence the sorting and fatemaking done by staff. A patient quickly learns that being up and dressed, participating in group meetings, and eating well and keeping out of bed are all viewed as "being pretty good."

Distributing

The community mental health legislation includes an official goal of moving mentally ill persons back into the community as rapidly as possible. Yet psychiatric professionals are constantly balancing this mandate against their perceived mandate to act as society's and the patient's protectors. Distributing is the final state of the dispatching process. It involves the dispersement of the discharged patient to one of a variety of aftercare placements or designating some alternative follow-up option like discharging the patients to their homes but with an outpatient clinic appointment. Distributing patients back into the community goes on under conditions of limited placement resources, most of which have lengthy criteria for accepting a patient. Some agencies want to "cream off" patients with whom they will not be successful. Others refuse to "put up with a lot of crap" (field note).

Strategies for distribution   Because of the conditions for distributing, a major strategy is that of matching the patient with the aftercare setting's criteria, often with some necessary and artificial adjustments.

> *A patient is brought in to change her meds because it's particularly hard to find an aftercare placement that will take a pregnant woman on phenothiazines. They are afraid of lawsuits (field note).*

For a different category of patients, the distributing decisions are virtually automatic, in that there are no options. These patients are distributed to the "last resort" facility, having used up all other possibilities in the past.

> *The foster home doesn't want B back. She was combative and assaultive. Our plan is just to get her into the state hospital. It is finally the only option for her. No facility will take him. He's going to one of the 'hotels' on Deepo Prolixin. Something should be attempted in the form of aftercare. It's part of our responsibility, but we've all had a lot of problems with him for a long time (field note).*

The analysis points not to the desirability of the old state hospital system but rather argues that the system originally set up as a competitive alternative to the state hospital has done so little to develop deinstitutionalizing alternative forms of residential care. Future research will undoubtedly be guided by the recognition that deinstitutionalization is less related to the locus of care and its funding arrangement than to the processes and patterns of interaction that limit self-care and self-determination wherever they occur (Wilson, 1982).

Some distributing decisions are bargained with patients. The consequence of this bargaining strategy is that the inpatient facilities play a vital role in educating society's troublesome elements about where the tolerance ranges lie.

The second major property of distributing is its link with the social control and guardianship roles delegated to the psychiatric professions.The options for aftercare placement include medication, follow-up groups, board and care homes, outpatient groups, locked facilities, shorter term treatment centers, conservatorships, etc. Staff must balance the options to preserve some semblance of patient's rights while keeping society's troublesome persons out of trouble. The psychiatric staff and public defender are further pitted against each other, each claiming to act in the patient's interests. The public defender is charged with defending the patient's civil rights, and the psychiatric profession is intent upon meeting his or her needs for treatment and protecting society, if necessary. Staff conclude that the pressures to move patients out in order to make bed space and keep within the law must be balanced with the pressures to keep patients in the hospital for their protection and safety.

CONCLUSION

Dispatching emerges as the central pattern of usual psychiatric treatment in American psychiatric inpatient units such as the setting for this research. Similar settings exist throughout the country. These locked units must fill the social control gap left by closing traditional state mental hospitals. The psychiatric professionals in these settings must become agents of the community. Regardless of how much the community may hope for and desire successful treatment of the mentally ill, it demands safe custody of those individuals it rejects.

Viewed in this light, the inpatient psychiatric facility must respond to multiple and contradictory messages. It stands at the intersection of community care ideology and legislation and the tradition of institutionalism with its emphasis on isolation and custodialism. It must protect the community but at the same time guarantee the patient's rights. It must provide for custodial needs of individuals whom society rejects and yet facilitate return as quickly as possible to the rejecting community.

Dispatching is a complex process. Among its consequences for the usual psychiatric treatment milieu are: (1) a very hectic and busy pace of work for staff members while the hours drift by for patients; (2) a low accessibility of staff for patients—sitting and talking with patients has very low priority in view of all the tasks that must be accomplished; (3) a substitution of technology for potential face-to-face contacts (eg, there is a mechanical cigarette lighter on the wall to discourage patients from bothering staff in report, team meetings, intake interviews, etc). Even ritualized staff-patient interaction sessions like "anger groups" and "feelings groups" are low on spontaneity and openness, and high on superficiality and control; (4) staff are the constants on the unit with patients only passing through—thus, a lot of energy is devoted to intra-staff interaction, conflict, problems, and the distribution of work.

The preceding analysis highlights America's community psychiatry movement's lack of true innovation. Lest it be used to justify a retreat from the principles of community psychiatry, it is placed in sufficient context to make these apparent criticisms understandable in light of the circumstances. Leaving aside these contextual considerations makes it easier to find community psychiatry's deficiencies sufficient to conclude that the whole thing was a mistake.

References

Abroms GM, Greenfield NS: *The New Hospital Psychiatry.* New York, Academic Press, 1971.

California Mental Health Services Act. California, Health & Welfare Agency, 1974.

Caudhill WA: *Psychiatric Hospital as a Small Society.* Cambridge, Massachusetts, Harvard University Press, 1958.

Glaser B, Strauss A: *The Discovery of Grounded Theory: Strategies for Qualitative Research.* Chicago, Aldine, 1967.

Goffman E: *Asylums.* New York, Doubleday, 1961.

Schatzman L, Strauss A: *Field Research.* Englewood Cliffs, New Jersey, Prentice-Hall, 1973.

Stanton A, Schwartz MS: *The Mental Hospital.* New York, Basic Books, 1954.

Wilson HS: (1982) *Deinstitutionalized Residential Care for the Mentally Disordered: The Soteria House Approach.* New York, Grune & Stratton, 1982.

Wilson HS, Kneisl CR: *Psychiatric Nursing,* ed 2. Menlo Park, California, Addison-Wesley, 1983.

16

Creating meaning: a grounded theory of NICU nurses

Sally A. Hutchinson

The ICU nurse works day-to-day in a setting where death is commonplace; where patients are desperately ill, mutilated and comatose . . . ; where the work load is demanding both intellectually and physically and the work space limited; where health care equipment is extremely intricate and malfunctioning may mean disaster in the form of patient lives; and where communication between peers and co-professionals is often strained or virtually nonexistent (Gentry et al, 1972, p 794).

Recognizing that intensive care units (ICUs) are indeed stressful for nurses, researchers have produced a growing body of literature that attempts to scientifically study stressors, ICU nurses, and coping methods (Hay, Oken, 1972; Huckabay, Jagla, 1979; Oskins, 1979; West, 1975). Literature that specifically examines neonatal intensive care units (NICU) focuses on nurses' stress and coping strategies (Jacobson, 1978; Marshall, Kasman, 1980); staff-parent communication (Bogdan et al, 1978; Perrault et al, 1979); and parent-infant bonding (Nugent, Goldsmith 1979). Price (1979) found that NICU nurses experience high levels of burnout; Duxbury and Theissen noted high staff turnover rates (1979); and both burnout

Reprinted with permission. Revised version of a paper published in *Nursing Outlook,* Vol 32, No 2, 1984, pp 86–90.

and turnover are viewed as being related to poor patient outcome (Duxbury et al, 1982).

Using NICU nurses' anecdotes and content analysis, Jacobson (1978) delineated five categories of "most stressful incidents." They include the following: (1) nurse-doctor problems; (2) understaffing and overwork; (3) sudden death or relapse of an infant; (4) insecurity about knowledge and competence; and (5) shock and impact of sights and smells. Marshall and Kasman (1980) discuss general individual and organizational strategies for dealing with these stressors; however, no researcher has yet addressed the social-psychological processes of providing care to critically ill newborns. An understanding of these processes should be useful in illuminating how NICU nurses do their work and how they get satisfaction within the constraints of a busy, stressful unit. The purpose of this chapter is to identify and describe the social psychological processes nurses use in a Level III Neonatal Intensive Care Unit.

THE NEONATAL UNIT

The research took place in a 20-bed Level III university hospital NICU. Level III units are designed to care for critically ill newborns with the most sophisticated technical equipment available. Babies arrived from the delivery room and by ambulance or helicopter from hospitals with Level I and II units. The average length of stay was 21 days. Thirty full-time nurses, four neonatologists, house officers, physicians' assistants, and respiratory therapists staffed the unit. Most of the babies were premature while others suffered severe birth defects. Death was not uncommon.

METHOD

Grounded theory methodology was used to generate a substantive theory explaining the basic social psychological process (creating meaning) inherent in a Level III NICU. Data collection methods included participant observation and interviews, both of which aided in understanding the nurses' perceptions of and meanings attributed to their NICU world. For 20 hours a week for four months, observations and informal and formal interviews involved nursing staff, physicians' assistants, physicians, and families. Interviews with nurses involved new and seasoned nurses, nurses on all shifts and in all positions of the hierarchy. Twelve in-depth interviews served to clarify and validate the observations.

Additional data came from staff meetings, a workshop on neonatal care, and helicopter and ambulance runs to pick up critical newborns. Experiences, observations, personal thoughts, and ideas about theory and method comprised field notes which were usually written in the unit and then expanded and typed later that day. Sensitivity to the participants and the affective tone of the unit occasionally required that the notes be written after leaving the unit. For example, if a baby had just died, or if the nurses were unusually angry or upset, the obvious writing of notes was inappropriate.

The wide left-hand margin of the double-spaced field notes allowed for substantive coding that began during the data collection process. Such codes are also called in vivo codes and may be the exact words that the participants (nurses) use. Examples of early substantive coding in this research were "checking the ventilator setting," "crying," "going sour," and "responding to the apnea alarm." Each sentence and each incident was coded into as many codes as possible to insure full theoretical coverage. For example, an incident was coded as both "checking the ventilator setting," and "watching the monitors."

With time and by working with and understanding the data, the substantive codes were collapsed into larger categories. "Checking the ventilator setting," "observing the baby's color," and "fixing the temperature probe" became the category of "monitoring." The incidents' codes and categories, via the constant comparative method, were compared again and again to each other until they were mutually exclusive and covered all behavioral variations.

Theoretical constructs, the third and highest level of codes, are derived from theoretical and clinical knowledge. Such constructs contribute theoretical meaning and scope to the theory (Glaser, 1978). Creating meaning, a theoretical construct in this research, essentially conceptualized the relationship between the three levels of codes and, therefore, became the basic social psychological process (BSP) of the theory.

Grounded theory coding methods are designed to help a researcher discover a basic social psychological process that is a response to the basic social psychological problem (in this case, horror). A BSP—creating meaning—is the main theme that illuminated the observed behaviors in the setting. A BSP, also called a core variable, reoccurs frequently in the data, links the various data together, and explains much of the variation in the data. All codes, categories, and theoretical constructs are related to the core variable. Creating meaning emotionally, technically, and rationally (the three stages of creating meaning), and their strategies, conditions, and consequences are all directly related to the BSP creating meaning. The structure of the theory is formed by the relationships among the component parts. Creating meaning functioned as a BSP since it explained so much of the behavioral variation in the data. It was used as a guide to selectively code the related data.

Certain questions asked during the coding process helped in discovering the BSP and its properties: (1) What is going on in the data? (2) What are these data a study of? (3) What is the basic social psychological problem these people must deal with? And (4) What basic social psychological process helps them cope with the problem? These questions essentially force theoretical thinking rather than empirical thinking.

Generating a theory requires theoretical sensitivity and the process of writing memos enhances such sensitivity. Writing memos involves recording ideas on index cards in an effort to capture the initially elusive and shifting connections.

Several hundred cards, headed by the emerging codes and categories, document the researcher's thinking process. For example, questions in this study included, "Is humanizing a strategy of attaching or a consequence of attaching? Is humor a kind of separate condition or is it a condition for creating meaning rationally?" Memos were written on legal pads to document lengthier ideas that demonstrate the evolution of the theory. Through writing memos, the conditions, causes, and consequences of the BSP and its stages became clear.

The sorting process, which follows memo writing, puts the "fractured data" (Glaser, 1978, p 116) together into a coherent theory and aids in forming the outline for the write up of the theory.

FINDINGS: NURSES' COPING STRATEGIES

In our society, the ideal infant is chubby, happy, healthy, and loveable. The NICU presents us with extreme violations of the ideal baby; this explains much of the horror nurses experience when working with abnormal, incomplete, unappealing, and dying infants. This problem of "horror," which was identified during data analysis, is especially evident in new NICU nurses. According to *The Random House Dictionary*, 1973, horror is "an overwhelming and painful feeling caused by something frightfully shocking, terrifying or revolting; a shuddering fear: to shrink back from a corpse in horror" (p 685).

Visual, aural, tactile, and emotional stimuli elicited horror and most nurses reported feeling horror at some time during their NICU experience, either as a new nurse, and/or when they were having a particularly difficult time coping. Jacobson described new and experienced nurses "being haunted day and night" by a baby's appearance or smells (p 149). One nurse expressed feeling "so unbelievably bad" when she had to take an anacephalic baby to the morgue: "I could feel the spinal cord in my hand," she said. One nurse lamented over the multiple problems a baby had suffered with—several surgeries, cardiac and respiratory arrests—and the mother had literally screamed with anguish on the unit. "Nobody deserves a child like this," the nurse moaned. A seasoned evening nurse came on duty, took one look at a new baby who had tubes coming from every organ and said with horror, "Oh, my God! Is this one for me?" One nurse who held a baby down so he could be stuck repeatedly by a resident said she could still feel his little fingers clutching her arm in desperation. This baby was going to die soon from a congenital heart defect and the nurse was opposed to the "unnecessary" blood work.

Other nurses described physical responses to the horror: "I felt my breath being taken away," "I felt my face contort," "I felt physically sick," and "I felt tears coming when I saw that baby gasp." Several nurses revealed dreams that were horrible. One nurse dreamed of the hum of the machinery and said that the beeping carts transporting people in airports reminded her of the NICU and the dying babies. Another nurse had a dream "of a baby being hooked up to a respirator on one of those big brown clipboards. The baby was on the kitchen sink, had hair coming off his body and was breathing really fast.''

The acknowledgement of horror forced the questions: In an environment of horror, how are nurses able to do their work? What allows them to survive and choose to work day after day?

The analysis of 300 pages of typed field notes helped formulate an answer: Nurses combat horror by *creating meaning*. Creating meaning is an active process requiring an expenditure of psychological energy by the nurse. Meaning does not merely exist within the unit. Rather, the nurse must create meaning for herself by reconstructing the NICU reality. By offering a new way of seeing, creating meaning reduces the NICU nurses' horror to manageable limits. These nurses create meanings both personal to themselves and shared by other NICU nurses. One nurse said exuberantly: "I love the tiny babies." Another said: "I feel anything I can do to help is better than nothing. I feel rewarded when babies get better." And another said, "My meaning comes mainly out of working with the parents—explaining everything to them so they feel okay about what we are doing." Those nurses who stay in the NICU believe in the value of their work.

Creating meaning is a three focused process: creating meaning emotionally, creating meaning technically, and creating meaning rationally. This process produces a mixture of perspective and awareness unique to NICU nurses. In any given situation, the nurse focuses on a selected cluster of stimuli and creates his or her own interdependent combination of emotional, technical, and rational meaning. Because these meanings are processes, they are never complete and they occur over time. After a period of socialization, when a nurse learns to create meaning, he or she continues to create meaning in all three ways (see Figure 16–1).

The three foci are indicative of differing levels of emotional distance from the baby. When a nurse creates meaning emotionally, she is closest to the baby; creating meaning technically, the nurse distances herself enough to function adequately; creating meaning rationally, she is most removed.

Creating Meaning Emotionally

Creating meaning emotionally demands affective involvement by the nurse. Nurses must acquire some degree of emotional investment in the infants in order to do their jobs well and feel good about their work. They create meaning emotionally by attaching and separating. *Attaching* is a cognitive/emotional process of attributing meaning to the babies for whom a nurse cares.

Manifestations of attaching include behaviors that are personalizing. "We make babies into people," said one nurse. Talking to babies demonstrates attaching: "You'd better be good;" "Hi, sweetie;" and "You are a very sick little baby" are examples. Touching, including patting, rubbing, kissing, and cuddling are attaching behaviors that are frequently seen. One physician laughingly told me after we saw a nurse kiss a baby on the top of the head, "I don't know if I should be glad to see that or if I should tell them not to do it because of the germs. I just look the other

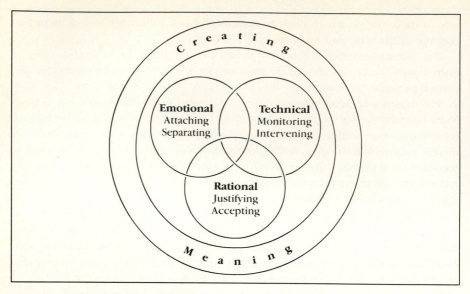

FIGURE 16–1.   Creating Meaning.

way.'' Toys in the isolette, jingle bells tied on a ribbon around a baby's wrists, or a mobile are examples of personalizing influences.

Because babies go home, are transferred, or die, nurses must not only attach but also separate. *Separating,* like attaching, is an emotional process and involves such feelings as grief, anger, guilt and, at times, relief that a baby has died or joy when he has gone home. The separating process is often painful; in order to create emotional meaning, a fine balance is required between attaching and separating. As one nurse stated

> *You get a baby that weighs a pound and a half or two pounds and the way you reason it out is if it doesn't make it, after all the things they go through, like a bleed and seizures and all that bad stuff, then you feel like it's a blessing that they go.*

Another nurse said she occasionally went to the funerals of "my babies." "I go for the parents, and for me, too." By creating meaning technically and rationally, nurses are helped with the separating process.

Conditions for Creating Meaning Emotionally

Conditions or "qualifiers" (Glaser, 1978, p 74) refer to these factors essential for the actualization of the social psychological processes under study. Conditions for creating meaning emotionally include the following:

Adequate staff   If a nurse is overworked by not having enough time off or by having to care for too many babies or too many critical babies (babies on respirators), attaching becomes more difficult. One needs time to get emotionally involved, to get to know the baby, and to personalize care.

Appearance   The appearance of the baby often affects the attaching process. The nurse's personal idiosyncracies determine which babies she responds to more quickly. For example, one nurse said she loved "the tiny scrappers" (very small preemies who are feisty).

Medical surgical crises   The degree of attachment is directly proportional to the number and severity of crises. Crises demand involvement and energy from the nurse which increases emotional involvement.

Strong positive or negative relationships with parents   If a nurse feels empathy and concern for the parents, there is a greater likelihood she or he will become emotionally involved with the baby. Anger towards the parents may also increase attaching behaviors. If a baby is being put up for adoption or is not visited by his parents, or if the mother was on drugs or known to be promiscuous, the nurse generally gets very involved with the baby.

Nurses, by evaluating the parents, essentially act as child advocates. A strong, positive identification with the parents or a negative identification requires energy that is directed toward the infant. Love and hate appear on one side of the continuum; apathy on the other.

Time   Time facilitates attaching behaviors. The longer a nurse cares for a baby, the more involved she becomes. Due to the necessity of these conditions for nurses to create meaning emotionally, it is possible that some nurses do not attach to the babies in their care. However, one nurse said, "With enough time, most nurses get involved with their babies."

Creating Meaning Technically

In order to create meaning technically, the nurse must learn to give the babies sophisticated technical care. And the nurse must derive meaning from her involvement in this care. The ability to give the care gives something back to the nurse. Nurses talk about feeling proud they "saved" a baby or "intubated" a baby in distress. They value their knowledge and skills and recognize that both are vital to babies' lives and to their own ability to work on the unit. The giving of technical care is the most time-consuming part of the nurses' work. Essentially, a nurse's eight-hour day is spent giving technical care.

Technical knowledge and skill are necessary for nurses to assess babies' conditions and make the appropriate interventions. The NICU demands a new way of seeing. A new nurse noticed a baby "sucking," as she called it, and "shivering." A seasoned nurse told her these were seizures. A new nurse noticed "teeth" in a newborn. In fact, they were not teeth but sucking blisters. A nurse has to know what she is seeing, the meaning and consequences of it, and possible interventions.

The nurse's skills are tested constantly by the vast amount of complex technical equipment she must use. Nurses need to understand the working of the equipment, its strengths and limitations, and be able to manipulate the myriad of tubes and devices that are part of most NICU babies' existence. Nurses' conversations often involve discussions of the equipment and what procedures they believe they can or cannot do well.

Certain nursing behaviors are vital to the ability to create meaning technically. *Monitoring* behaviors involve listening and observing the babies and the equipment. Monitoring is an on-going omnipresent watchfulness by the nurses. They listen for any sound that indicates a baby in distress. Such sounds may be the alarm of an apnea monitor signaling cessation of breathing or the temperature alarm warning of a change in temperature. While observing, a nurse may notice a tube that has become detached, unexpected bleeding, or a baby turning blue. Being alert requires the expert use of all five senses. Note the following examples:

> Sight: *"You watch color and chest movement."*
> Smell: *"You can smell a septic baby. They smell like they look—green."*
> Hearing: *"You listen for wheezing which may be a sign of pneumonia, and grunting which means a baby is gasping for air."*
> Touch: *"On a newborn you check the grip and the sucking reflex. With certain babies, you check for pitting edema. The feeling of the skin changes right before death."*
> Taste: *"If you kiss a baby and he taste salty (they smell salty, too), you suspect cystic fibrosis."*

A nurse must use her senses masterfully in checking on the technology. Often the alarms are malfunctioning or are "too sensitive," filling the NICU with a cacophony of sounds. The nurses rely on their expertise via their senses to assess when and if a problem exists.

Observations provide nurses with a systematic basis for decisions about nursing interventions.

> *The baby turned blue and the nurse who was across the room noticed he was having apnea. She quickly sat him up, patting him vigorously. "We'd better keep an eye on him. The apnea alarm would have gone off in another 20 seconds."*

Intervening behaviors may be the mere readjustment of a temperature probe, an alteration in a heart monitor, or a call to a physician to discuss a change. The physician may come to check the baby and order a medication or diagnostic test to obtain further information. More drastic intervening behaviors involve lifesaving maneuvers.

> *A nurse discovered a baby had no blood pressure and very little heart rate. The baby was intubated but no ventilator was available so they "bagged" him. The nurse tried to start an art line but the arteries clamped down. She then tried to start an IV but the vein collapsed. The baby arrested and wouldn't respond to cardiac massage and bagging. The nurse gave intracardiac adrenalin but the baby was dead.*

To monitor accurately and to intervene appropriately requires much technical knowledge, skill, and judgement. If an NICU nurse is not competent in these areas, babies will suffer unnecessarily and can die. The ability to use technical knowledge and skill is translated into meaning of great significance by nurses who choose to work in the NICU. The refinement of this ability is the avenue by which the nurse creates meaning technically.

Conditions for Creating Meaning Technically

Adequate knowledge and skill   A nurse can only create meaning technically if he or she is aware of what is going on with the babies and if he or she is able to decide what to do about it. Recognizing the meanings of blood gas values and their relationship to ventilator settings, specific behaviors that indicate neurological damage, or the necessity of constantly checking the umbilical line are a few examples of knowledge that is essential to being a competent technical NICU nurse. Processing this information and deciding what to do or who to call is the next step. A nurse could be deficient in either part and would then be unable to make technical meaning.

Functional equipment   The nurse is only as good as the equipment. If a certain brand of respirators consistently fails to function adequately, the baby will suffer and the nurses will spend their time working with the machine. Detail workers are frequently in the unit demonstrating new equipment and checking on existing equipment. Nurses' feedback is vitally important.

Necessary information from other professionals   Physicians and respiratory therapists are in and out of the unit writing orders and adjusting the monitoring equipment. Frequently, they do not communicate with the nurse about changes in the baby's care. Or, for example, a respiratory therapist may change a ventilator setting without informing the nurse and this directly affects the nurse's monitoring and intervention with the baby. This uncommunicated intervention by respiratory therapists and physicians is the source of many problems and much frustration for the nurses.

Creating Meaning Rationally

Creating rational meaning out of the NICU experience enables the nurse to maintain a functional mix of compassion and technical competence. By creating meaning rationally, nurses impose a sense of reason or logic on the realities in the NICU. A belief in the triumph of technology prevails. Many occurrences in the NICU may appear absurd, nonsensical, or irrational to observers (for example, the repeated drawing of blood for studies that are useless since the baby is dying; keeping babies with multiple deformities alive artificially). Nurses must make "sense" of these occurrences in order to survive in the unit. "Working here, you have to reason some way or you would go crazy," said one nurse.

Justifying helps nurses create meaning rationally. For example, nurses frequently perform procedures that are painful to babies; they are able to do this because they believe such procedures are necessary for the child's survival. One nurse remarks,

> *"Poking for IVs is gruesome, but you have to have them to keep the baby alive. Did you ever see their poor little feet? Sticking their feet for blood gas analysis is necessary so we can evaluate oxygen levels or they might get brain damage."*

Occasionally a baby who is near death is placed in the NICU.

> *A baby is brought in from the delivery room to die. The nurses go about their work while the baby slowly dies in the corner. Social conversation continues. They made sense of this by saying the baby would not be able to live anyway and they were told by physicians to let it die.*

To tolerate these daily realities and to keep from being overwhelmed emotionally, nurses must create sense or reason. The justification process is a major basis for the creation of sense or reason in an environment filled with abnormality.

Accepting human and technical errors and limitations allows nurses to create meaning rationally. In the NICU, human errors will occur—errors of commission, omission, and timing. Judgement calls are made continuously. For example, a nurse may wean a baby from a respirator too quickly. The nurse may be wrong and may have to live with that reality. Technical errors are a real source of fear and are likely to occur. An arterial line can get disconnected and the baby can "bleed out" (die) in a minute. The failure to turn on the temperature control or accidentally bumping it up or down can cause severe injury. Such accidents do occur and will continue to occur. When many babies are hooked up to multiple monitors and are subject to many tests and procedures, the inevitability of errors is obvious.

Human and technical limitations are revealed in situations in which there are no errors but a baby dies. One nurse relates a case:

> *"We had a baby one time that was almost a year old and he was going home on Saturday. The mother had ordered a cake and everything. He died three or four days before going home. It was terrible."*

The technical equipment and heroics were just not enough to save his life. An accepting attitude prevails: "We did everything we could but the baby still died." The underlying belief of nurses' ability to create meaning rationally could be stated as, "We do the best we can under the most difficult circumstances" (note the justifying and accepting). "Sometimes we have to settle for less but at least we are there trying to make a difference" (creating meaning). The nurse who is able to create meaning rationally believes that all crises eventually end and believes in the healing nature of time.

Conditions for Creating Meaning Rationally

An aerial or transcendent view   Nurses who are able to make sense out of caring for these babies have a longitudinal perspective that transcends the day-to-day traumas. They have knowledge of statistical successes and failures; they believe their care works in most cases. They learn, as one seasoned nurse told me, to know there are only so many bad things that can happen and there are certain correct ways of responding to them. And, they "have seen it all." Acquiring this perspective takes time but is clearly present with most of the "old timers," those nurses who love the NICU and have been there for five or more years.

Black humor   Black humor, an appreciation for the absurd or the bizarre, allows nurses to detach from extremely stressful situations, survive emotionally, and continue to give good care. Such humor is often a source of embarrassment to the staff, in that it makes them question their own feelings of tenderness and caring. On the other hand, they all readily admit the humor permits them to survive and serves as a cohesive force in the unit during times of stress.

Being able to create meaning emotionally, technically, and rationally allows nurses to find meaning when confronted with the painful realities and stresses of the NICU. For each focus a nurse makes a different type of meaning that has its own rewards: feeling concerned and involved, becoming technically competent, and believing that the work makes sense.

Integrating and Balancing

The ability to create meaning focused in one or two ways is not enough. Rather, a nurse must be able to integrate the types of meaning. If a nurse is upset because a baby died, she must, within a short period of time, be able to focus on the technical needs of the other babies, and she must, for her own self, be able to carry on and to continue to find some sense in her work.

An example of what it is like to be a nurse in the NICU demonstrates the necessity for integrating the three types of meaning.

> *A nurse was caring for a very sick baby who would probably die within the day. She worked with the many tubes attached to the baby, discussed the respirator setting with a respiratory therapist and helped put in an arterial line (technical). The baby's grieving parents came in and she talked with them. She finally left the unit, cried for a while, and returned (emotional). Later she said, "This baby really should die. No one deserves a child as sick as this and these parents have had a terrible time. There is nothing more we can do for him" (rational).*

Integrating the three ways of creating meaning is the essence of an NICU nurse's daily work. Integrating allows the nurse to transcend the initial horror of death and the struggle for life by creating meaning in several different ways.

At any minute in the unit, a nurse has the opportunity to create emotional, technical, or rational meaning. In such an overstimulating environment, many stimuli compete for one's attention. The emotional tone of the unit or one's own mood and personal idiosyncrasies make it easier or more difficult to focus on some stimuli rather than others.

Equally important to survival in the NICU is the art of balancing these three processes of creating meaning. If a nurse becomes a technician, devoting all his/her energies to learning about the new equipment and its functioning, and the putting in of arterial lines, etc, other processes of meaning will remain elusive and he/she will only be able to give technical care. The nurse will lack the humanness necessary for babies and parents. He/she may also lack an ability to make sense or meaning of his/her work. Suffering from tunnel vision, technical success may become a dream. One may become a "machine" nurse (a derogatory term used by nurses to describe one doctor), gearing care and attention to machinery rather than to the babies. A balance of all processes is necessary for effective nursing care.

Creating meaning is a complex set of interrelated processes and, as such, is never completed. NICU nurses at every level of experience are always attempting to create meaning by integrating and balancing their responses.

Causes and Consequences of Nurses' Inability to Create Meaning

Occasionally, the integrating and balancing processes of creating meaning fail; this failure is inevitably due to nurses suffering extreme emotional distress. Inadequate staff, overattachment to a baby, multiple deaths over a short period of time, chronic arguments with co-workers, or a breakdown in any of the conditions necessary to creating meaning can cause meaning to be elusive.

If nurses are overworked by not having enough time off or by having to care for too many babies or too many critical babies (babies on respirators), creating meaning is impossible. They cannot relate emotionally to the babies, cannot give safe technical care and surely cannot make sense out of their work. The picture is one of harried frustration and real regret and guilt that "we are not doing what we should be doing," or "it doesn't make sense anymore." One nurse said, "When it gets to the point that I can't give minimally safe care, I'm leaving. And it's getting to that point."

When a nurse becomes overattached to a baby and the baby dies, meaning escapes. For example, one nurse said, "I felt I was Susie's mother. I even called her by my daughter's name. I brought her presents. I thought about her when I was home, and I loved her for five months, night and day." When the baby died, the nurse was distraught and had difficulty functioning for some time. She said later,

"I know I cannot let myself get that attached again. It is too painful and it doesn't work."

If there are many deaths on the unit over a short period of time, nurses question the meaning of their work. When I arrived, 19 babies had just died over a period of three weeks. The nurses and the attending physician talked freely about the despair they felt, how they could barely move to carry out the care for the other babies, and how no explanations for what happened made any sense. The shared grief increased their cohesiveness and appreciation for one another but sapped them of their physical stamina.

Chronic and intense arguments with other nurses, respiratory therapists, and/or physicians can cause severe problems. Complaining, crying with frustration and anger, and violent verbal fights caused some nurses' ability to create meaning to fail. "Going to work is like going to a free-for-all, or slugging contest," said one nurse.

A failure to create meaning over a period of time has severe consequences for the nurses, co-workers, patients, and families. Nurses who feel emotionally drained are chronically unhappy. This negative affective tone directly affects the morale on the unit. Nurses may quit their jobs or get fired. One nurse's letter of resignation said, "I need a break. My whole family is falling apart because of my work here. I'm emotionally dead." Another letter said, "I'm leaving because I'm tired. I'm tired of working in an environment where the staff nurses receive no positive reinforcement from anyone. I'm tired of inadequate supplies, understocked medications, and having to do the aide's work." A nurse was fired for leaving the unit to go bowling with her team. Her shift was over, but a replacement for the nurse did not show up, so she was expected to stay until another nurse arrived. At that point, bowling was more important to her than her job.

IMPLICATIONS

The grounded theory method of theory generation made possible the exploration and illumination of the NICU culture. After hundreds of hours of observing, interviewing, and analyzing the international processes of the NICU, a transcending meaning emerged. Creating meaning with its three elements is a means of professional survival. NICU nurses should be educated about this process and encouraged to develop innovative strategies for creating meaning. Adequate preparation for the essence of NICU nursing—confronting horror and resolving it through creating meaning—should serve to decrease staff turnover, low morale, and stress. According to Eisner, the "validity of this research is the product of the persuasiveness of a personal vision: its utility is determined by the extent to which it informs" (1981, p 6).

References

Benfield G, Lieb S, Vollmen J: Grief response of parents to neonatal death and parent participation in deciding care. *Pediatrics* 1978;62:171–177.

Bogdan R, Brown, MA, Foster S: Be honest but not cruel: Staff/parent communication on a
neonatal unit. *Hum Organiz* 1982;41:6–16.

Duxbury M, Henley G, Armstrong G: Measurement of the nurse organizational climate of
neonatal intensive care units. *Nurs Res* 1982;31:83–88.

Eisner E: On the differences between scientific and artistic approaches to qualitative research.
Educ Res 1981; 10:5–9.

Gentry WD, Parkes K: Psychological stress in intensive care unit and non-intensive care unit
nursing: A review of the past decade. *Heart Lung* 1982;11:43–47.

Glaser B: *Theoretical Sensitivity.* Mill Valley, California, The Sociology Press, 1978.

Hay D, Oken D: The psychological stress of intensive care unit nursing. *Psychiatr Med*
1972;34:109–119.

Huckabay L, Jagla, B: Nurses' stress factors in the intensive care unit. *J Nurs Admin*
1979;9:21–26.

Jacobson S: Stressful situations for neonatal intensive care nurses. *Matern Child Nurs J*
1978;3:144–150.

Marshall R, Kasman C: Burnout in the neonatal intensive care unit. *Pediatrics* 1980;65:1161–
1165.

Nugent J, Goldsmith J: Parent/infant bonding in a neonatal intensive care unit. *J Louisiana
State Med Soc* 1979;131:235–239.

Oskins S: Identification of situational stressors and coping methods by intensive care nurses.
Heart Lung 1979;8:953–960.

Perrault C, Collinge J, Outerbridge E: Family support in the neonatal intensive care unit.
Dimens Health Serv 1979;56:16–18.

Price ME: Why NICU nurses burn out and how to prevent it. *Contemp Obstet Gynecol*
1979;13:37–46.

The Random House Dictionary of the English Language. New York, Random House, 1973, p
685.

Roget's International Thesaurus. New York, Thomas Crowell Publishers, 1977, p 158.

West N: Stress associated with ICU's affect patients, family, staff. *Hosp* 1975;49:62–63.

17

Getting around with emphysema

Shizuko Y. Fagerhaugh

A major problem for patients with advanced emphysema is their great difficulty in getting around physically because of extreme oxygen shortage. Sociability may be restricted, too, because their respiratory disability interferes with talking, laughing, and crying. In this analysis of the process patients used to cope with problems of physical mobility and sociability, the data are from interviews with 22 patients, 18 men and four women, with advanced emphysema. Most were indigent; and most were divorced, single, or widowed. The majority were elderly.

Time, energy, and money are three basic resources which people—whether sick or well—draw on for physical mobility and sociability. All people have varying amounts of these basic mobility resources (BMRs) that they can juggle and balance for physical mobility and sociability.

Usually, a generous supply of money and energy—wealth and health—enables a person to use time for a high degree of physical and social mobility. If illness or old age decreases a person's energy but he has ample funds, his money can purchase other people's BMRs. His own time and energy can be saved. BMRs may still be balanced when a person has a short supply of both energy and money, but has friends and family.

The majority of the patients I interviewed had meager energy because of old age and advanced emphysema. Several had other chronic conditions.

GAUGING OXYGEN AND ENERGY

The mobility problem in emphysema is primarily the inability to get enough oxygen to produce energy. Patients with advanced emphysema have a limited oxygen reserve that is difficult to maintain. These patients become short of breath with minimal physical activity and require long and frequent periods to "recoup" their diminished oxygen reserve. Recouping oxygen is not an accurate physiological term but was used by one patient I interviewed.

These patients must gauge the oxygen requirement for various activities and relate it to their recoupable supply. Misgauging can result in extreme physical distress—a sense of suffocation, a chance of losing consciousness, and of course, great fatigue. In fact, many patients expressed a sense of panic in misgauged mobility situations.

People with normal lungs ("normals") can carry out several activities simultaneously—walking, talking, and holding a parcel. The patient with advanced emphysema cannot. This patient must consider where he will expend his meager air supply for sociability or other uses. Interviewing these patients can be rather taxing for them and the interviewer because their typical conversation pattern is to talk a bit, pant, talk a bit, and pant. Some patients stated they decreased interactions with others because they sensed their discomfort.

Social situations that provoke anxiety tend to bring on attacks of shortness of breath. A characteristic of emphysema is that anxiety triggers dyspnea which brings on more anxiety, and a vicious cycle develops (Dudley et al, 1968). Therefore, over the long haul, these patients tend to isolate themselves as a defense (Dudley et al, 1969).

All people, whether sick or well, choosing the location of their residence consider the availability of BMRs—work, family, social life, and social values. A person may decide to live in the suburb rather than the city or a certain section of the city by weighing the advantages and disadvantages of the schools, rental costs, time and money for commuting to work, social prestige, proximity to friends, and so forth.

Depending on his BMRs and his life-style, a patient with emphysema must set priorities regarding residential features and topography. The features of both are as follows: (1) terrain of the location—whether flat or hilly, and terrain of the residence itself—first floor, elevator or no elevator, and so forth; (2) distance and terrain from residence to public transportation; (3) distance and terrain to such essential places as a grocery store, cafe, laundromat, and bank; (4) propinquity of mobility assistants (family members and friends).

A patient with money can afford taxis and have groceries delivered. A patient with reliable friends and family with an automobile is less concerned about location of his residence and public transportation than a patient without such friends and family. Patients with limited money often are unable to afford a costly oxygen-saving residence. Moreover, because of limited energy, they frequently cannot do extended residence hunting. Consequently, they settle for whatever meets their oxygen-saving specifications. These patients have to tolerate some bad housing and territorial features in exchange for other features judged more essential in their lifestyle. A few examples follow.

TWO MEN: TWO STYLES

Mr B., a widower, had always lived in an apartment. Unable to afford an apartment in a building with an elevator, he settled for a second-floor apartment within his financial means. It was located on a slightly inclined terrain but he could manage with his oxygen reserve. This apartment was close to a grocery store. He liked to cook and stretched his money by doing his own cooking.

His social interactions were limited primarily to the apartment tenants and the manager. All acted as mobility assistants by picking up a quart of milk or the newspaper for him while doing their own errands. A particularly important person among the tenants was a man with a car. He was useful for the difficult travel situations like getting to the medical clinic. Public transportation to and from the medical clinic meant considerable expenditure of time and energy and required several bus transfers. The patient was careful not to abuse the help of his friend, limiting the mobility requests to those which seemed legitimate and reasonable.

At one time, he was placed on inhalation therapy and this necessitated daily trips to the clinic. Feeling unjustified in requesting daily mobility assistance, he managed the visits by public transportation. After a week of treatment, he stopped therapy because the time and effort spent getting to and from the clinic left him too exhausted to do other necessary tasks—cooking, keeping up the apartment, and doing laundry.

In contrast, a bachelor with a network of casual acquaintances who met regularly at the neighborhood bar chose his residence and how to expend his oxygen quite differently. Due to his deteriorating respiratory and financial conditions, he moved to poorer and poorer residences in the neighborhood where he had lived for many years. One move was from a nice apartment to a single room on the second floor in an inexpensive hotel, which had no elevator.

He reasoned that a room was preferable to a residence with cooking facilities because he hated to cook. Accessible eating places with reasonable prices (he ate only two meals a day to save money) and the neighborhood bar were most important. A goodly amount of air was expended at the bar, as he put it, "shooting the breeze with the guys." The bartender and patrons had known him for many years and his credit was good. He could buy an occasional drink on credit and borrow money from friends. Here he could call on his friends with cars for especially difficult mobility situations.

DISLOCATED LIVES

When life situations change as emphysema progresses, mobility needs and residential locations are altered also. For example, an elderly patient who had lived most of his life in a downtown hotel preferred to remain downtown even after several acute respiratory episodes. The territory was familiar, and public transportation and eating places were close. He was also able to continue living alone by enlisting the aid of an elderly sister. She handled his laundry, ran errands, and invited him to Sunday dinner.

A major change was locating himself in a moderate-cost hotel which had 24-hour clerks. Clerks were important as interceptors of SOS signals should immediate medical attention be needed. Also, they become familiar with a tenant's daily mobility routines and checked if these changed.

Events such as razing an apartment building for urban redevelopment where a patient has several tenant mobility assistants or the loss of mobility agents through illness and death can create difficulties not only in mobilization, but in balancing BMRs as well. For example, an elderly man who lived for many years in an economical boarding house run by an interested and concerned landlady and friendly, long-term boarders, was able to manage on his BMRs. Unfortunately, the landlady developed arthritis and could no longer run the boarding house. The patient could not find comparable housing within his financial means and the loss included his major mobility assistants and his major source of sociability.

For many patients with little money and progressive disease, more and more energy and time are eaten up in bodily subsistence. Cultivation of mobility assistants becomes increasingly crucial. Friendly, likable patients who live in hotels with lobbies where tenants gather to watch television, read, or chat, are more likely to cultivate and recruit mobility assistants than less sociable patients who live in hotels without natural gathering places for tenants.

ROUTING: PROCESS AND STRATEGIES

All people, whether ill or healthy, deal with problems of mobility by routing. The dimensions involved in routing are as follows: (1) anticipation of the number and types of activities in terms of available BMRs; (2) judgments whether to drop or postpone some activities or to condense by combining several activities; (3) sequential ordering of activities in terms of the importance, distance, time, and energy involved in each activity; and (4) anticipation of possible obstacles.

Efficiency in routing depends on the mode (walking, public transportation, another person's car) and on the degree of control over the mode. Efficiency also depends on how much of other people's time is needed to complete an activity. Situations where a person can condense activities in the shortest time are (1) those where one has control over the mode of routing—having money for taxis, owning a car, or having dependable friends or family with an automobile; (2) having control over the sequence and time involved for activities—such as having a prior appointment; and (3) having sufficient energy to combine activities. When a person has no control over mode of routing, efficiency, nevertheless, may be attained by stringent control of sequence or expending more energy to hasten the routing process by running and generally moving fast.

PLANS TO AVOID OVEREXERTION

In emphysema with its characteristic mobility problems, a patient's anticipation and planning of his route are essential if he is to avoid the consequences of overexertion and anxiety. For example, Mr P. lives on the second floor. Before venturing outside, he carefully plans all the necessary paraphernalia and errand lists, and he gauges the time and energy required to reach the bus stop. If he is late for the bus, he cannot run to catch it.

Patients state that when they have forgotten their grocery list, drug prescription, a form for the social worker, or whatever, they become anxious. Their anxiety is due, in part, to irritation with themselves, but also to their dread of making the trip home for the forgotten item or, worse still, climbing the stairs again.

Planning for an ordinary activity like shopping for groceries becomes long and complicated. A patient lives on the second floor; he must recoup oxygen after walking a single block even when it is a flat surface. The route to the grocery store is uphill, so after half a block he must rest to catch his breath.

If he chats with the grocer, he must rest for the trip home. If he carries a bag of groceries, he expends more oxygen than if he did not. So, even though the route home is downhill, he can go only three-fourths of the block before getting winded. Once at home, there is a flight of stairs. Twelve steps can be taken with his usual oxygen supply. If he is carrying groceries, he must stop to get his wind back every six to eight steps. What normals can do in 20 minutes is stretched out to one hour or more.

When he lacks money and, therefore, has little control over mode of routing, the patient may use his time as his chief mobility resource. He expends small amounts of energy over an extended period of time. He may take the roundabout bus route. For example, a patient on a steep terrain walks downhill to catch a bus. After taking care of his business, he transfers to two buses to catch a third bus which stops uphill from his house. Another patient's most direct route to the clinic entails crossing a wide thoroughfare with heavy traffic. Before he gets across, he runs out of breath. He manages his routing by taking a time-consuming, round-about bus route which crosses the unmanageable thoroughfare.

An important routing concern that these patients face is to find appropriate ways to recoup oxygen by locating appropriate "puffing" stations (another descriptive term used by a patient). Sitting down is the preferred way to "get the wind back," but seats are seldom available in public. In public, the prevalent strategy is to start recouping oxygen while one can still stand. Sitting on a street curb can cause a public scene. Moreover, in a skid row area, one might be mistaken for a drunk. Walls, telephone poles, or mailboxes to lean against are considered good puffing stations.

Both cardiac and respiratory patients have stated they do not shop downtown because appropriate puffing stations are lacking. One patient shopped exclusively at a particular department store because the ladies' lounge was easily accessible.

When routing, emphysema patients must weigh the weather more carefully than do healthy persons because they must avoid catching cold. Windy weather is said to increase breathing problems. Also, there is the questions of a tail wind or head wind. And of course, smog greatly increases their dyspnea.

They must also anticipate other unforeseen obstacles. For example, patients living in deteriorated areas of the city where there are many predators tend not to venture outside too often. Should they be accosted, they could not run or have enough air to yell for help.

PLANNING FOR CYCLIC ACTIVITIES

All people have varying daily, weekly, and monthly routing routines. Patients with emphysema must carefully plan theirs. Frequently, they live in difficult terrains (such as the second or third floor) and must plan to avoid unnecessary stair climbing.

Thus, a man who eats all his meals in restaurants planned his daily route so that, once downstairs for breakfast, he delayed climbing the stairs until after supper. This, of course, required locating time-killing and rest stations like coffee shops and park benches.

Another patient who did her own cooking made an every-other-day trip to the grocery store. This not only gave her a change away from her apartment, but also enabled her to socialize with the grocer and her neighborhood acquaintances. Also, the grocery bag was lighter than the weight from once-a-week shopping.

Routing must be planned so that on days that require an increased energy output (cleaning the apartment), shopping is not considered. Healthy people tend to think of routing only when great distances are involved, but not emphysema patients. One patient who becomes short of breath after a few steps requires two or three hours to dress. She gets up and goes to the bathroom, rests, washes while sitting in a chair, and takes several rest periods. She then walks back to the bedroom, rests, and dresses with frequent rest periods.

Another patient who mops his kitchen floor every week worked out an elaborate routing pattern. He gathers the cleaning paraphernalia and puts it and a chair in the middle of the room. He then mops a few strokes and sits to rest.

When I was arranging for interviews, patients not only specified certain days, but time of day. "Come in the morning around ten because I'll be too tired to talk in the afternoon," or "Come by in the afternoon. I rest after lunch and will be less tired."

MEDICAL REGIMEN AND MOBILITY

The long-term medical regimen for emphysema patients aims primarily to hold the line and to compensate for irreversible lung damage. The regimen includes preventing further lung deterioration (by treatment); preventing acute respiratory infections; and helping patients breathe easier by using drugs and inhalation therapy, ridding their lungs of accumulated mucus by postural drainage and drugs, and conditioning themselves to breathe more efficiently by breathing exercises and breath control (Berdixen et al, 1965; Boren, 1965; Farber, Wilson, 1968; Kinney, 1967; Nett, Petty, 1967; Petty et al, 1969).

How well a patient complies with treatment is determined in part by how much the regimen interferes with his life-style and mobility needs. In part, it also depends on how well he comprehends the uses and effects of therapy.

Sometimes a patient's condition warrants extended inhalation therapy. This may require daily outpatient clinic visits, or inhalation equipment may be sent to the home. Patients may not see the value of daily outpatient visits when they consider the time and energy spent in reaching the clinic. When professionals send respirators to a residence, their well-intentioned help may not be perceived as helpful. Inhalation therapy is often ordered two to three times a day. For patients who live on the second floor and must limit stair climbing, a two- to three-times-daily treatment means virtual imprisonment or maneuvering the stairs several times a day. Confinement in their rooms is often depressing. Several patients thought inhalation therapy was a big nuisance and requested the doctor to discontinue it.

Sometimes drugs via aerosol spray are prescribed for immediate relief of periodic respiratory distress. These drugs may be ordered three to six times a day at a maximum because of undesirable side effects (Eisenstadt, 1969). When an activity requires prolonged oxygen expenditure, there is a likelihood of drug overdose since these sprays supply the extra energy to complete an activity. One patient patted his portable nebulizer, stating it was his "lifesaver" as it gave him the needed energy spurt in difficult routing situations. Although he had been warned by the physician about overdosing, he unfortunately did not know the symptoms of overdose.

Bronchodilator drugs help breathing but often cause nervousness and sleeplessness. Sometimes the sedatives required to counteract these side effects leave the patient groggy. Not infrequently, balancing of the two drugs can become a problem. When health professionals are not attentive to a patient's drug balance problems, he may doubt the usefulness of the therapy and the competence of his physician.

Patients' criteria for therapeutic effectiveness are based on how well the therapies help them to be mobile in their daily routing schedules. They may omit a drug to see what difference it makes. A man whose daily route included a walk to the park tested the therapy by judging its effect on his ease in walking to the park and over its various kinds of terrains. This is in contrast to the elaborate laboratory criteria used by professionals and to the inaccurate standards found in patients' medical charts: "Gets short of breath after one block, two blocks."

One of the more disheartening facts uncovered by the interviewing was that professionals neglect to teach rehabilitation measures to patients, such as respiratory exercises, respiratory hygiene, and conditioning for more efficient breathing.

In my experience, the current emphysema medical scene primarily emphasizes the critical respiratory episode treated in acute care facilities. There are heroic efforts to mobilize patients for survival but no real assistance to help them effectively mobilize for living once the acute episode is over.

OTHER CHRONIC DISORDERS

In short, the general process by which emphysema patients cope with physical mobility include (1) calculating the availability of basic mobility resources—time, energy, and money; (2) gauging oxygen requirement (energy) in relation to the physical and psychosocial consequences of misgauging; (3) making choices and setting priorities about what to be mobile about (which are determined by life-styles and life conditions); (4) developing routing strategies for mobilization which take into account calculating basic mobility resources, physical and psychosocial consequences of misgauging energy requirement, and the particular life-style and social conditions; and (5) weighing whether to follow or disregard the medical regimen in terms of how the regimen impinges on life-styles.

This way of looking at emphysema patients' process for managing mobility needs could be useful in other chronic disorders where lessened energy hampers physical mobility.

Whatever the long-term disability, one would have to consider how the quality and nature of the patient's mobility problem and the treatment regimen impinge on his basic mobility resources and his life-style.

For example, a patient with ulcerative colitis has low energy because frequent diarrhea prevents proper absorption of food. More important, diarrhea interferes with mobility because routing requires locating toilets. His time is preempted by his symptoms, which means that routing requires conserving and scheduling time (Reif, unpublished data, 1971).

In a chronic disorder like arthritis, pain on physical movement is a major factor. This patient must learn to gauge his pain threshold and allow increased time for mobilization.

In neurological disorders such as multiple sclerosis, patients have mobility problems due to loss of energy and motor control. They may require crutches and wheelchairs. This creates other BMR imbalances and life-style changes, which in turn necessitate other routing strategies (Davis, 1970). In addition to BMR imbalances caused by the disease, the psychosocial dimension—for example, shame and embarrassment because of physical disfigurement or clumsy movements—may be a major routing concern.

Cardiac disease and emphysema involve different organs and pathology, but in both conditions energy for physical mobilization is decreased because of oxygen reduction to the body tissues. Selected interviews with cardiac patients indicate that they use routing strategies somewhat similar to those of the emphysema patient. However, in certain cardiac conditions, the results of misgauging one's BMRs are more likely to be fatal than they are for emphysema patients. Cardiac patients have more anxiety related to testing and gauging their energy threshold. This difference is apt to create different life-style changes from those emphysema creates. In other diseases, ulcerative colitis, for instance, the consequences of misgauging may be primarily shame and embarrassment.

The types of questions to ask if a nurse wants to assist patients in mobilization and in improving the quality of their lives are as follows:

- What are the patient's basic mobility resources?
- How do the disability and the medical regimen impinge on his life-style and basic mobility resources?
- What are the physiological and psychosocial consequences of misgauging?
- What are the patient's life-style conditions that shape his mobility needs and priorities?
- What are his daily, weekly, and monthly mobility routines?
- Who are the mobility agents?
- How available and reliable is their assistance?
- What kind of life-related routing assistance would help the patient mobilize best and improve the quality of his life?

Accumulating answers should provide approaches to vital concerns as developing assessment tools, patient education, and social support of outpatients.

References

Bendixen HH, et al: *Respiratory Care.* St Louis, C. V. Mosby Co, 1965.

Boren HG: Pulmonary emphysema: Clinical and physiological aspects, in Baum GL (ed): *Textbook of Pulmonary Diseases.* Boston, Little, Brown and Co., 1965, pp 412–447.

Davis MZ: *Transition to a Devalued Status: The Case of Multiple Sclerosis,* doctoral dissertation, University of California, San Francisco Medical Center, 1970.

Dudley DL, Martin CJ, Holmes TH: Dyspnea: Physiologic and psychological observations. *J Psychosom Res* 1968; 11:325–339.

Dudley DL, Verhey JW, Masuda M et al: Long-term adjustment, prognosis and death in irreversible diffuse obstructive pulmonary syndromes. *Psychosom Med* 1969; 31:310–325.

Eisenstadt WS: Some observations on a new syndrome—respiratory mendicamentos. *Ann Allergy* 1969; 27:188–190.

Farber SM, Wilson RH: Pulmonary emphysema. *Clin Symp* 1968; 20:2.

Kinney M: Rehabilitation of patients with COLD. *Am J Nurs* 1967; 67:2528–2535.

Nett LM, Petty TL: Effective treatment for emphysema and chronic bronchitis. *J. Rehabil* 1967; 33:10–11.

Petty TL, Vett LM, Finigan MM et al: Comprehensive care program for chronic airway obstruction. *Ann Intern Med* 1969;70:1019–1020.

Reif L: *Beyond Medical Intervention: Strategies for Managing Life in the Face of Chronic Disease,* unpublished paper. University of California, San Francisco Medical Center.

18

Entry into a
nursing home
as status passage:
A theory
to guide
nursing practice

W. Carole Chenitz

*When new patients come in here, they often feel abandoned by their families. They
don't understand why they have to be here.* They either lash out or they become
depressed.
*We watch them closely. You have to move quickly, to get to know them and so that
they will trust you. At the first sign from them, you must be there to respond, to get
them to interact. Otherwise it's all over. You can never reach them. They will just be
here and waste away (Chenitz, 1978).*

This nurse was describing how some elders react to their admission to a nursing
home. Because that situation has troubled practitioners for the past twenty-five
years, I undertook a study to generate nursing practice theory that could guide
nursing interventions with elders who are experiencing difficulty in making the
transition to a nursing home. Four specific questions were raised: (1) What are
elders' responses to admission to a nursing home? (2) What conditions lead to
negative responses? (3) What are the consequences to the elder, staff, and family

when elders respond negatively to the nursing home? (4) What are successful and unsuccessful nursing interventions with clients who respond negatively?

Literature review indicated that most early studies measured the effects of relocation in terms of mortality. In comparison to the mortality rates of elders who had not moved recently, higher rates were found among elders recently relocated from home to hospital, from community residential setting to a hospital, and from home to a nursing home (Caramago, Preston, 1945; Costello, Tanaka, 1961; Lieberman, 1961).

Higher mortality rates also were found during mass transfers of elders from one institution to another (Jasnau, 1967; Aldrich, Mendkoff, 1963; Aleksandrowiez, 1961), and even within the same institution (Killian, 1970). Some studies reported higher mortality for specific subgroups of elders (Bourestom, Tars, 1974; Markus et al, 1971). Other studies showed no increased mortality following relocation (Borup et al, 1978, 1980; Gutman, Herbert, 1976; Zweig, Csank, 1976).

Several factors have been identified that affect the outcome of relocation for elders:

- the voluntary or involuntary nature of the move which encompasses decision making (Beaver, 1979);
- the predictability of the move and degree of control elders have over events surrounding it (Schulz, Brenner, 1977);
- the extent of environmental change as a result of the move (Gutman, Herbert, 1976; Bourestom, Tars, 1974);
- the physical and mental health of elders at the time of the move (Kowalski, 1978; Markus et al, 1972; Kral et al, 1968);
- the degree and type of preparation for the move (Jasnau, 1967).

Bourestom and Pastalan point out that "the question no longer is whether relocation has negative (or positive) effects but under what conditions and with what kinds of populations are those negative (or positive) effects most likely to be observed" (Bourestom, Pastalan, 1981, p 7).

METHODS AND PROCEDURE

I used grounded theory methodology: collecting and analyzing data from the actual experiences of those engaged in the move to a nursing home. Data were gathered through observation, formal and informal interviews, and review of medical records.

Data were stored in notes and on tape. Theoretical memos, generated through line-by-line study of the field notes, became capsules of the total analysis. These memos stored principal categories and themes that recurred in the data. Further analysis led to a linking of the memos by a basic process that seemed to explain the events and the experiences of those engaged in these events. The linked memos became the foundation for a theory regarding elders and their entry into nursing homes.

Thirty elders admitted to two nursing homes were interviewed from the time of their admission and several times each week for six to nine months thereafter. These 22 women and eight men were between 63 and 96 years old. The mean age was 79.

In addition to observations of the elders' care and informal interviews with them, their families, the staff in the nursing homes, and physicians the elders' medical records were reviewed.

All 30 elders were alert and oriented on admission. After I had explained the study to them completely, all consented to participate.

The facilities chosen were considered typical of proprietary (the majority of facilities) skilled nursing facilities in the San Francisco Bay area in terms of size, ownership, and method of payment by residents.

Comparative data were collected by observation and interviews with 30 elders receiving home care from visiting nurses. Interviews with elders, staff, and physicians in an intermediate care facility and several other skilled nursing facilities provided additional data for verification and correction of the emerging theory.

DATA ANALYSIS

For theory to assist nurses in their practice, it must meet two prerequisites: it must frame information with enough specificity to guide practice in particular situations and also be generalizable to a variety of situations with different clients. To provide this framework, terms were generated to describe the experiences that emerged. Together, these terms appeared through analysis to capture the process under study. The first such term is *basic condition*; other terms are defined as they arise throughout the chapter.

Basic conditions are the circumstances affecting elders' responses to nursing home admission. These conditions are both global and specific, for example, societal beliefs about family relations and an individual's relationships with immediate family members.

These conditions set the stage for future events and are explanatory of these events. As defined in this study, events are the specific behaviors and occurrences observed. Because human life is complex, both conditions and events lead to a given response to a situation. In this study, these conditions and events are interwoven. The value placed on them by the persons involved lead to the subsequent consequences.

Analysis of these elders' experience in entering a nursing home indicated that before the actual entry, a series of events, situations, and relationships was shaping their responses. Each person responded to the nursing home admission based on his or her individual characteristics, perception, and understanding of this event and his or her relationship with significant family members and friends and personal coping style. In spite of individual differences, however, conditions that appeared basic to the elders' responses to the nursing home, and appeared basic to nurses' understanding of these responses emerged from the analysis. The importance of each condition varied with individuals but the universality and impact of these conditions on the elders in this study suggest they are of principal importance.

The impact of these basic conditions became evident in each elder's subsequent behavior in the nursing home. Hence, in order to understand their response, these conditions will first be discussed separately, then illustrated in the elders' response patterns.

CONDITIONS PRODUCING RESPONSES TO NURSING HOME ADMISSION

A basic condition affecting the elders' response was the *centrality,* or importance, of the admission in their struggle for independence and autonomy, control over their life, or control over how and where they would die. An elder's perception of the degree of disruption that nursing home admission would produce in his or her control was central.

Another basic condition was the desirability of the move. Unfortunately, despite many improvements, the negative image of nursing homes still prevails. This image, combined with the strong desire of today's elders for self-sufficiency, makes becoming a nursing home resident highly undesirable (Hirschfield, Dennis, 1979; Sussman, 1976). To accept admission may mean that elders view themselves as unwanted, dependent, near to death, or worse, senile (Butler, 1975).

For an elder to accept a nursing home admission, *legitimation* must occur. Legitimation is the finding of a plausible reason for the admission that allows elders to see themselves as other than a "typical nursing home patient."

Legitimation for these elders came from a variety of sources: family, friends, physicians, social workers, nurses, or the elders themselves, and usually from a combination of these sources. Legitimation hinged on the reasons for admission: physical, social, familial, medical, financial, and usually on a combination of these reasons.

Legitimation was another essential condition because it provided an incentive. Once the reason for the admission was explained and accepted by the elder, entry into the nursing home was legitimated. The move could be made voluntarily because the elder had accounted for it in his or her self-perception.

Not all elders received legitimation. Time and problematic or distant family relationships were two main factors that hindered legitimation. The elder's physical health was another intervening factor among time, family relationships, and legitimation.

A common route into an American nursing home is by way of the acute care hospital. During the average 10-day stay, elders with flareups of chronic disease, acute illness, or trauma are in varying states of physical, mental, and emotional health. For several study subjects legitimation did not occur because they took no part in the decision-making process.

Family members or physicians may believe an elder is in no condition to make this decision or that doing so would be frightening. Hospitalization can upset the delicate balance carefully maintained by elders between their management of chronic illness and their dependency. This disruption of independent management through the occurrence of acute illness, unusual behavior, and temporary confusion (as an iatrogenic complication of the hospital stay or a result of physiological imbalance) may signal to families that either temporary or long-term nursing home care is necessary. Worried relatives may ask physicians for their opinion.

One physician in this study said about his role of fatemaker: "You have to protect yourself. Often that means you can't send them home if the family says they're worried that the person can't manage at home." Another physician avoided this role by passing it on. "I repair broken hips. I keep telling the social workers to send them home. They say they can't, and keep sending them to nursing homes."

If families were not in daily contact with their elderly relatives, they were more apt to be alarmed by their appearance in the hospital. Other families with long-standing difficulties apparently used the hospitalization as an excuse to make their relative's institutionalization seem plausible.

A woman newly admitted to a nursing home said of her family's role, "I fall many times at home. I begged my daughter not to call the ambulance. I was not hurt [after a fall]. I was so mad when I heard the ambulance come."

Lack of participation in the decision-making process meant that some elders had no way to make sense of this event. For them the nursing home admission was not only undesirable but illegitimate and involuntary.

While time affected both legitimation and the voluntary or involuntary nature of their admission, time was important to these elders in another way. It was translated into the duration of their stay in the nursing home. "How long will I be here?" "When can I go home?" "How much time do I have left [before death]?" were cues to their search for duration.

Families and health care personnel often handled such questions with reassurance that "it is only for a little while" or "until you are strong enough." These evasions did little to convince elders and they pressed for more specifics. When honest answers about duration were not given, they suspected their stay would be irreversible—that they could never leave.

When irreversibility was combined with undesirability, lack of voluntary participation, and no legitimation, the elder resisted. Figure 18–1 shows the interaction of these conditions and elders' responses, that is, acceptance or resistance to admission.

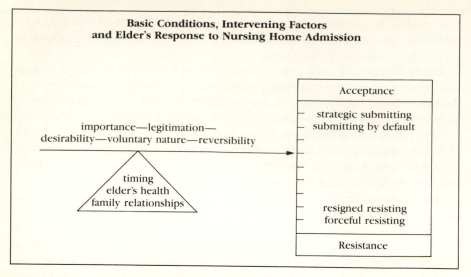

FIGURE 18–1.   To varying degrees, elders accept nursing home admission if they believe it is legitimate, desirable, the result of their own decision, and for a short time. Elders who see admission as undesirable, involuntary, and permanent usually resist.

ACCEPTANCE

A change in any of the conditions that produced resistance to the nursing home could lead to acceptance. Elders demonstrated acceptance by what is called *strategic submitting* or by *submitting by default.*

The majority of elders in the strategic submitting category were in the nursing home for a short time. They submitted as they would to an acute hospitalization. Inconveniences were dismissed, lack of privacy ignored, and other life concerns temporarily put aside while they concentrated on being ready for discharge.

One woman put it this way, "I just have to get to the bathroom. If I can do that it means I can go home. I won't be able to leave my apartment but I *have* to be able to get to the bathroom."

This woman, only 63, had generalized arthritis with several hip fractures and revisions of her hip pinnings. She knew that eventually she could not remain at home. "At the rate I'm going, I won't have a cent in a few years," she said.

Like her, some elders who submitted strategically needed long-term care and realized they would live out their lives in the nursing home. They had painstakingly stretched out their options over time, knew their physical care requirements, and did not want to burden family members or friends. The nursing home was a carefully considered choice among other shrinking options. They focused their energy on making a life in the nursing home that was continuous with their past life.

A former executive secretary, for instance, posted the facility newsletters, was active on the residents' council, and served as the informal receptionist on weekends.

A retired registered nurse who had been a recluse for years before admission obtained a private room, furnished it with small articles from home, and had a companion come in five days a week. She never socialized with others and was able to continue her life of seclusion in the nursing home.

The distinguishing characteristic of the elders who submitted by default was their preoccupation with another, usually catastrophic, life event. Ms C. entered the nursing home two months after the death of her husband of 50 years. His sudden death left her alone and unable to manage because she had advanced Parkinson's disease. She sold her home, moved in with her ailing sister, and quickly discovered that this arrangement was not workable. Ms C. focused almost exclusively on the loss of her husband and home for months after her admission.

Other preoccupations of the elders included physical pain, worry about an illness, or concentration on life review. Admission to the nursing home seemed to be a marker along another course that they were more concerned about or another event that flooded out even the entry to the home.

Elders who accepted the nursing home had satisfied more than one of the basic conditions (desirability, legitimation, voluntary nature, reversibility). Reversibility may be the most important condition, especially for those who submit strategically. However, for elders who knew their functional disabilities and natural support system strengths and who accepted their need for care, a gradual playing out of their options over time enabled them to decide to enter a nursing home. They carefully weighed and balanced alternatives. For these elders, the voluntary nature of the admission based on *their decision* seemed a more important condition than reversibility or desirability.

RESISTANCE

Nursing home resistance occurred when one or more of the basic conditions was not met positively.

Analysis of the interviews showed that resistance took two forms: resigned resisting or forceful resisting. The type depended on the individual's usual methods of dealing with stress.

Resigned resisting was characterized by a range of behaviors from brief withdrawal, crying, and sadness to expressions of profound hopelessness and helplessness. These elders were described by staff and family members as "giving up the will to live" or as "just waiting to die."

Family members of elders who manifested resigned resistance felt powerless, guilty, angry, and grief stricken.

If they could, some would have taken their relatives home. Full-time jobs, children, their own age and health, and numerous other life situations made this impossible. They often turned to staff either in anger, "I thought you said my mother would be happy here" or for support and guidance, "What do I do when my father won't speak to me when I visit?"

Staff were aware of their responsibility to reverse the process of resigned resisting. These elders, by their apparent distress, caused staff to feel upset and sad. They, in turn, might be impatient with family members.

On the other hand, family members and staff who aligned to intervene in the elder's resignation provided a supportive wall around the elder.

This was the case with Ms D. who packed her bag every day for several weeks after admission. She would then sit in her room, weeping quietly. Her daughter visited daily. The staff, aware that she could not take her mother home, were tireless in their efforts to entice Ms D. to converse or take part in activities. After several months, they succeeded; Ms D. became content in the nursing home.

Unfortunately, not all elders have an attentive family and not all staff have the interpersonal skill and personal warmth or the administrative support that provides enough personnel and time to make this type of intervention possible.

Forceful resistance is more difficult for all involved. It was manifested by angry silence and refusal to bathe and eat or accept help with such activities, by refusing medications, or by verbal and physical abuse, usually directed at the staff.

Verbal abuse included name calling and screaming. Physical abuse could be finger twisting, pinching, hitting, spitting, and throwing food and other objects.

These elders were angry, believed they had been betrayed or were being punished unjustly for something they had not done. They distrusted their family and physicians for the "conspiracy" that put them in the nursing home and the staff for keeping them there.

"They can make me stay here," one interviewee said. "There's no way for me to leave in my condition now, but they can't make me be nice. I've been a lady all my life and it's brought me to this. I will show them. They will know I do not want to be here."

Other forceful resistors offered money to staff and visitors to "get me out of here." When the request was denied, it was met with angry rejection of all other overtures.

How, where, and when they would die were the foremost concerns for resisting elders aware of a terminal disease. Therapeutic regimens—even daily care—represented interference with the dying course they were attempting to control. Believing death was near, they angrily rejected the dependence and prolongation of life offered by the staff.

Strategies to ward off staff efforts might be a stream of verbal abuse or total disregard for safety. Mr G., a 90-year-old with terminal cancer, complained about the staff, screamed at them, refused to eat or use his call bell. He was found dead in the bathroom during the night. Apparently he had climbed over his siderails and made his way there alone.

A nursing staff has limited resources to treat forceful resistors therapeutically. The central issue becomes management of the elder's behavior in order to deliver essential care. Some options available to manage forceful resistance are interpersonal, such as humor, confrontation, serious discussion, avoidance, working in teams, or assessing the elder as confused and therefore not responsible. Other options are physical: restraint, medication, transfer, or a combination of these.

A forceful resistor displaying openly aggressive behavior can demoralize a staff. Staff, knowing their efforts at control are not the answer, are not sure what the answer is. After being assigned to a forceful resistor, a nurse's aide said, "If I have that lady tomorrow, I'm not coming in. I don't care if they fire me. I spent the whole morning with her and all she did was call me names and shout at me."

Since none of the interventions available to staff resolve the elder's conflict, consequences for a forceful resistor are negative: transfer to a more restrictive facility, sedation and restraint, permanent confusion, or death. In these cases, everyone is caught in a downward spiral. No one is satisfied with the results and everyone feels impotent to change the situation.

A PRACTICE THEORY

Understanding elders' responses and the conditions that produce them is essential for accurate nursing assessment. Theory to guide subsequent nursing interventions is equally important. This study generated the theory that entry into a nursing home is a relocation that may precipitate a crisis.

Entering a nursing home is not a discrete, time-limited event. Elders repeatedly discussed their entry as an ongoing adjustment. Even those who knew they would spend the rest of their lives in the nursing home discussed the prolonged transition and its effects on them. The central process they were engaged in can be termed a status passage. Status passage is a formal sociological theory that is employed to explain movement, the passage, from one of life's resting places, the status, to another (Glaser, Strauss, 1971).

Passages may be theoretical, such as the developmental stages of life, or they may be actual, such as retirement or widowhood. People manage to juggle several passages at the same time, for example, learning to live with a chronic illness while embarking on a second career. However, a passage may be so overwhelming that it floods out everything else, even other passages. This type of passage is called a crisis (Glaser, Strauss, 1971).

Hospitalization for a life-threatening illness is a passage that can flood out all else and represent a crisis. Admission to a nursing home can also be this type of passage.

Entering a nursing home can occur rapidly and when an individual's resources are at a low ebb, it can be the result of careful planning done over time, or it can be somewhere in between. In any case, acceptance of the nursing home depends on the basic conditions surrounding this event and the individual's ability to cope with the passage.

If contemplation of entry into a nursing home requires coping abilities beyond the elder's resources, tension will build. In this study, the elders' official admission to the home was the stressor event that released their tension. Release of tension was evident in the elders' behavior, characterized as response patterns in this analysis.

Theoretically, since all elders entering a nursing home are engaged in a major life passage, some degree of stress is expected, even in elders who accept their admission. A clinical crisis will present as resistance to the nursing home if elders are overwhelmed by the preceding circumstances and the admission itself, and cannot handle this passage by employing their usual coping skills.

The elder in crisis—the resistor—will attempt to slow down or change the course of this passage. He or she simply is unable to cope with the present situation (Figure 18–2).

A careful assessment of the elder's response pattern will determine whether a full-blown crisis exists or merely transitional difficulties.

Using crisis theory to conceptualize the passage into the nursing home leads to several guidelines for intervention. First, the elder displaying resistance is in crisis. Elders displaying acceptance need assistance, but helping them through the passage into a nursing home may not be the central focus of intervention. Often, as with a grieving widow, the primary nursing intervention is to help resolve loss and grief; the secondary focus is on easing the passage.

Second, crisis resolution usually is achieved in about eight weeks. Intervention is aimed at understanding how the person is experiencing this crisis, reinforcing usual coping skills, and assisting with resolving the crisis while learning new skills. Crisis work is intense and directed specifically to the individual's resources and strengths. If the crisis is not resolved, the elder continues to function maladaptively.

Third, trust in the nurse-patient relationship is necessary for any intervention to succeed. In psychiatric settings, the nurse uses himself or herself as a therapeutic agent, actively engaging with the elder while acting as an adviser for staff and family. In nursing homes, because registered nurses are usually supervisors, the nurse acts as a consultant to the staff, providing outlets for their frustration, guiding their work through case conferences, and reinforcing their interventions.

The multidimensional role of the nursing home nurse is complex: negotiation between resident and staff, staff and family, and often resident and family. Indeed, elders in crisis may require consultation from one of the mental health disciplines to assist with assessment, planning of care, and intervention.

CONCLUSION

Undoubtedly, other researchers might have analyzed these experiences differently. This is the principal limitation of qualitative research. However, this study provides the process to further our understanding of the relocation of elders into a nursing home. The nursing practice theory ties nursing assessment to elders' responses,

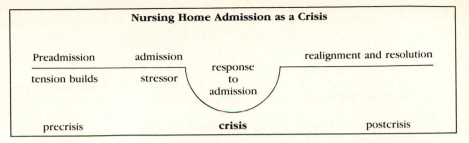

FIGURE 18–2.   Resolution of the crisis of nursing home admission will restore the elder to a higher than usual level of functioning because of the new skills learned. If resolution fails, the elder continues to function maladaptively.

and joins nursing interventions with assistance to elders as they make the passage that nursing home admission represents.

The test of the theory is whether it will assist nurses to frame their practice with elders entering nursing homes and assist educators who teach nurses about long-term care. If it proves specific enough to guide nursing action with a particular client yet generalizable to other similar situations, the theory of nursing home passage will serve its purpose. Its use by nurses can refine, elaborate, and correct this theory as both the art and the science of gerontological nursing practice steadily advance.

References

Aldrich CK, Mendkoff E: Relocation of the aged and disabled: A mortality study. *J Am Geriatr Soc* 1963; 11:185–194.

Aleksandrowiez DR: Fire and its aftermath on a geriatric ward. *Bull Menninger Clin* 1961; 25:23–32.

Beaver ML: The decision making process and its relationship to relocation adjustment in old people. *Gerontologist* 1979; 19:567–574.

Borup JH, Gallego DT, Heffernan PG: Relocation: Its effect on health, functioning and on mortality. *Gerontologist* 1980; 20:468–479.

Borup JH, Gallego DT, Heffernan PG: *Geriatric Relocation.* Ogden, Utah, Weber State College Press, 1978.

Bourestom N, Pastalan L: The effects of relocation on the elderly: A reply to Borup, Gallego and Heffernan. *Gerontologist* 1981; 21:4–7.

Bourestom N, Tars S: Alterations in life patterns following nursing home relocation. *Gerontologist* 1974; 14:506–510.

Butler RN: *Why Survive? Being Old in America.* New York, Harper and Row Publishers, 1975, pp 260–261.

Caramago O, Preston GH: What happens to patients who are hospitalized for the first time when over 65. *Am J Psychiatry* 1945; 102:168–173.

Chenitz WC: Registered nurse interview, in *Acceptance of the Standards of Geriatric Nursing Practice and Perceptions of Satisfaction and Stress in Practice by Geriatric Nurses,* doctoral dissertation. New York, Teachers College, Columbia University, 1978, pp 148–150.

Costello JP, Tanaka GM: Mortality and morbidity in long term institutional care of the aged. *J Am Geriatr Soc* 1961; 9:959–963.

Glaser BG, Strauss A: *Status Passage: A Formal Theory.* Chicago, Aldine Publishing Co, 1971.

Gutman GM, Herbert CP: Mortality rate among relocated extended care patients. *J Gerontol* 1976; 31:352–357.

Hirschfield IS, Dennis H: Perspectives, in Ragin PK (ed): *Aging Parents.* Los Angeles, University of Southern California Press, 1979, pp 1–10.

Jasnau KF: Individualized versus mass transfers of nonpsychotic geriatric patients from mental hospitals to nursing homes, with special reference to the death rate. *J Am Geriatr Soc* 1967; 15:280–284.

Killian EC: Effects of geriatric transfers on mortality rates: Stockton (Calif.) State Hospital. *Soc Work* 1970; 15:19–26.

Kowalski NC: Fire at a home for the aged: A study of short term mortality following dislocation of elderly residents. *J Gerontol* 1978; 33:601–602.

Kral VA, Grad B, Berenson J: Stress reactions resulting from the relocation of an aged population. *Can Psychiatr Assoc J* 1968; 13:201–209.

Lieberman MA: Relationship of mortality rates to entrance to a home for the aged. *Geriatrics* 1961; 16:515–519.

Markus E, Blenker M, Bloom M, Downs T: The impact of relocation upon mortality rates of institutionalized aged persons. *J Gerontol* 1971: 26:537–541.

Markus E, Blenker M, Bloom M, Downs T: Some factors and their association with postrelocation mortality among institutionalized aged persons. *J Gerontol* 1972; 27:376–382.

Schulz R, Brenner G: Relocation of the aged: A review and theoretical analysis. *J Gerontol* 1977; 32:323–333.

Sussman M: The family life of old people, in Binstock RH, Shanas E (eds): *Handbook of Aging and the Social Sciences,* New York, Van Nostrand and Reinhold Co, 1976, pp 218–243.

Zwieg JP, Csank JZ: Effects of relocation on chronically ill geriatric patients on a medical unit: Mortality rates. *J Am Geriatr Soc* 1975; 23:132–136.

19

From grounded theory to clinical practice: cases from gay studies research

Robert J. Kus

Terry, a 21-year-old man, was admitted to a large West Coast psychiatric unit because "voices" were telling him he was no good. Paul, a 28-year-old man, visited his family physician with numerous somatic complaints, not the least of which was "heart pain." Skip, age 20, found himself on a psychiatric unit after overdosing on Quaaludes, a suicide gesture. Tony, a 31-year-old doctoral student at a large midwestern university, complained of an inability to concentrate on his studies. Rick, a 34-year-old Missouri priest and workaholic, would burst into tears for no apparent reason. And Lance, a 28-year-old high school teacher, was admitted to a southern hospital after an auto accident caused by his alcoholism.

At first glance, each of these cases would seem to lead to diverse nursing diagnoses and treatment plans. However, each of these men was found to be stuck in the gay coming out process. And while their presentations of self were diverse, the treatment each received was rather simple: each man was helped to move through the coming out process as quickly as possible thus eliminating the problematic symptoms. The term "coming out" will be defined in "The Methods" section.

But how was this possible? How could such a diverse collection of individuals be diagnosed and treated in the same way by nurses and physicians? The answer is this: The treatment plan for each was based on knowledge gained from a grounded theory study, "Gay Freedom: An Ethnography of Coming Out" (Kus, 1980). This study not only identified the stages of the coming out process that gay Americans experience but also identified the common health picture seen in each stage. Furthermore, based on informants' accounts and the literature about the subject, the study suggested gay treatment modalities to help the gay client move through the early stages of the process. The early stages of coming out often cause multiple health problems; in the latter stages, however, the health status is usually positive.

In this chapter I will report briefly on the methods used in "Gay Freedom" and then discuss 6 case reports concerning young men who were diagnosed and treated using the knowledge generated by the study.

THE METHODS

"Gay Freedom" used ethnographic procedures to generate grounded theory. The core of the study consisted of in-depth interviews with 25 gay men and six lesbians in Missoula, Montana and Seattle, Washington.

Early interviews were structured yet flexible enough to allow the informant to discuss relevant material. All of the formal interviews were tape recorded and typed verbatim. Content analysis (see chapter 10) was then done on each group of five to six interviews to generate categories. Subsequent interview questions were designed to focus on specific categories until saturation was reached, that is, until no new information was forthcoming.

In addition to the formal interviews, data were gathered from gay music lyrics, cartoons and comic strips, newspapers and magazines, poetry, and gay fiction and nonfiction writings such as biographies, autobiographies, plays, self-help books, political tomes, humor books, and spirituality books. Non-homophobic behavioral science writings and historical works were also used. Field notes were kept in a log to record personal observations, questions, reflections, flashes of insight, jokes, anecdotes, and relevant information picked up informally in gay bars, restaurants, board meetings, and parties.

Because I am a gay researcher as well as a nurse-sociologist, I was concerned that I might use words not understood by "straight" (heterosexual) readers. To prevent this, a committee of three straight readers read my study and pointed out "gay words" not adequately defined for straight readers.

But how, one may ask, can a clinician go from grounded theory research findings to clinical practice? After all, grounded theory studies often use small samples. Aren't large samples needed to generalize effectively? And what about the fact that grounded theory uses theoretical sampling? Aren't statistical samples needed before one may safely apply scientific knowledge? Although the quantitative, logical-positivist approach to scientific knowledge requires statistical sampling and large numbers to yield valid results, the qualitative perspective of grounded theory research offers different bases for validity.

The first answer lies in the nature of "saturation," the concept of a category of newly generated theory being full or complete; no new knowledge is forthcoming to change the category's nature. In this study, for example, there were only so many ways persons "passed as straight," and further interviews revealed nothing new to contribute to one's understanding of it.

Second, validity is achieved by taking the finished study to non-informant members of the category of people under study, in this case gay men and women. When a gay man or woman in Iowa agrees with a statement made by a gay person in Washington one assumes that the statement is indeed valid.

Finally, validity was tested by having my work read by a four-person panel of non-informant gay men and women who had completed the coming out process. Consistently strong affirmative responses indicated that the goal of the ethnographer was achieved; that is, the life process of a people was portrayed both adequately and accurately.

THE RESULTS

Coming out is a dramatic, powerful, and complex life process experienced by the 10% of our population who are gay or lesbian. Before examining the stages of this process and the health picture found in each of the stages, definitions will be provided and sample characteristics given.

Definitions

Certain terms apply specifically to the gay experience and may require definition for the general readers. The first is "coming out." While the term "coming out" has many meanings in popular culture—such as self-disclosure of gay identity, first same-sex sexual experience, and so forth—based on this study's findings, "coming out" as a gay life process is defined as

> *that process by which a gay individual identifies self as gay, changes any preconceived notions of gays or homosexuality, accepts being gay as a positive state of being, and acts on the assumption that being gay is a positive state of being (Kus, 1980, pp 52–53).*

The four stages of coming out in this model are Identification, Cognitive Changes, Acceptance, and Action.

Homosexuality comes from the Greek *homo* which means *same*. It is not derived from the Latin *homo* meaning man. *Homo* refers to a state of being rather than something one "does." It is defined as "an unchosen, lifelong, and irreversible predominant physical (sexual) and psychological attraction to members of one's own sex as opposed to the opposite sex" (Kus, 1980, p 37). Thus, the gay person may have exclusively heterosexual sexual experiences in life, same-sex sexual experiences, or live a celibate lifestyle. The thing that makes one gay is not sexual activity but is rather one's sexual orientation.

The term "homosexual" as a noun is rarely used by gay and lesbian Americans. It has come to be seen in the gay and lesbian communities as an outdated, heterosexually chosen word. In fact, many gay and lesbian Americans are offended by this word and consider someone who uses it lacking in awareness and sensitivity, much as one would wonder about an American who used the word "colored" or "Negro" rather than "black."

Although I use the term "gay" to refer to both men and women with same-sex sexual orientation in deference to space concerns of this book, in actual practice I never do so; gay (men's) society, culture, reality, and oppression are radically different from lesbian (women's) society, culture, reality, and oppression. The one similarity shared by both gays and lesbians, however, is the coming out process and, therefore, "gay" will here stand for both unless otherwise noted.

The word "lover" has different meanings for gays and straights. In the straight world, a lover implies a type of sexual side affair. For gays, the term lover is more analogous to the straight term "spouse." Thus, a gay with a lover is "coupled," as opposed to "single," in gay/lesbian jargon (Kus, 1985, p 193).

Sample Characteristics

The ages of the informants ranged from 20 to 66 years; the average age was 33.5. All 31 informants had at least a high school education and 29 had post high school education including 15 with bachelor's degrees, four with master's degrees, and one with a doctorate. At the time of the interview, eight persons defined themselves as Protestant, six were Roman Catholic, four were agnostic, one was a nonpracticing Jew, and 11 considered themselves "unaffiliated."

Informants' home states were California, Georgia, Idaho, Illinois, Indiana, Maryland, Minnesota, Missouri, Montana, New Jersey, Pennsylvania, Ohio, Tennessee, Texas, Washington, West Virginia, and Wisconsin.

Occupations of the informants were diverse. In addition to four students, there were two Protestant ministers, a Roman Catholic nun, a mental health specialist, a psychiatrist, a social worker, an armed forces paramedic, a hairstylist, a field representative for a boys' group, a vocational counselor, an unemployment determiner, a banker, a retired railroad person, a public relations specialist, a gay bar owner, an auditor, a national gay leader, an unemployed postal worker, a journeyman cutter, a forester, a retail store assistant manager, a criminal justice counselor, a gay activist organizer, a nurse-counselor, a clinical audiologist, a farm laborer, and one self-described "jack-of-all-trades."

STAGES OF COMING OUT

Stage One: Identification

In the stage of identification, the gay undergoes a radical identity transformation ("Who am I?"). Even though one's sexual orientation is set well before age three

(Money, Ehrhardt, 1972), if not before birth, the gay infant and child must usually wait until the teenage years before recognizing his or her gay or lesbian identity. Gay men usually recognize their true identity earlier than do lesbians (Jay, Young, 1979).

Unlike racial or ethnic minority children, gays grow up unaware they are members of a minority. This lack of anticipatory socialization often produces a profound sense of aloneness when one learns of his or her gay identity.

Identifying self as gay often occurs after reading gay literature, from hearing talk about gays and exploring this, or falling in love with a member of one's own sex.

Early in this stage, the individual may experience opposite-sex sexual experience which is described as feeling "unnatural" or "abnormal." The gay may erroneously define self as "bisexual," confusing sexual orientation (a state of being) with sexual behavior (action). This false labeling occurs more frequently among lesbians than gays (Jay, Young, 1979).

Once identification is achieved, the most commonly heard type of statement goes something like this: "In retrospect, I've always been gay. I always knew as a child I was somehow 'different' from other people, but I didn't know how I was different. Now I know!"

Because the gay often has been taught negative ideas about gays, while growing up, his or her health might suffer. Informants' accounts and literature report that in this first stage, the gay often experiences severe guilt and low self-esteem, a sense of loneliness arising from the feeling of aloneness, stress and its physical manifestations such as ulcers, depression symptoms such as insomnia or its reverse, and the inability to concentrate on everyday tasks. Suicidal ideation, estimated to have occurred in 40% of the gay population (Jay, Young, 1979) can be seen in this stage. Likewise, drinking alcohol excessively may begin here and lead to alcoholism which is the foremost health problem in both the gay and lesbian communities. Fear of rejection by family, friends, and others is also experienced in the first stage of coming out. In very rare cases, an acute psychotic episode can occur in gay men.

Stage Two: Cognitive Changes

While a radical identity change is the criterion of stage one, the criterion of stage two is changing one's negative notions about gays and homosexuality yet still not accepting being gay as a positive state of being.

Having learned a straight reality all through childhood, the gay must now learn a gay reality, a new way of seeing and explaining the world and one's place in it. Thus, this stage is analogous to going to school.

The hallmark of this stage is passing as straight while exploring what it means to be gay. Passing is done out of fear—fear of rejection, fear of violence, fear of loss. And although informants report the fear of self-disclosure of gay identity is often worse than the actual disclosure, one must remember that this is the century that has produced such anti-gay figures as Anita Bryant, Jerry Falwell, Adolf Hitler, and Joseph Stalin as well as such anti-gay groups as the Nazis, the Ku Klux Klan, and the Moral Majority.

Passing as straight takes many forms, the most common being dating the opposite sex and entering into male-female marriages. The most damaging form of passing is becoming an anti-gay crusader. In this situation, the gay may enter into
conservative political causes or fundamentalist religious cults or sects which seek
the persecution or extermination of gays.

Often a geographic dimension of coming out is seen in this stage as the gay
moves from his or her home in order to be freer to explore the gay world. The gay
individual wants to be away from friends or family who might learn of his or her
gay identity. Rural gays might move to urban areas where there is a greater gay
support system.

To change negative notions, the gay often enters the gay or lesbian community.
Often, the gay is unsophisticated in the beginning and is unable to accurately discern what would be best to explore. For example, a lesbian may erroneously start
working for a gay community center which appeals only to gay men, while an
apolitical gay man might join a gay political group when he would be happier in a
gay bowling league.

While some gays report changing their notions through reading positive gay
literature or counseling, all agree that the very best way of getting through this
stage is getting to know many gay people.

The stage of passing as straight has its share of health problems. First, there is a
tremendous waste of energy being an actor 24 hours a day. Second, passing can
lead to stress and the host of physical and mental problems arising from stress.
Third, pretending to be straight to retain the advantages of straight status leaves one
open to blackmail. Fourth, passing may hurt others especially if the gay is stringing
along someone of the opposite sex merely to create a "set." Furthermore, there is
a moral-ethical problem in passing, especially for professionals such as priests,
nurses, professors or physicians who are gay. By passing as straight, the gay is
denying colleagues and clients a positive gay role model as well as a ready reference source to help gay clients.

Finally, there is a sense of paranoia about being "discovered." Such paranoia
can creep into all aspects of life including not signing out a gay library book for
fear that someone will see the name on the library card.

This is not to be confused with what Clark calls "benign paranoia" (1977, pp
36–37). Benign paranoia is a healthy awareness that all gays must possess to recognize homophobia which can manifest itself at any time. For example, many of my
informants reported that they would be leery around a stranger who used the word
"homosexual" rather than "gay."

But as one changes negative ideas, it becomes simply too difficult to pass as
straight and feel negative about oneself. It is a radical assault on one's identity, self-
worth, and sensibilities. One begins giving clues as to gay identity such as object-
ing to anti-gay jokes. The serious closet passing begins to fade and one moves to
stage three.

Stage Three: Acceptance

Of all the stages, none is more joyful than the stage of acceptance. In this stage, the gay accepts being gay as a positive life force; the "bad news" becomes "good news." As a result, the gay can now move toward self-actualization as self-esteem is raised to new heights.

The essense, or criterion, of this stage is the beginning of a special type of freedom—a gay freedom. One's initial war with self is over. A peacefulness descends. As Fisher says:

> *The inner conflict is over and one is suddenly free to be himself. More important, one is no longer at war with himself. The energy which was devoted to denying one's self can now be directed toward building a happy life (1972, p 24).*

The health picture is vastly improved over the previous two stages. First, there is an overwhelming sense of relaxation which translates into decreased stress. Second, self-esteem is raised to new heights as one becomes free from the guilt seen earlier. This results in a sense of general well-being. And third, depression and its cluster of symptoms such as suicidal ideation disappears.

Now that "gay is good" and "gay is proud" become internalized, the gay must now decide what he or she will do about it. Stage four is entered.

Stage Four: Action

The essence, or criterion, for this stage is engaging in behavior which results from accepting self as gay in a positive light. Such action may be highly visible, such as making the irreversible statement "I am gay," or hidden such as a gay Trappist monk making a silent prayer of thanksgiving for his new-found peacefulness.

Common types of action seen in this stage include self-disclosure, expanding one's circle of friends to include more gays, modifying or rethinking religious beliefs, becoming politically involved in gay causes, volunteering for gay groups such as community centers, raising one's occupational sights, and speaking or writing about gay issues. Further, the gay is now free to "talk gay," to be open about aspects of his or her life which are important.

The health picture seen in this stage is generally positive, but a few problems may occur. The gay may experience rejection by family, friends, or co-workers leading to a crisis situation. Usually, family and others will move toward acceptance of the gay in time. I found no incident of a family member going from acceptance to non-acceptance.

Another possible problem is that gays often become "overachievers." This is due to many factors—the growth and development pattern of gay children that is unique and just now being described, the perceived need to compensate for being gay, etc. On the one hand, this overachieving can lead to great career success; on the other hand, it can lead to workaholism and the problems that entails.

With the tremendous burst of energy unleashed from no longer passing as straight combined with the excitement of self-acceptance, one often becomes a "professional gay" for a period of time (Rochlin, 1979). In this phase, the gay temporarily loses perspective and being gay is all-encompassing. For example, in this phase, any non-gay activity is seen as irrelevant, the gay person talks only about gay issues, self-discloses to virtually everyone he meets, becomes emerged in gay political or social activities or both, and has a difficult time concentrating on non-gay concerns, and the like. This phenomenon is both healthy and natural and it will run its course.

Before showing how these findings about the four stages were applied clinically, three points need to be made.

1. Not all gay persons make it through each stage of the coming out process; many get stuck permanently in stage two and never reach the joyfulness found in stages three and four.
2. Each stage of coming out has a time dimension different for each person; one informant took 25 years getting from stage two to stage three, while another reported completing the entire process in three weeks.
3. Accepting self in a positive light (stage three) is the essence of coming out, not merely self-disclosure of gay identity. It is possible to say, "I'm gay" while not actually seeing being gay as a positive thing. Such a person has not completed the process.

Having briefly looked at the stages of coming out and the common health picture seen in each stage, we now look at how the knowledge generated from "Gay Freedom" was used in clinical practice. For some clinicians, especially those who are gay, lesbian, or straights sensitive to gay/lesbian needs and concerns, the directives for action emerging from this study will be no surprise. Rather, this study will simply provide scientific confirmation of their already existing practices. For other clinicians, however, the prescriptions for action may not be familiar. Prescribing positive gay literature, for example, might not have been considered in helping the gay or lesbian client. But whether these prescriptions are familiar or foreign, most clinicians will find them to be simple to use and effective for their gay and lesbian clients.

CLINICAL CASE REPORTS: "GAY FREEDOM" APPLIED

The following case studies were chosen to represent a wide variety of persons stuck in the coming out process, the problems they experienced as a result, and how each was treated. None of the case studies presented here were part of this study, and all of the examples are of men since all of the clients I have seen suffering as a result of the coming out process were men. Lesbian clients seeking help were doing so for other reasons, usually as a result of breaking up with a lover.

Perhaps the overrepresentation of men is due to the more severe and rigid social-ization men receive. At any rate, such hypothesizing is beyond the scope of this chapter.

Case One: Skip

Skip, a 20-year-old white man, was taken to the emergency room of a large West Coast hospital after overdosing on Quaaludes. He is presented here since his expe-rience is "typical" of gay men in crisis in stages one and two.

I was called from the psychiatric unit to evaluate him for possible admission to the unit. Strapped to the stretcher, he was crying and was obviously drunk. He was happy to see me as he had been lying there for quite some time waiting for lab work to be completed. He took my hand and squeezed very hard.

Following a short interview, Skip admitted he was gay but hated it. In fact, he was very adamant that he was "not gay, there's nothing gay about it. I'm a homo-sexual, a queer." Because of his openness in sharing his feelings and because our unit was particularly sensitive to the needs of gay clients, he was admitted.

As with any gay client, Skip was assessed for alcoholism. It was found that his intoxication on admission was unusual for him; he had drunk that night after sitting home alone thinking how "awful" it was he was gay. Another highly rele-vant piece of datum in assessing him was his refusal to use the word "gay" in referring to himself and using, instead, the straight clinical term "homosexual." This behavior is often seen in gays in stage one or early stage two and it indicates a non-acceptance of being gay as a positive thing.

On the unit, the medical staff agreed not to prescribe anti-depressants until he had received some individual counseling about his gay identity. The nursing staff, which had had a workshop on this study in the recent past, was more than willing to be supportive toward Skip. He was provided frequent individual counseling sessions with me and other gay staff as well as some straight staff. He was given Clark's *Loving Someone Gay* (1977). In these sessions, Skip was encouraged to share his feelings about being gay, encouraged to read positive gay literature, and taught the stages of coming out as found in this study. The staff believed that by teaching Skip the findings of this study, he would see his current dislike of being gay as a natural, yet temporary, state which would pass. Further, it would show him that indeed what he was experiencing was not unique in any way, but rather, was a phenomenon experienced by millions of fellow Americans.

Within four days he was proudly talking about being gay, trying out gay humor, wanting more positive gay literature, and using the gay staff as a resource to answer his questions. He was discharged on the fifth day.

As a follow-up, Skip was advised to join a gay men's group at a local counseling center and he was encouraged to make gay friends. Like many gays reaching stage four of the coming out process, he said upon leaving the hospital, "I feel like a ton of bricks has been lifted off my back!"

Case Two: Paul

A 28-year-old married man and father of a 3-year-old daughter, Paul made an appointment to see his family physician in his Ohio town. Paul had complaints of intermittent chest pain, insomnia, fatigue, and general malaise.

After carefully listening to Paul's complaints, the physician, who had just finished reading "Gay Freedom," had a hunch that perhaps Paul was gay and stuck in stage two of the coming out process. The physician admitted that he did not know why he had this "hunch," but perhaps it was due to Paul's meeting his stereotypes of gay men—that is, Paul was good looking, concerned with taking care of his body, friendly, sensitive, and so forth. When asked, Paul admitted that he was gay and had never told anyone and that this was causing him a great deal of stress. He feared losing his daughter as well as his wife should his sexual orientation become known.

To be on the safe side, Paul's doctor gave him a complete physical examination including extensive heart tests; all were within normal limits. Because of Paul's symptoms and his being closeted about his gay identity, the doctor assumed Paul to be in stage two of the coming out process. Further, because Paul's physician knew that contact with other gays is the best way to help the gay move into stages three (acceptance) and four (action), he recommended that Paul see a gay counselor and that he get to know more gay people with whom he could share his concerns.

Not only did Paul see a gay counselor, but he was fortunate to find a gay fathers' rap group in his town. As he began meeting more and more gay men with whom he could share self, Paul began to see himself in a positive light. Several weeks after first meeting with his doctor, he returned for a follow-up visit. Paul's earlier symptoms had disappeared, he appeared much more relaxed and had a brighter affect. Also he was planning on telling his wife about his gay identity.

Before looking at the next case study, it must be pointed out that health histories for teens and adults should always explore sexual orientation. Done in a professional way, the health history interview usually does not offend the client. Rather, clients see this as relevant data, especially since the advent of diseases such as acquired immune deficiency syndrome (AIDS). Generally, getting this information is done by the clinician asking questions such as "Do you have sex with men or women or both?" Or, if the person answers affirmatively to the question "Are you coupled?" she or he is asked "Do you live with him or her?" (Note that the clinician asks about being coupled rather than married. Information about marriage should be obtained later for insurance and legal purposes.) By asking such questions and by keeping one's affect completely neutral, the client is made aware of the clinician's acceptance. In terms of sexual behavior, which is sometimes harmonious with one's sexual orientation, the clinician may ask a man, for example, if a rectal swab for venereal disease testing needs to be done. If the man says yes, the clinician may explore the man's sexual orientation with him.

Case Three: Rick

Rick, a 34-year-old priest, was first seen by me at his monastery. I had met him while visiting another priest in the order, and I was asked by my friend to "visit Rick and see what you can make of him." My friend felt that Rick's "crying jags" had to do with his frustration over hiding his gay identity. I found Rick to be an extremely interesting and dynamic individual, a person forever concerned with "bettering" himself through study, writing, and working. Further, he was the ideal client in terms of his willingness to be open with me.

The assessment revealed Rick to be a workaholic to the point of being unhappy when he was not in a whirlwind of activities. He admitted to driving himself unmercifully to the point of fatigue. In our first session, he admitted to being gay only after hedging around a bit with, "Well, I think I might be bisexual . . . no, that's not true, I'm gay." He said that I was the first person he had told that to and expressed a great deal of relief. After his self-disclosure, his expression, like so many other gays had used before him, was "I feel like a ton of bricks has fallen off my shoulders." I recommended that he read positive gay literature as well as investigate a Catholic organization of gay priests. He followed both of these prescriptions.

Several months later, I learned that Rick's crying jags had stopped, that he was more relaxed, and his presentation of self was that of a man happy with himself. My friend, Rick's fellow priest, said "You wouldn't believe the change in Rick! It's as though he's reborn. Whatever you did or said to him surely did the trick."

This example is important in that it shows that persons in need of help in coming out most often do not end up in a hospital or physician's office. Rather, they are functioning in the world as best they can, even though this existence could be made so much better if they could go through the coming out process more rapidly, and thus reduce the negative aspects felt in a lengthy stage two.

Case Four: Terry

The following case story is presented here for three reasons. First, it is an excellent example of the rare situational psychotic state which can occur in gay men who have entered stage one of the coming out process. Second, it shows that non-gay persons can use knowledge gained from this study to effectively help a client move through the coming out process. And third, it demonstrates vividly the need to be very careful in labeling a client schizophrenic without first ruling out situational psychoses.

Terry, a 21-year-old man, was admitted to the same psychiatric unit where Skip had been. He complained of feeling worthless and said that "the voices" were telling him he was no good. He had frequent nightmares, poor eye contact, never initiated conversation, and seemed suspicious of other patients. When taken down to the cafeteria by a straight nursing staff member, Joe, Terry demanded to be taken back to the unit because "everybody is staring at me and saying I'm a queer."

Fortunately, Joe had just attended the workshop on this study and he correctly remembered that such a client may be either gay or schizophrenic and not gay.

The assessment revealed that Terry had many friends, was an excellent worker in his job, had a college degree, and had no previously psychiatric history. Further, until this episode, he was seen by his friends as a "happy, warm" person.

In an individual counseling session with Terry, Joe said, "You know, Terry, if you're gay that's okay. Lots of my friends are gay and I think they're really neat people." Following this opening, Terry began opening up to Joe. After much questioning to test Joe's trustworthiness, Terry admitted that he was gay. This admission of gay identity led to a tremendous catharsis for Terry. He began sharing with Joe his innermost thoughts and feelings, fears and hopes. Within 24 hours, all psychotic symptoms disappeared. He became his usual self within 48 hours and was discharged on the third hospital day. He agreed to get involved in the gay community, to read positive gay literature, and to seek counseling at the gay counseling center when needed.

Such a dramatic recovery is not unusual in this form of situational psychosis once self-disclosure occurs and the person to whom the gay is disclosing is supportive.

A final note about this case. When non-gay therapists begin dealing with this phenomenon in clients, they often need positive reinforcement from gay staff that indeed, they are doing a good job. Otherwise, they are too self-conscious and feel that "only gays can do this right."

Case Five: Tony

Tony, a 31-year-old doctoral student, came to see me at a large midwestern university. He said he thought he needed counseling because, as he put it, "I might be a bisexual . . . maybe." Through questioning he finally said, "Well, I'm not really bisexual, I'm gay."

The assessment revealed that Tony was having a difficult time concentrating on his studies because he was so ashamed of being gay. He also indicated how frustrated he felt passing as straight and how much of a "phony" he felt by passing.

I prescribed several things: (1) take a gay studies class at his university; (2) become active in a gay group on his campus; and (3) read some positive gay literature. He carried out each prescription with good results.

However, the gay studies course made him get in touch with anger directed toward straight society. He was able to deal with this by putting much energy into working for the gay community, speaking on gay issues in university classes, and generally becoming a low-key gay activist. In short, he was exhibiting the "professional gay" phase.

Tony did some soul-searching about whether or not the pursuit of a doctorate, which he felt he needed to be "as good as" straights, was worth the effort. After a vacation with his European lover, Tony decided to finish his doctorate but move to Europe to be with his lover. Further, he not only decided to finish his doctorate, but to do a gay studies research project in his discipline for his dissertation. His newfound gay pride, therefore, benefited him personally and professionally.

Case Six: Lance

Lance, a 28-year-old high school teacher, was admitted to a big city southern hospital after overdosing on "downers." His blood alcohol level was dangerously high. When admitted he was yelling, "It's too much! I just can't cope any more. I wish I was dead."

After being stabilized medically, he was transferred to the psychiatric unit where I was working. He was referred to me after he told the other nurses that they "wouldn't understand" because they were not gay.

The assessment revealed that he was feeling overburdened at his school, frustrated that all of his gay friends lived outside of the town where he lived, and that alcohol had become a problem in his life. In fact, he admitted that he had several drunk driving citations.

Through the problem-solving process of crisis intervention, Lance identified his problems as threefold: alcoholism, lack of freedom to share self because of being "in the closet," and lack of assertiveness in the workplace. He said that he accepted being gay as a positive thing. However, because recent research has shown that gay alcoholics who have not experienced sobriety do not fully accept their sexual orientation as a positive thing (Kus, 1985), we cannot say that Lance was in stage three. Rather, I put him in stage two and ready for stage three if sobriety was chosen.

Through problem solving, he agreed that alcoholism was his main problem and the only solution was total abstinence. With his permission, gay Alcoholics Anonymous (AA) members were called to visit and he began attending gay AA meetings. His friends from all over the country visited him and, with this support, he came out to his family as well as to his school board, principal, and fellow teachers. He had his work load at school reduced as the principal agreed that indeed, he was shouldering more than his fair share.

When he was discharged, his eating, sleeping, and concentration were back to normal. His affect was bright and his outlook on life positive. His psychiatrist hugged him on discharge and said she wished all her patients could be like him. In 1983, Lance celebrated his first AA birthday.

Lance's story is important for two reasons. First, while he was sharing his gay identity with gay friends, his non-disclosure to significant straight friends was leading him into trouble. Second, this case report shows that alcoholic gays must choose sobriety before they can truly experience stage three and live happy lives.

END NOTE

In this chapter we saw how a profound life process called coming out, unique to gay and lesbian people, can create havoc on physical and mental health. We also saw that nurses and other health professionals can help gay people move through the process more quickly in order to reduce the negative consequences sometimes found in the process. And although most gays go through this process without nursing intervention, it behooves nurses to be aware of this process in order to help not only gay clients in clinical settings, but also to be able to help gay sons, lesbian friends, gay spouses, and others.

Not all symptoms such as insomnia or lack of concentration seen in gay clients have to be the result of the coming out process, however. They may be present because of breaking up with a lover, economic problems, and the like. Therefore, one must be cautious in applying the knowledge presented here without first assessing that the gay person's problems do, indeed, stem from the coming out process.

As demonstrated by the application of the findings of this research study on the gay experience of coming out, grounded theory is not only a means of obtaining information from clinical and non-clinical settings, it also provides knowledge that can be effectively applied in those same settings. In the case of the psychosocial problems experienced by gay men, grounded theory was an appropriate research methodology because the focus of study was the felt experience of individual lives. It was in relation to this felt experience that these gay men manifested health problems, and so it was through the understanding of that experience—as assisted by the grounded theory study—that the health professionals could help resolve the health problems. It is perhaps through such clinical validation that grounded theory research most clearly demonstrates its value to nursing.

References

Clark D: *Loving Someone Gay.* Millbrae, California, Celestial Arts, 1977.

Fisher P: *The Gay Mystique.* New York, Stein & Day, 1972.

Jay K, Young A: *The Gay Report.* New York, Summit, 1979.

Kus RJ: *Gay Freedom: An Ethnography of Coming Out,* thesis. University of Montana, Missoula, Montana, 1980.

Kus RJ: Stages of coming out: An ethnographic approach. *West J Nurs Res* 1985a;7:177–198.

Kus RJ: Gay alcoholism and non-acceptance: The critical link. Presented at the nursing research conference, Honolulu, June 21, 1985.

Money J, Ehrhardt AA: *Man and Woman, Boy and Girl: Differentiation and Dimorphism of Gender Identity from Conception to Maturity.* Baltimore, Johns Hopkins Press, 1972.

Rochlin M: Becoming a gay professional, in Berzon B, Leighton R (eds): *Positively Gay.* Millbrae, California, Celestial Arts, 1979, pp 159–170.

Bibliography

QUALITATIVE RESEARCH

Archbold P: An analysis of parentcaring by women. *Home Health Care Serv Quar* 1982; 3: 5–26.

Artinian B: Conceptual mapping: The development of the strategy. *West J Nurs Res* 1982;4:379–393.

Artinian B: Role identities of the dialysis patient. *Neph Nurs* 1983;5:10–14.

Barnes JA: Some ethical problems in modern fieldwork, in Filstead WJ (ed): *Qualitative Methodology.* Chicago, Markham Publishing Co, 1970, pp 235–251.

Becker HS: Whose side are we on? in Filstead WJ (ed): *Qualitative Methodology.* Chicago, Markham Publishing Co, 1970, pp 15–26.

Becker HS, Greer B: Participant observation and interviewing: A comparison, in McCall GJ, Simmons JL (eds): *Participant Observation: A Text and a Reader.* Reading, Massachusetts, Addison Wesley Publishing Company, 1969, pp 322–331.

Benoliel JQ: Grounded theory and qualitative data: The socializing influences of life threatening disease on identity development, in Wooldridge PJ, Schmitt MH, Skipper JK, Leonard RC (eds): *Behavioral Science and Nursing Theory.* St Louis, Missouri, CV Mosby, 1983.

Blumer H: *Symbolic Interactionism: Perspective and Method.* Englewood Cliffs, New Jersey, Prentice Hall, 1969.

Blumer H: Society as symbolic interaction, in Rose AM (ed): *Human Behavior and Social Processes.* Boston, Houghton Mifflin Company, 1962.

Byerly EL: The nurse as a participant observer in a nursing setting, in Brink PJ (ed): *Transcultural Nursing.* New York, Prentice Hall, 1976, pp 230–236.

Byerly EL: The nurse researcher as a participant observer in a nursing setting. *Nursing Research* 1969;18:230–236.

Cassell J: Risk and benefit to subjects of fieldwork. *Am Sociologist* 1978;13:134–143.

Charmaz K: The grounded theory method: An explication and interpretation, in Emerson RM (ed): *Contemporary Field Research: Collection of Readings.* Boston, Little Brown and Co, 1983.

Chenitz WC, Swanson JW: Surfacing nursing process: A method for generating nursing theory from practice. *J. Adv Nurs* 1984;9:205–215.

Corbin J: Protective governing: *Strategies for managing a pregnancy-illness,* doctoral dissertation, University of California, San Francisco, 1980.

Davis MZ: The organizational, interactional and care oriented conditions for patient participation in continuity of care: A framework for staff interaction. *Soc Sci Med* 1980;14A:39–47.

Davis MZ: *Living with Multiple Sclerosis: A Social Psychological Analysis.* Chicago, Illinois, Charles C Thomas Publishers, 1973.

Davis MZ: Transition to a Devalued Status: The Case of Multiple Sclerosis, doctoral dissertation. University of California, San Francisco Medical Center, San Francisco, 1970.

Davis MZ: Some problems in identity in becoming a nurse researcher. *Nurs Res* 1968;17:166–168.

Dean JP, Eickhorn L, Dean R: Fruitful informants for intensive interviewing, in McCall GJ, Simmons JL (eds): *Issues in Participant Observation: A Text and a Reader.* Reading, Massachusetts, Addison Wesley Publishing Company, 1969.

Dean JP, Whyte WF: How do you know if the informant is telling the truth?, in McCall GJ, Simmons JL (eds): *Issues in Participant Observation: A Text and a Reader.* Reading, Massachusetts, Addison Wesley Publishing Company, 1969.

Denzin NK: *The Research Act: A Theoretical Introduction to Sociological Methods.* Chicago, Aldine Publishing Co, 1970.

Deutscher I: Words and deeds: Social science and social policy, in Filstead WJ (ed): *Qualitative Methodology.* Chicago, Markham Publishing Co, 1970, pp 27–51.

Eisner E: On the differences between scientific and artistic approaches to qualitative research. *Educ Res* 1981;10:5–9.

Emerson EM (ed): *Contemporary Field Research: A Collection of Readings.* Boston, Little Brown and Company, 1983.

Evanseshko V, Kay MA: The ethnoscience research technique. *West J Nurs Res* 1982; 4:49–64.

Fagerhaugh S, Strauss A: *The Politics of Pain Management: Staff-Patient Interaction.* Menlo Park, California, Addison-Wesley, 1977.

Fagerhaugh S: Getting around with emphysema, in Strauss A (ed): *Chronic Illness and the Quality of Life.* St Louis, Missouri, CV Mosby, 1975, pp 99–107.

Fagerhaugh S: Getting around with emphysema. *Am J Nurs* 1973;73:94–99.

Fox RC: *Experiment Perilous.* Philadelphia, University of Pennsylvania Press, 1959.

Glaser BG: *Theoretical Sensitivity: Advances in the Methodology of Grounded Theory.* Mill Valley, California, The Sociology Press, 1978.

Glaser BG, Strauss AL: *Status Passage: A Formal Theory.* Chicago, Aldine Publishing Co, 1971.

Glaser BG, Strauss AL: *Time for Dying.* Chicago, Aldine Publishing Co, 1968.

Glaser BG, Strauss AL: *The Discovery of Grounded Theory: Strategies for Qualitative Research.* Chicago, Aldine Publishing Co, 1967.

Glaser BG, Strauss AL: The purpose and credibility of qualitative research. *Nurs Res* 1966;15:56–61.

Glaser BG, Strauss AL: *Awareness of Dying.* Chicago, Aldine Publishing Co, 1965.

Goffman E: *Stigma: Notes on the Management of Spoiled Identity.* Englewood Cliffs, New Jersey, Prentice-Hall, 1964.

Goffman E: *Asylums.* New York, Doubleday, 1961.

Gussow Z: The observer-observed relationship as information about structure in small group research: A comparative study of urban elementary school classrooms. *Psych* 1964; 27:230–247.

Hoeffer B, Archbold P: Interfacing qualitative and quantitative methods. *West J Nurs Res* 1983;5:254–257.

Jackson BS: An experience in participant observation. *Nursing Outlook* 1975;23:552–555.

Jacobson SF: An insider's guide to field research. *Nursing Outlook* 1978;26:371–378.

Kaplan A: *The Conduct of Inquiry: A Methodology for Behavioral Science.* Scranton, Pennsylvania, Chandler, 1964.

Katz J: A theory of qualitative methodology: The social system of analytic fieldwork, in Emerson RM (ed), *Contemporary Field Methods: A Collection of Readings.* Boston, Little Brown and Co, 1983, pp 127–148.

Krassen-Maxwell E: *Modeling Life: A Qualitative Analysis of the Dynamic Relationship Between Elderly Models and Their Proteges,* doctoral dissertation. University of California, San Francisco, 1979.

Kus RJ: Stages of coming out: An ethnographic approach. *West J Nurs Res* 1985;7:177–198.

Kus RJ: Gay alcoholism and non-acceptance: The critical link. Presented at the nursing research conference, Honolulu, Hawaii, June 1985.

Kus RJ: *Gay Freedom: An Ethnography of Coming Out,* doctoral dissertation. University of Montana, Missoula, Montana, 1980.

Light RJ: Numbers and narrative: Combining their strengths in research reviews. *Harvard Educ Rev* 1982;52:1–26.

Lofland J: *Analyzing Social Settings: A Guide to Qualitative Observation and Analysis.* Belmont, California, Wadsworth Publishing Co, 1971.

Lofland J: *Doing Social Life.* New York, John Wiley, 1976.

Maxwell EK, Maxwell RJ: Search and research in ethnology: Continuous comparative analysis. *Behav Sci Res* 1980;15:219–243.

May KA: Three phases in the development of father involvement in pregnancy. *Nurs Res* 1982;31:337–342.

May KA: A typology of detachment/involvement styles adopted during pregnancy by first time expectant fathers. *West J Nurs Res* 1980;2:445–453.

Mead GH: *Mind, Self and Society.* Chicago, University of Chicago Press, 1934.

Melia KM: "Tell it as it is"—qualitative methodology and nursing research: Understanding the student nurses' world. *J Adv Nurs* 1982;7:327–335.

Morris MB: *An Excursion into Creative Sociology.* New York; Columbia University Press, 1977.

Munhall P: Nursing philosophy and nursing research: In apposition or opposition? *Nurs Res* 1982;31:176–177.

Oiler C: The phenomenological approach in nursing research. *Nurs Res* 1982;31:178–181.

Oleson V, Whittaker E: *The Silent Dialogue: A Study in the Social Psychology of Professional Socialization.* San Francisco, Jossey Bass, 1968.

Quint JC: The case for theories generated from empirical data. *Nurs Res* 1967;16:109–114.

Quint JC: *The Nurse and the Dying Patient.* New York, Macmillan Company, 1967.

Quint JC: The case for theories generated from empirical data. *Nurs Res* 1967;16:109–114.

Roth JS: Comments on "secret observation," in Filstead WJ (ed): *Qualitative Methodology.* Chicago, Markham Publishing Co, 1970, pp 278–280.

Roth JS: *Timetables.* New York, The Bobbs-Merrill Company, 1963.

Rubin L: Sociological research: The subjective dimension. The 1980 SSSI distinguished lecture. *Symbolic Interaction* 1981;4:97–112.

Schatzman L, Strauss, AL: *Field Research Strategies for a Natural Sociology*. Englewood Cliffs, New Jersey, Prentice-Hall, 1973.

Spradley JP: *The Ethnographic Interview*. New York, Holt, Rinehart and Winston Inc, 1979.

Stern PN: Affiliating in stepfather families: Teachable strategies leading to stepfather-child friendship. *West J Nurs Res* 1982;4:75–89.

Stern PN: *Integrative Discipline in Stepfather Families,* doctoral dissertation. University of California, San Francisco, 1977.

Stern PN: Grounded theory methodology: Its uses and processes. *Image* 1980;12:20–23.

Stern PN: A comparison of culturally approved behaviors and beliefs between Filipino-immigrant women, American-born, dominant-culture women, and Western-female nurses: Religiosity of health care, in Leininger M (ed): *Proceedings of the 1980 Transcultural Nursing Conference,* vol 6. Salt Lake City, University of Utah Press, 1980.

Stern PN, Tilden VP, Maxwell EK: Culturally induced stress during childbearing: The Filipino-American experience. *Iss Health Care Women* 1980;2:129–143.

Stern PN: Grounded theory methodology: Its uses and processes. *Image* 1980;12:20–33.

Stern PN: Stepfather families: Integration around child discipline. *Iss Ment Health Nurs* 1978;1:50–56.

Strauss AL: *Qualitative Analysis*. Cambridge, England, Cambridge University Press, 1986.

Strauss AL, Schatzman L, Bucher R, Ehrlich D, Sabshin M: Field tactics, in McCall GJ, Simmons JC (eds): *Participant Observation: A Text and a Reader.* Reading, Massachusetts, Addison Wesley Publishing Company, 1969.

Strauss AL: *Psychiatric Ideologies and Institutions*. Glencoe, Illinois, Free Press, 1964.

Swanson J: Privatized discovery: The process of finding contraceptive options, presented at Sigma Theta Tau Tri-Chapter Conference, San Francisco, California, April, 1983.

Swanson J, Corbin C: The contraceptive context—a model for increasing nursing's involvement in family health. *Maternal-Child Nurs J* 1983;12:169–183.

Swanson J: Qualitative research using grounded theory. Presented at the Second Annual Patient Education Research Seminar, University of California, San Francisco, December 1980.

Swanson JM, Chenitz WC: Why qualitative research in nursing? *Nurs Outlook* 1982;30:244–245.

Swanson T: Knowledge, knowledge, who's got the knowledge? The male contraceptive career. *J Sex Educ Ther* 1980;6:51–57.

Tilden V: Ethical considerations in qualitative research: A new frontier for nursing, in Davis AJ, Krueger J (eds) *Patients, Nurses, Ethics*. New York, American Journal of Nursing Co, 1980.

Wax ML: On fieldworkers and those exposed to fieldwork: Federal regulations, moral issues, rights of inquiry. *Hum Organiz* 1977;36:321–328.

Wilson HS: *Deinstitutionalized Residential Care for the Mentally Disordered: The Soteria House Approach*. New York, Grune and Stratton, 1982.

Wilson HS: Usual hospital treatment in the USA's community mental health system: A dispatching process. Presented at the American Public Health Association Meeting, Los Angeles, Nov 1981.

Wilson HS: Limiting intrusion—social control of outsiders in a healing community: An illustration of qualitative comparative analysis. *Nurs Res* 1977; 26:103–111.

Woodward B: A Descriptive Study on the Phenomenon of Revaluing Self in Colostomates, masters thesis. California State University, Los Angeles, 1982.

GENERAL

Abroms GM, Greenfield NS: *The New Hospital Psychiatry.* New York, Academic Press, 1971, p 3.

Aldrich CK, Mendkoff E: Relocation of the aged and disabled: A mortality study. *J Am Geriatr Soc* 1963;11:185–194.

Aleksandrowiez DR: Fire and its aftermath on a geriatric ward. *Bull Menninger Clin* 1961;25:23–32.

Allen G: A note on interviewing spouses together. *J Marriage and the Fam* 1980;42:205–210.

American Nurses Association: *Nursing: A Social Policy Statement.* Kansas City, Missouri, American Nurses Association, 1980.

Ashley JA: *Hospitals, Paternalism and the Role of the Nurse.* New York, Teachers College Press, 1976.

Beaver ML: The decision making process and its relationship to relocation adjustment in old people. *Gerontologist* 1979;19:567–574.

Bendixen HH, et al: *Respiratory Care.* St Louis, C.V. Mosby Co, 1965.

Benfield G, Lieb S, Vollmen J: Grief response of parents to neonatal death and parent participation in deciding care. *Pediatrics* 1978;62:171–177.

Benton DA, White HC: Satisfaction of job factors for registered nurses. *J Nurs Admin* 1972;2:55–63.

Bernard J: *Remarriage: A Study of Marriage.* New York, Dryden, 1956.

Bingham WD, Moore BV: *How to Interview,* ed 4. New York, Harper and Row, 1959.

Bogdan R, Brown MA, Foster S: Be honest but not cruel: Staff/parent communication on a neonatal unit. *Hum Organiz* 1982;41:6–16.

Bohannan PJ: Stepfathers and the mental health of their children, in *Final Report of NIMH,* La Jolla, California, Western Behavioral Science Institute, 1975.

Bohannan PJ, Erickson R: Stepping in. *Psychol Today,* January 1978, 53–59.

Boren HG: Pulmonary emphysema; clinical and physiological aspects, in Baum GL (ed): *Textbook of Pulmonary Diseases,* Boston, Little, Brown and Co, 1965, pp 412–447.

Borup JH, Gallego DT, Heffernan PG: Relocation: Its effect on health, functioning and on mortality. *Gerontologist* 1980;20:468–479.

Borup JH, Gallego DT, Heffernan PG: *Geriatric Relocation.* Ogden, Utah, Weber State College Press, 1978.

Bourestom N, Pastalan L: The effects of relocation on the elderly: A reply to Borup, Gallego and Heffernan. *Gerontologist* 1981;21:4–7.

Bourestom N, Tars S: Alterations in life patterns following nursing home relocation. *Gerontologist* 1974;14:506–510.

Bower FL: *The Process of Planning Nursing Care.* St Louis, C.V. Mosby, 1982.

Bowerman CE, Irish DP: Some relationships of stepchildren to their parents. *Marr Fam Living* 1962;24:113–121.

Bozett F: Practical suggestions for the use of the audio cassette tape recorder in nursing research. *West J Nurs Res* 1980;2:602–605.

Browne GB, Pallister RM: Introduction to the research process, in Williamson YM (ed): *Research Methodology and its Application to Nursing.* New York, John Wiley and Sons, 1981, pp 43–63.

Burns P: Learned helplessness in the renal patient. *Neph Nurs* 1983;5:14–16.

Butler RN: *Why Survive? Being Old in America.* New York, Harper and Row Publishers, 1975, pp 260–261.

California Mental Health Services Act. California, Health and Welfare Agency, 1974.

Campbell DT, Stanley JC: *Experimental and Quasi-Experimental Designs for Research.* Chicago, Rand Mc Nally, 1966.

Capra E: *The Tao of Physics.* New York, Bantam Books, 1975.

Caramago O, Preston GH: What happens to patients who are hospitalized for the first time when over 65. *Am J Psychiatry* 1945;102:168–173.

Card JJ: The correspondence of data gathered from husband and wife: Implications for family planning studies. *Soc Biol* 1978;25:196–204.

Caudhill WA: *Psychiatric Hospital as a Small Society.* Cambridge, Massachusetts, Harvard University Press, 1958.

Caudhill WF et al: Social structure and interaction processes on a psychiatric ward. *Am J Orthopsychiatry* 1952;22:314–334.

Chenitz WC: Registered nurse interview, in *Acceptance of the Standards of Geriatric Nursing Practice and Perceptions of Satisfaction and Stress in Practice by Geriatric Nurses,* doctoral dissertation. Columbia University, New York, 1978, pp 148–150.

Clark D: *Loving Someone Gay.* Millbrae, California, Celestial Arts, 1977.

Cook TD, Campbell DT: *Quasi-Experimentation: Design and Analysis Issues for Field Settings.* Boston, Houghton Mifflin Company, 1979.

Costello JP, Tanaka GM: Mortality and morbidity in long term institutional care of the aged. *J Am Geriatr Soc* 1961;9:959–563.

Craig S: Theory development and its relevance for nursing. *J Adv Nurs* 1980;5:349–355.

Downs FS: What's going on here? editorial. *Nurs Res* 1982;31:323.

Duberman L: Step-kin relationships. *J Marr Fam* 1973;35:283–292.

Dudley DL, Verhey JW, Masuda M et al: Long term adjustment, prognosis and death in irreversible diffuse obstructive pulmonary syndromes. *Psychosom Med* 1969;31:310–325.

Dudley DL, Martin CJ, Holmes TH: Dyspnea: Physiologic and psychological observations. *J Psychosom Res* 1968;11:325–339.

Duxbury M, Henley G, Armstrong G: Measurement of the nurse organizational climate of neonatal intensive care units. *Nurs Res* 1982;31:83–88.

Eisenstadt WS: Some observations on a new syndrome—respiratory mendicamentos. *Ann Allergy* 1969;27:188–190.

Farber SM, Wilson RH: Pulmonary emphysema. *Clin Symp* 1968;20:2.

Fast I, Cain AC: The stepparent role: Potential for disturbances in family functioning. *Am J Orthopsychiatry* 1966;36:485–491.

Fawcett J: A declaration of nursing independence: The relation of theory and research to nursing practice. *J Nurs Admin* 1980;10:36–39.

Fisher P: *The Gay Mystique.* New York, Stein and Day, 1972.

Flaskerud JH, Halloran EJ: Areas of agreement in nursing theory development. *Adv Nurs Sci* 1980;3:1–7.

Gentry WD, Parkes K: Psychological stress in intensive care unit and non-intensive care unit nursing: A review of the past decade. *Heart Lung* 1982;11:43–47.

Goode WJ: *The Family.* Englewood Cliffs, New Jersey, Prentice-Hall, 1964.

Gorden RL: *Interviewing: Strategy, Techniques, and Tactics.* Homewood, Illinois, The Dorsey Press, 1975.

Gordon T: *P.E.T., Parent Effectiveness Training.* New York, Plume, 1970.

Gray BH: *Human Subjects in Medical Experiments: A Sociological Study of the Conduct and Regulation of Clinical Research.* New York, John Wiley and Sons, 1975.

Green R (ed): *Human Sexuality—a Health Practitioner's Text.* Baltimore, Williams and Wilkins, 1975.

Gutman GM, Herbert CP: Mortality rate among relocated extended care patients. *J Gerontol* 1976;31:352–357.

Hay D, Oken D: The psychological stresses of intensive care unit nursing. *Psychiatr Med* 1972;34:109–119.

Henderson V: The nursing process: Is the title right? *J Adv Nurs* 1982;7:103–109.

Hirschfield IS, Dennis H: Perspectives, in Ragin PK (ed): *Aging Parents.* Los Angeles, University of Southern California Press, 1979, pp 1–10.

Huckabay L, Jagla B: Nurses' stress factors in the intensive care unit. *J Nurs Admin* 1979;9:21–26.

Jacobson S: Stressful situations for neonatal intensive care nurses. *Matern Child Nurs J* 1978;3:144–152.

Jacobson DS: Stepfamilies. *Child Today* 1980;9:2–6.

Jasnau KF: Individualized versus mass transfers of nonpsychotic geriatric patients from mental hospitals to nursing homes, with special reference to the death rate. *J Am Geriatr Soc* 1967;15:280–284.

Jay K, Young A: *The Gay Report.* New York, Summit, 1979.

Keith J: *Child-Rearing Attitudes and Perceived Behavior Patterns of Natural Parents and Stepparents,* doctoral dissertation. North Texas State University, Denton, Texas, 1977.

Kerlinger FN: *Behavioral Research: A conceptual approach.* New York, Holt, Rinehart and Winston, Inc, 1979.

Kerlinger FN: *Foundations of Behavioral Research,* ed 2. New York, Holt, Rinehart and Winston, Inc, 1973.

Killian EC: Effects of geriatric transfers on mortality rates: Stockton (Calif.) State Hospital. *Soc Work* 1970;15:19–26.

King IM: *Toward a Theory For Nursing: General Concepts of Human Behavior.* New York, John Wiley and Sons, Inc, 1971.

Kinney M: Rehabilitation of patients with COLD. *Am J Nurs* 1967;67:2528–2535.

Kowalski NC: Fire at a home for the aged: A study of short term mortality following dislocation of elderly residents. *J Gerontol* 1978;33:601–602.

Kral VA, Grad B, Berenson J: Stress reactions resulting from the relocation of an aged population. *Can Psychiatr Assoc J* 1968;13:201–209.

Kubler-Ross E: *On Death and Dying.* New York, Macmillan Publishing Co, 1969.

Langner TS, Michael ST: *Life Stress and Mental Health.* New York, Free Press, 1963.

Lieberman MA: Relationship of mortality rates to entrance to a home for the aged. *Geriatrics* 1961;16:515–519.

Longest B: Job satisfaction for registered nurses in the hospital setting. *J Nurs Admin* 1974;4:46–52.

Markus E, Blenker M, Bloom M, Downs T: The impact of relocation upon mortality rates of institutionalized aged persons. *J Gerontol* 1971;26:537–541.

Markus E, Blenker M, Bloom M, Downs T: Some factors and their association with post-relocation mortality among institutionalized aged persons. *J Gerontol* 1972;27:376–382.

Marshall R, Kasman C: Burnout in the neonatal intensive care unit. *Pediatrics* 1980;65:1161–1165.

Maslow AH: *Motivation and Personality.* New York, Harper and Row, 1954.

May KA: The nurse as researcher: Impediment to informed consent? *Nurs Outlook* 1979;27:36–39.

McFarlane EA: Nursing theory: The comparison of four theoretical proposals. *J Adv Nurs* 1980;5:3–19.

Medeiros J: *Relationship Styles and Family Environment of Stepfamilies,* doctoral dissertation. California School of Professional Psychology, San Francisco, 1977.

Messinger L: Remarriage between divorced people with children from previous marriages: A proposal for preparation for remarriage. *J Marr Fam Couns* 1976;2:193–200.

Messinger L, Walker K: Remarriage after divorce: Dissolution and reconstruction of family boundaries. *Fam Process* 1979;18:185–192.

Mims FH, Swenson M: *Sexuality: A Nursing Perspective.* New York, McGraw-Hill Book Co, 1980.

Money J, Ehrhardt AA: *Man and Woman, Boy and Girl: Differentiation and Dimorphism of Gender Identity from Conception to Maturity.* Baltimore, Johns Hopkins Press, 1972.

Mowatt MH: Group psychotherapy for stepfathers and their wives. *Psychother Theor Res Prac* 1972;9:328–331.

Nelson KS: The nurse in a methadone maintenance program. *Am J Nurs* 1973;73:870–874.

Nett LM, Petty TL: Effective treatment for emphysema and chronic bronchitis. *J Rehabil* 1967;33:10–11.

Newman M: *Theory Development in Nursing.* Philadelphia, FA Davis, 1979.

Nugent J, Goldsmith J: Parent/infant bonding in a neonatal intensive care unit. *J Louisiana State Med Soc* 1979;131:235–239.

Nye FI: Child adjustment in broken and in unhappy unbroken homes. *Marr Fam Liv* 1957;19:356–361.

Orem D: *Nursing: Concepts of practice,* ed 2. New York, McGraw-Hill, 1980.

Oskins S: Identification of situational stressors and coping methods by intensive care nurses. *Heart Lung* 1979;8:953–960.

Palermo E: Remarriage: Parental perceptions of steprelations with children and adolescents. *J Psychiatr Nurs Ment Health Serv* 1980;18:9–13.

Paterson J, Zeewald L: *Humanistic Nursing.* New York, John Wiley, 1976.

Perdue B, Horowitz J, Herz F: Mothering. *Nurs Clinics North America* 1977;12:491–501.

Perrault C, Collinge J, Outerbridge E: Family support in the neonatal intensive care unit. *Dimens Health Serv* 1979;56:16–18.

Petty TL, Velt LM, Finigan MM et al: Comprehensive care program for chronic airway obstruction. *Ann Intern Med* 1969;70:1019.

Piaget J: *The Origin of Intelligence in Children.* New York, International University Press, 1952.

Platt JJ, Lebate C: *Heroin Addiction: Theory Research and Treatment.* New York, John Wiley and Sons, 1976.

Population Reference Bureau. *New York Times,* November 27, 1977.

Price ME: Why NICU nurses burnout and how to prevent it. *Contemp Obstet Gynecol* 1979;13:37–46.

Rallings EM: The special role of the stepfather. *Fam Coord* 1976;25:445–449.

Ransom J, Schlesinger S, Derdeyn A: A stepfamily information. *Am J Orthopsychiatry* 1979;49:36–43.

Rochlin M: Becoming a gay professional, in Berzon B, Leighton R (eds): *Positively Gay.* Millbrae, California, Celestial Arts, 1979, pp 159–170.

Rogers ME: *The Theoretical Basis of Nursing.* Philadelphia, F.A. Davis, 1970.

Roget's International Thesaurus. New York, Thomas Crowell Publishers, 1977.

Roosevelt R, Lofas J: *Living in Step.* New York, Stein and Day, 1976.

Rounsaville HJ, Glaser W, Wilber CH, et al: Short term interpersonal psychotherapy in methadone maintained opiate addicts. *Arch Gen Psych* 1983;40:629–636.

Satir V: *Peoplemaking.* Palo Alto, California, Science and Behavior Books, 1972.

Schlotfelt R: On the professional basis of nursing. *Nurs Forum* 1974;13:16–31.

Schulz R, Brenner G: Relocation of the aged: A review and theoretical analysis. *J Gerontol* 1977;32:323–333.

Seligman M: *Helplessness.* San Francisco, WH Freeman Co, 1975.

Slocum JW, Sussman GI, Sheridan JE: An analysis of need satisfaction and job performance among professional and paraprofessional hospital personnel. *Nurs Res* 1972;21:338–341.

Stanton A, Schwartz MS: *The Mental Hospital.* New York, Basic Books, 1954.

Stevens BJ: *Nursing Theory: Analysis, Application, Evaluation.* Boston, Little Bown and Co, 1974.

Stycos J: A critique of focus group and survey research. *Stud Fam Plan* 1981;12:450–456.

Sudman S, Bradburn NM: *Asking Questions: A Practical Guide to Questionnaire Construction.* San Francisco, Jossey-Bass Publ, 1982.

Sullivan HS: *The Psychiatric Interview.* New York, W.W. Norton and Co, 1954.

Sullivan HS: *The Interpersonal Theory of Psychiatry.* New York, W.W. Norton, 1953.

Sussman M: The family life of old people, in Binstock RH, Shonas E (eds): *Handbook of Aging and the Social Sciences.* New York, Van Nostrand and Reinhold, 1976, pp 218–243.

Swanson J, Corbin J: The contraceptive context—a model for increasing nursing's involvement in family health. *Matern Child Nurs J* 1983;12:169–183.

Sweeney MA, Olivieri P: *An Introduction to Nursing Research.* Philadelphia, J.P. Lippincott, 1981.

The Population Council. A manual for surveys of fertility and family planning: Knowledge, attitudes and practice. New York: The Population Council, 1972.

The Random House Dictionary of the English Language. New York, Random House, 1973.

Visher EB, Visher JS: *Stepfamilies: A Guide to Working With Stepparents and Stepchildren.* New York, Brunner/Mazel, 1979.

Webb EJ, Campbell DT, Schwartz RD, Sechrest L: *Unobtrusive Measures: Non-Reactive Research in the Social Sciences.* Chicago, Rand McNally College Publishing Co, 1966.

West N: Stress associated with ICU's affect patients, family, staff. *Hospitals* 1975;49:62–63.

White CH, Maguire MC: Job satisfaction and dissatisfaction among hospital nursing supervisors. *Nurs Res* 1973;22:25–30.

Wilson HS: *Research in Nursing.* Menlo Park, California, Addison-Wesley, 1985.

Wilson HS, Kneisl CR: *Psychiatric Nursing,* ed 2. Menlo Park, California, Addison-Wesley, 1983.

Wilson KL, Zurcher L, McAdams DC, et al: Stepfathers and stepchildren: An exploratory analysis from two national surveys. *J Marr Fam* 1975;37:526–536.

Wood P, Schwartz B: *How To Get Your Children To Do What You Want Them To Do.* Englewood Cliffs, New Jersey, Prentice Hall, 1977.

Woods NF: *Human Sexuality in Health and Illness.* St Louis, C.V. Mosby, 1979.

Zweig JP, Csank JZ: Effects of relocation on chronically ill geriatric patients on a medical unit: Mortality rates. *J Am Geriatr Soc* 1975;23:132–136.

Index

AUTHOR INDEX

ISBN 0-201-12960-4

9 780201 129601

90000

12960